TAKING
BACK
AMERICA

The Revolution Begins!

by

Michael William Haga

TAKING BACK AMERICA
The Revolution Begins!

By Michael William Haga

Published in the United States by Acclaim Publishing Co., Inc.

Library of Congress Cataloging-in-Publication Data
Haga, Michael William
TAKING BACK AMERICA
The Revolution begins, by Michael William Haga
1. United States--History
2. Religion
3. Feminism
4. Politics
5. Racism
6. Environmentalism
7. Education
8. National Characteristics, Americans
Library of Congress Catalog Card Number: 94-74475
ISBN 1-881872-17-3

Design by Roger Rockenbach

Manufactured in the United States of America

TO
Clara, Margaret, David, Mickey, Cathy, Molly, and Mandy
my loving family

A very special thank you to
Marilyn Brannan, Larry Bates, Thomas McConnell, and M. Kenneth
Creamer who provided excellent articles for use in this book

For all *concerned* Americans

A Note From The Author

Many people may consider this book inflammatory and reactionary; it is neither, nor is it meant to be racist, although racial matters are discussed in common sense terms. Although it may seem I am targeting such controversial groups as feminists, environmentalists, the federal government, and today's educational system, (or lack thereof) I do so from the standpoint of rationality and reason. Unfortunately, in a world, seemingly gone mad, reason and rationality are rarely encountered today..

If we, as individuals and as a nation, do not end the insanity of today's welfare system, stop the influx of illegal aliens, break the strangle-hold of environmentalists, feminists, politicians, and educators who graduate children who can neither read nor write, then we as a nation are doomed.

Prior to the Republican Rout in the recent Congressional elections, I was convinced that America and all Americans faced a very bleak future of complete moral decay and total governmental control. Today, I have *some* hope, although it will be a Herculean task to take back America and to make America great once again, we must do it!

Let the Revolution begin!

TAKING
BACK
AMERICA

The Revolution begins!

by

Michael William Haga

Other books by Michael W. Haga

ON THE BRINK
How To survive the Coming Great Depression

IS THE AMERICAN DREAM DYING?
Voices of Americans

Monthly Publications By Michael Haga

THE ECONOMIC OUTLOOK

For information on any of the above call 1-800-323-3523

Contents

INTRODUCTION

Introduction

"Congress shall make no law . . . abridging the freedom of speech, or of the press."
                                        - First Amendment to the U.S. Constitution

"The American people need to understand the American government is in the business of taking what belongs to one American and giving it to another. Typically, when we do that privately, we call that theft."
                                        - Dr. Walter Williams

America is in the midst of a social revolution. The success or failure of this revolution will determine not only the future course of America but whether America, as we know it, will exist in the Twenty-First Century.

Everywhere you look, its sleaze, scandals, and putrefaction, interspersed with hollow-sounding reassurances that *"all is well"* emanating from Babylon by the Potomac. While most Americans instinctively know that *"all is not well"* in America, most do not understand why our country is in chaos. By the time you finish reading this book, hopefully you will understand why America is in chaos and what must be done to stop the destruction of America.

Most Americans say they trust members of the 104th Republican dominated Congress more than they do President Clinton, to make good decisions on major social issues, but most remain uninformed about the Republicans *Contract With America*. While there is broad public support for substantial change, and, in general, for limiting the welfare system, balancing the federal budget, allowing organized prayer in public schools, the support splinters on how to achieve the goals. For instance, nearly two-thirds of Americans favor permitting organized prayer in public schools, but about the same number say they would not want to change the Constitution to allow prayer in public schools.

Unfortunately, the only way we can allow prayer in public schools is to change the Constitution. This is because the liberalized Supreme Court of the United States, after one hundred and seventy some years, decided that the Constitution forbade prayer in schools, in a ruling that would have astonished some of our great Presidents like, George Washington, Thomas Jefferson, James Madison, and Abraham Lincoln (who, by the way, are no longer mentioned by today's educators utilizing the new history standards which are discussed, dissected, and condemned later in this book).

While many Americans continue to sing the praises of the Republican Rout in the November, 1994, elections, whether the Republican dominated Congress will live up to the terms of its *Contract With America* remains to be seen. At the present time American citizens are witnessing a lot of political posturing coming from Washington but whether that posturing will result in real reform also remains to be seen. I believe the Republican shift represents the last chance to avoid total chaos in America. While we need to pay attention to the Republicans recently elected to Congress, it is more important to pay attention to all those Republicans at the state level who won office. Many of these legislators are quite radical in the pursuit of liberty and in the pursuit of States' rights. While this is a beginning, it is not going to happen until *all* working Americans start demanding it.

Thomas Jefferson said, "When all government, domestic and foreign, in little as in great things, shall be drawn to Washington as a center of power, it will render powerless the checks provided by one government over another, and it will become just as venal and oppressive as the government from which we separated. (Meaning Great Britain).

Many Americans, feeling the systems of checks and balances has broken down completely, believe we will witness armed and open conflicts between the states and the federal government in the coming years. Citizens in Wisconsin, Ohio, Texas, Arizona, Idaho, etc., are forming state militia's in preparation for such armed conflicts, while Washington bureaucrats continue to push for gun control in a thinly disguised attempt to disarm all Americans; to make all Americans helpless. In Florida, the sheriff of a small town recently deputized the entire populace to circumvent compliance with the Brady Bill. This is just the beginning.

In Washington, many bureaucrats continue to talk about the necessity of maintaining social safety nets for the poor. Many bureaucrats believe that corporations and individuals alike must be made to understand the importance of sending their tax dollars to Washington to support single mothers with children, the uneducated, the illiterate, the dependent, lazy vermin of society in spite of the fact that during the past forty years Americans have sent trillions of dollars to Washington to alleviate the suffering of the poor, only to see an *increase* in poverty and illiteracy in America. *The American people need to understand the American government is in the business of taking what belongs to one American and giving it to another. Typically, when we do that privately, we call that theft.*

In the heartland and on the coasts, Americans are tired of being forced to hand over their hard earned dollars to support what they consider the lazy, the unwilling, the arrogant who expect to be paid to do nothing. While bureaucrats discuss the needs of the poor, the working class is fed up with paying high taxes which causes them, in turn, to become poor. Working people feel they have become little more than slaves being forced to hand over their hard earned income to support the non-productive members of our society.

Most people no longer care about how deserving the poor are. While they do care about the innocent children, whatever happens to those children is not worth enslavement; it is not worth being forced to labor to provide for them.

While I berate the welfare system and Aid to Dependent Families with Children throughout this book, these handouts amount to only a tiny portion of the total handouts in this country. Congress could cut a lot from the deficit by mandating that no person with income or assets greater than one million dollars could receive one penny from the United States government. Most people haven't a clue of just how much spending this would reduce. Take for instance the handouts to farmers; the handouts to Boeing and Lockheed and Chrysler through the Export Import Bank; the handouts to big companies to do advertising overseas. To cut welfare will be good too. We have made poor people dependent on handouts' as a way of life.

The Federal Department of Education is waging war on the very concept of educating our young. Bureaucrats say that every black or brown kid thrown out of school has somehow been discriminated against by the mean heartless Caucasians and the sell-out Uncle Toms and Uncle Julios. I find that attitude to be disgustingly wrong. The bleeding heart bureaucrats should be forced to spend time in all schools, to witness first hand just how out of control our children are.

Why should American citizens be forced to pay to educate illegal aliens who contribute nothing to the cost of the educational system? We should send the bleeding heart bureaucrats to Chapas, Mexico. That's where they should be defending people. The poor Indians in Mexico are on the verge of genocide yet they say that we, the American people, have been trying to genocide everybody but Caucasians. Why is it that we house, feed, clothe, and educate illegal Mexican aliens in America but when Americans go to Mexico they are met with "Go home, Yankee!"

Why should our tax dollars be funneled into defunct public school systems rife with administrators who won't allow teachers to discipline unruly students? In being forced to conform to dysfunctional educational policies, our teachers can do little but try to maintain order in classrooms where hoodlums hold teachers and students alike hostage. I'm talking about grade school students; children who are eleven years old. Liberalism created the crisis in the classroom and now the liberals want to implement national educational standards which will ensure the complete destruction of our educational system. If we do not stand up and take back our public school systems and begin teaching our children the basics, our children are doomed. Remember this: teachers can only academically train children. That's all they can do. Teachers cannot teach children morals and values. Morals and values come from the home.

Liberalism brought hordes of third world citizens into America, creating the chaotic mess we currently find ourselves mired in. America does not need illegal aliens; we should be sending them back, turning them away. We need to send back everyone who just wants welfare, because we can't afford the price. In supporting illegal aliens, we have been draining our coffers dry. We have reached the point where legal residents will not be able to obtain Social Security benefits even though legal residents contributed to the system.

Jessie Jackson advocates the formation of a third party. Jackson says democrats cannot afford to embrace the tenets of the Republicans. According to Jackson, all Republicans are little more than ultra racists. Jackson says he will create a party that will keep alive the democratic promises made to the working class of this country. Jackson is a liberal. Jackson wants the government to take care of all people even though the government has failed miserably in this task for forty years. Jackson is a racist! Jackson would promote skin color over hard work and honesty. Jackson would keep all Blacks in servitude by making them dependent on the government for support. Dependence is the root of racism. Jackson tells all Blacks the Republican control of Congress will be short lived and will cause chaos in America. While Jackson may well be correct in his belief that Republican control will be short lived, we must not allow him an unlimited forum to fuel the fires of hatred that will come with weaning people off the public dole. Jackson is not a preacher! Preachers do not preach hatred! Jackson is nothing more than a parasite feeding on the ignorant masses.

While it is true that at one time in America Blacks did not have the benefits of equality, they have equality today. For this reason, the NAACP must fade in the coming years. The majority of blacks are no longer in favor of forced busing. The majority of blacks now support the death penalty. The majority of blacks realize they have equal rights. It is only the black leaders like Jessie Jackson who keep harping on equal rights and racialism.

Affirmative action, quotas, are an insult to black Americans. Blacks have come to dominate basketball because they can do a three hundred-sixty degree turn right in front of your face. Whites can't do that. We do have some serious racial issues in America but these issues can only be corrected by correcting the fraudulent educational system in this country; a system which fosters racism. In the real world, people of all races can achieve greatness *if they have the intellect, the desire, and the drive to achieve greatness*. We never hear Jessie Jackson talk about the achievements of blacks, only the failures. I suspect that for every failure, there is an even greater success.

Members of the liberal media establishment love the Jessie Jackson's of this world. That's because the media elite views all Americans as little more than ignorant fodder to be molded for political purposes. It's true. Do you realize that members of the media elite, when talking with each other, refer to the masses as *"John and Jane six-pack."* Think about the meaning of that statement. It means the media elite think Jack and Jane, you and me, are nothing more than beer swilling pigs. Disgusting isn't it?

Later in this book you will read about the great fraud the media elite committed on all Americans by promoting the passage of the General Agreement on Tariffs and Trade (GATT). You will learn that members of the media will be paid, by the federal government, over one billion dollars in the coming years. That money, which comes from your taxes, is the pay-off for the successful promotion and ultimate passage of GATT.

The truth is we didn't need GATT. For many years many good people in America have built bridges between the former Soviet Union, Communist China, and other Eastern European countries. Mr. Clinton gets up on the stage and talks about free trade and the benefits of GATT, but when it comes right down to it, the Department of the Treasury is not giving out the permits for people to import foreign commodities because their products are not politically correct. I'm referring to just about all types of firearms, sporting goods, machine parts, different products coming out of China and the former Soviet Union. These products are in the Trade agreement but importers cannot get the permits to bring them into this country. Exporters often face the same run around from the Department of the Treasury. We could see an exponential increase in exports if our government would allow it. Many politicians continue to talk out of both sides of their mouths. We, of course, know that our famous President Bill Clinton is one of those politicians.

That fact should make you angry. You should also be

angry that Rush Limbaugh went right along with the great GATT fraud. Many people look to Rush for leadership. Did Rush know what was going on beneath the surface? One would certainly think so. Rush touts the fact he knows all. Was Rush bought off? Is Rush leading his flock to the cliff? Only time will tell. The point to remember here is not to put your faith in any one man. Men will always let us down. We need to return our faith to a belief in our Creator. If we fail to do this then we are a doomed civilization, bound to follow in the footsteps of the Romans who watched their empire collapse because they put their faith in men.

The point I am trying to make is the lack of leadership, the lack of spine in this country is sickening. If you have an opinion, state it! Whether you are right or wrong, whether you are politically correct or not, say what you think and what you feel. This leads to leadership. If you believe strongly in something and you state your views, you will anger some people. That's ok! At least you are taking a stand. Unfortunately this is not happening right now in America. Our current leaders have the back bone of Gumby. What we need in this country is a group of people in leadership positions who are willing to stand up to the politically correct idiots out there and tell them where to get off. To tell them that we refuse to sacrifice our country, our affairs, our streets, our shops, our schools, for you people! To tell them that they have no idea what they are talking about.

I believe kids that do better in school come from families that care; from parents that love their children. When we talk about urban black and brown communities, clearly we cannot deny that there are high numbers of children being raised by children. Children have no business raising children. How can children instill in children the basic values of right and wrong? Especially when the children raising children are wards of the state, dependent on a welfare system that fosters dependence and anger. Parental involvement does not exist in welfare dependent black and brown neighborhoods. This is why most of today's problems stem from children living in black and brown neighborhoods.

The issues that go on within the inner cities where most of the brown and black kids reside, affect all the outlying communities and suburbs of the cities. people need to be aware of this. People need to understand why people are moving out of our cities. It's because the schools and the school administrators and the mayors and the police cater to black trash, brown trash, and rif-raf. That's why our cities are falling apart. But the spill-over affects the suburbs of all cities. That's why children in suburbs are being taught in portable buildings to alleviate overcrowding because people are pouring into the suburbs because they cannot live in the cities. Understand how it's all connected. You can run but you cannot hide. When the first black families moved into middle class neighborhoods in our cities, many of them had crosses burned on their front lawns. By the time these same blacks began leaving the inner-cities they were running from the Crypts, the Bloods, the Brims, and this and that. Blacks and Browns are now running from dysfunctional black and brown trash that mayors and governors won't talk about.

We've tolerated gang activity so long in our cities that it's beginning to spread to suburbia. Complacent parents have sent a signal to children of all colors that it's all right for all children of all colors to act like hoodlums; to destroy property and degrade dignity. Is it any wonder our children have become cold, jaded, cynical and arrogant? All adults are told that if they see a child with a mark on his or her body and they don't report it, they are somehow responsible if something bad has happened. In today's world, my parents would be in San Quentin doing hard time for the whippings they gave me. My mother used to beat me senseless when I acted up. There were times I had to cut the switch that she used on me. Discipline, like morals, has to come from the home.

Since most welfare dependent parents don't seem capable of disciplining their children, society must step in and do it now while there's still time. If children are suspended from school, they should be forced to work on street crews until they decide it's better to sit quietly in warm classrooms. If children continue to fail courses they should perform manual labor until they realize it is much better to exercise the mind than the body. We need to work these kids until they drop, then they will want to do better and they *will* do better. The state of Florida recently instituted a boot camp for dysfunctional school children. Every other state should do the same.

We have got to stop listening to the likes of Jessie Jackson and the NAACP talk about how racist the whites are in America today. White people aren't dumb, deaf, stupid or dysfunctional when it comes to race. They see what every black and brown person sees in black and brown neighborhoods, schools, churches, and streets. Blacks and browns have crime, drive by shootings, crack and everything else. Seventy per cent of all black births today are to unwed teenage mothers. When was a black or brown child killed in a drive by shooting done by a white kid? I'm not saying all black and brown people are bad although I am sure that is the way Jessie Jackson will interpret it.

Why isn't Jessie Jackson attacking the Black Entertainment Channel. You can turn on BET at any time of the day and I'll guarantee you there's some black thug talking about bitches, whores, niggers, and everything else. If I'm doing a disservice to blacks and browns by writing about the problems in our society, then tell me why Jessie Jackson won't pick up the telephone and call BET to protest having such trash shown on the television? If Jackson and the NAACP are going to protest anybody then they had better protest BET in Washington D.C., the chocolate city that's dying, and tell them they have no right, how dare they have the audacity to have people on television like Snoop Doggie Dog talking about bitches, whores, and niggers. That's where Reverend Jackson should focus his energy.

What is wrong with the vision that disproportionality across races is probative, as they say in the courts, of discrimination and something has to be done about it? Around the world, in every country, there are enormous disparities between any two groups you talk about: by race, by social class, by anything you want to mention. Among blacks, for example, women with IQ's over 120 outnumber men by three to one. This is legally fascinating because black men and black women have the same genetic background. Everywhere you look, in our court systems, our laws, our policies, our university admission systems, are all based on the assumption that if people are not evenly distributed there must be something wrong.

Look at coffee production. For as many years as there are statistics, over half of the coffee in the entire world is grown on less than fifteen per cent of the land in one plateau in one state in Southern Brazil. In other words, there is no evidence for proportionality across races or anything else. In fact there are all kinds of disproportionality, even in situations in which you know there is no possibility of discrimination. For example, back in the 1960s, Chinese minorities in Malaysia earned over four hundred degrees in engineering. The Malay majority earned 4 degrees during the entire decade. The Malay majority had complete control of the universities. This shows the Chinese were not discriminated against by the Malays. It had to do with the fact that the Chinese people simply liked engineering. In South Africa, the Africans are mostly in the army and the British are mainly in the navy.

This is in a country the Africans run. As I said earlier, turn on any basketball game and you can see there is not a proportionality of races. Black athletes make up seventy per cent of professional basketball players and are also the highest paid ones. If you look at the National Hockey League you find very few blacks. In the history of the League, there has only been one black. If you break it down by geography you will find very few hockey players coming out of Florida or Southern California.

However, in our courts we continue to think that if we don't find equal distribution between the races in all areas, something is wrong. How many times have we heard the argument that blacks make up sixteen percent of the population and yet only two per cent of the engineers, for instance. It just does not make sense. The underlying fallacy of legal reasoning is that courts utilize statistical theories based on random events. Life is not a random event. People do things for a purpose. People are able to do some things because of circumstances. In other words, the races that originated in the Himalayan Mountains do not become great seamen. This is why people in Florida are not experts in ice hockey, and on and on......

With such diverse things as child rearing and entertainment, where these are voluntary acts and it is impossible for anyone to discriminate against someone, that there are still racial differences. Even when you find Japanese and Jewish kids with the same IQ, if you break down the different sections of the IQ test, the Japanese do their best on the part of the IQ test where the Jewish kids do the worst. What I am trying to say is that it is impossible to level the playing field and to make everyone equal. There will be differences between races and between peoples of the same race regardless of affirmative action plans to level the playing field. In fact in the chapter titled Racism you will find an in-depth analysis of why affirmative action plans for colleges have been a miserable failure.

Jessie Jackson loves to state that slavery was a peculiar institution to America. Slavery was a peculiar institution in the United States only because the United States was founded on the premise of freedom. Historically, slavery was one of the most common institutions in the world for thousands of years. There was slavery in the Western Hemisphere before Columbus came to America. There was slavery in Africa. There was slavery in Asia. There was slavery everywhere there was human beings. As a matter of fact the word slave comes from Slav in Arabic, German, Spanish, and Italian. *One of the peculiarities about Western slavery is that the West was the first to end it.* It was the sight of the Union Jack on the high seas that helped end slavery in the Western world. Why doesn't Jessie Jackson talk about this?

It is amazing how little attention is paid to this. When I was researching this book I had no trouble assembling shelves of books on slavery in the United States, or slavery in the Western Hemisphere. But it was the hardest thing to find even articles on slavery in the Islamic world where the number of Africans enslaved exceeded the number of slaves in the Western Hemisphere, not to mention the enslavement of hundreds of thousands of Russians, the enslavement of Bosnian Serbs, and so on. In fact slavery is going on today. One of the most outrageous things was a story that appeared several months ago discussing finding thirty thousand African slaves currently in Mauritania in North Africa. By all indications from international agencies they are treated terribly. Why was there no outcry about this from the Jessie Jackson's of this world? I'll venture an educated guess. The same people that go ballistic when someone makes a racist remark don't care anything about the thirty thousand African slaves because their real concern is not about slavery, their real concern is about inducing guilt and getting political chips from it. In fact, to a certain degree slavery still exists in the United States. Slavery in the United States comes in the form of taxes. Every working American is currently enslaved by governmental taxes. But, if the recent shift in the political landscape is to carry forward, this type of slavery is about to change for the better.

The Republican Congress is considering scrapping the current income tax structure and replacing it with a flat tax. Think of how many Americans will stand up and shout "free at last," if this happens. While a flat tax will severely diminish the public treasury and entitlement programs in general, all Americans will be freed of oppressive government. If we are to take back America, we must continue to push for the abolition of all taxes.

There is also a move to abolish the Federal Reserve. It is the Federal Reserve that has enabled the government to enslave all Americans. One man's view of the Federal Reserve System is discussed in this book. I consider the author of this segment to be right on target.

There is also a move to abolish the Environmental Protection Agency, the Forest Service, The Clean Air and Clean Water Act, and all other such regulatory agencies that have been usurping individual property rights guaranteed by the Constitution. In fact, recently, members of the Forest Service tried to prevent a land owner from developing some land in New Mexico. The land owner challenged members of the Forest Service and went right on with his plans. While there was a confrontation, the land owner, to date, has been winning.

Behind the Republican proposal to change the legal system is the correct belief that people sue too much, lawyers manipulate the system, witnesses lie, and in the end, juries make excessive awards and judges do little to check abuses.

The House Republicans *Common Sense Legal Reform Act*, would create disincentives for lawsuits, including making losers pay winners court costs. It would preempt state laws with a *federal standard* (which I do not like) for claims against companies whose products maim or otherwise harm people; reduce the liability of retailers who unwittingly sell defective products and cap punitive damages which courts impose to punish malicious business practices. To make sure juries are not misled, the GOP plans would restrict expert witness statements and disallow comments from those whose pay depends on the client winning the case.

Separately, the ninth proposal in the GOP's ten point *Contract With America*, would limit lawsuits brought by shareholders whose stock purchases have gone sour, possibly through fraud. "The bottom line is to restore accountability to the legal system and to reduce costs to Americans," said Representative Jim Ramstead, Republican of Minnesota, the proposal's lead sponsor. Ramstead characterized the current system as being abused and overused. Judgments are based solely on emotions. A perfect example of an outrageous judgment based solely on emotion was the award of millions of dollars to a woman who spilled hot coffee in her lap when exiting from the drive through at McDonald's. The woman claimed the coffee was too hot. The jury agreed and awarded her millions of dollars. McDonald's then lowered the temperature of the coffee it sells. Those of us who enjoy a cup of hot coffee now wistfully remember when McDonald's used to be the place to get it.

These are good ideas, whether or not they comport with the Ninth and Tenth Amendments to the U.S. Constitution is something else again.

In Washington, Transportation Secretary Fredrico Pena recently moved to put tighter regulations to enhance the safety of commuter airlines? At least Pena has experience. Look at how many planes he grounded with Denver International Airport, his $3.8 billion dollar airport project in Denver, Colorado. Pena is another fine example of what incompetence our President has surrounded himself with in Washington.

Recently former President Jimmy Carter has been traveling around the world, attempting to resolve various crises and conflicts. We've seen Carter travel to Haiti, North Korea, and Bosnia to meet with various diplomats and rebel leaders, attempting to quell unrest and warring fractions. Has Carter been successful? Not really. Not for anyone other than Carter that is. In fact the only one who has benefitted from these meetings is Carter who has managed to garner the media limelight.

For most conservatives, Carter's travels seem laughable. Most conservatives remember Carter as the President who presided over a nation beset with the constant threat of gasoline shortages, ruinous interest rates, failed social and foreign policies. Most remember heaving a sigh of relief when Carter left office. Most do not understand how Carter could even command the attention of the press or foreign diplomats and/or rebels. In fact, when Carter was discussed on a national talk show recently, the host said, "Jimmy Carter is going to Bosnia. My God! We've sent in our deadliest weapon; deadliest to us."

Even I had to laugh when Carter, jubilant from what he viewed as his success in Bosnia, offered his negotiation skills to help resolve the national baseball strike. When Carter's offer was politely but bluntly declined, my faith in the rationality of Americans was somewhat restored.

A few Blacks and Browns are beginning to take a stand, to speak out about all of the insanity that has gripped our nation. A few whites are beginning to take a stand, too. Hopefully, others will soon follow. What each of us must remember is that as long as we allow our leaders to distract us with the small details, we will fail in our quest to take back our country. When I speak of the small details, I am speaking of racial issues, entitlement spending, taxes, education, punishment, and gun ownership. We must not let our leaders distract us from our mission. If we do, then American will continue to sail down the current river of hopelessness that will end in destruction.

And make no mistake, there will be more deceptions thrown at each of us in the coming years than any of us can hope to understand. Most of these deceptions will continue to come from members of our nation's media elite who have a vested financial interest in maintaining the status quo. There are many Americans who believe the members of our media elite are involved with our governmental leaders in a conspiracy to create a one world government based on Socialism. While I continue to remain skeptical of the conspiracy theories, I have begun to wonder if there might not be some validity to the theories, especially after completing the research necessary for a chapter entitled A Case For Conspiracy later in this book.

I am concerned about the hypocrisy of Newt Gingrich. One hand Newt is willing to chastise all Americans for not standing up and embracing the basic rights of freedom and equality this country was founded on, only to turn right around and give back a $4.5 million dollar book advance in an effort to silence critics. Why does Newt Gingrich care what critics say about income he makes if that income is the product of legitimate work that market forces place a high value on? America was founded on the premise that every individual should celebrate hard work and celebrate the fruits of prosperity that come with hard work. Giving back money earned from a legitimate business venture should be celebrated not shunned to silence critics. If Newt makes these types of compromises in his private legitimate business affairs. how can we trust him to make honest decisions that will ultimately affect the rights of all hard working business people attempting to achieve the same level of financial success?

Newt tells Americans he is giving up his $4.5 million book advance because his book contract is with Harper Collins, a major publishing house controlled by Rupert Murdock who also has an interest in major communications industry legislation to be taken up by Congress. Because Newt is a member of Congress, Newt feels many Americans might consider his acceptance of money from a company controlled by Murdock as unconscionable. What a bunch of bunk.

If all Americans adhered to this type of flawed reasoning, no one would do business with anyone because at some point in every business decision someone could find evidence of what appears to be a conflict of interest. Its just amazing to me how politicians manage to operate on two levels of morality.

But then, so much of what we see today is based on smoke and mirrors.......

1

Is America Dying?

"Every nation becomes great based on the belief off and adherence to the values of integrity, family, and the work ethic. At the height of every great country, people turn away from the values that made the country great. A long process of decline then commences, ending with a collapse of the nation. All nations that are resurrected start back at square one."

- Mike Haga

Jim Nelson Black recently wrote a terrific book entitled *When Nations Die, America on the Brink, Ten Warning Signs of a Culture in Crisis*, a very well written book that accurately portrays many of America's most pressing problems.

The premise of Black's book is not that America is dead or dying, but that there are symptoms which can be seen in great cultures, including our own, and going all the way back as far as ancient Egypt, which point to decline.

Black tries to list factors, which can be seen throughout history; factors which have contributed to the declines of great civilizations, seeing if any of those factors are operative in America today.

According to Black there are ten factors comprised of social, cultural, and moral ideas which influence the decline of a civilization. Black says all ten factors are active in our culture today. A scary thought.

For example, if you allow a culture to inflate its money supply, it will not be able to resist the temptation to keep inflating. If you open up certain doors of taxation, it will not be able to resist doing more of it. If you open up certain changes in the culture, it will almost invariably wind up in a certain place.

The two best chapters in Jim's book are the two middle chapters. The first examines the weakening of cultural foundations, the second examines the loss of tradition. In reviewing these chapters, we understand that everything from lawlessness to the loss of Religious belief come with the loss of the foundations of our culture. When the view of self reliance supersedes the belief in The Creator, a strong view of right and wrong begins to fade. As the underlying belief of right and wrong begins to fade, people begin to lose to faith in the nation, and faith in the family structure. When those things begin to slide, and we lose our attachment to the institutions that made our nation great, culture goes into a decline.

Today, America's cultural foundation is crumbling. Anything that is old is bad; anything that is new is good. The result? Chaos! To understand the tremendously destructive result of the loss of our cultural foundation, we simply have to look back in history to another culture once caught in the same cultural collapse we face today.

In France, during the French Enlightenment of the Seventeenth and Eighteenth Centuries, promiscuity rose to the point people either died of sexually transmitted diseases or became sterile. The result? There was an immediate drop in population because promiscuity made childbirth not only undesirable but often impossible. During this period, the French people discovered science. The scientific method came along just prior to the Enlightenment. It made people believe in a new form of authority. People believed that things happened because of purely natural and mathematical purposes. People turned away from the belief in a Creator. They began to think they could do away with God.

The result was a change in authority from the traditional belief that God ruled the world and people were responsible to him to one where people believed that science held all the answers. We can follow this same trend right through the Twentieth Century and into our classrooms, major universities, and individual households today. We have replaced the belief in God with the belief in man and the state. It is a very dangerous process.

What we have, as a result, is a collision of the traditional philosophy with the ascendent philosophy which has left a large trail of wreckage in its wake. We call it the culture wars. We have one side, the Christians, standing for traditional family values, and another side, the Liberals, that stand for changing traditional values to something else to be changed as circumstances dictate. Liberalism basically is a doctrine of change simply for the sake of change. The result is chaos. This is why we now live in a nation of chaos.

In the beginning, America became what it was because people came here looking for freedom for their souls. To express themselves and to worship God. I believe God blessed this nation in a very special way. When the enlightenment turned away from faith in God and said, "God is dangerous and we don't need him anymore," they introduced factors into culture which have been very destructive.

Today, America is not a religious nation. There is chaos. Back in the 1940s, when seventy-five percent of Americans would say they were not only religious but Christian, did we have astronomical rates of crime? Did we have drive by shootings? Did we have a government out of control? Did we have bureaucracy running our lives? Did we have taxes at the rates we currently have? Did we have continual scandals emanating from Washington and even from the White House? Did everybody claim to be a victim of something and therefore not responsible for their own actions?

Today most people say America is not a Christian nation and that religion does not matter. Look around; what do we see? Crime is rampant! The economy is in decay! The bureaucracy is out of control! Our educational system is worthless!

Which is better, morality or chaos? How much influence was Christianity on morality? We must infer, based on today's circumstances that America was a much better country when we adhered to traditional values. Of course, the feminists, the blacks, the homosexuals, the Hispanics, the politicians, and so forth, argue that the reason America is in chaos today is because no one had rights before liberalism gained the upper hand. This is hogwash! We have reached the point where everybody is now attempting to assert rights which are superior to everyone else's. The result is chaos.

Non Christians argue that the Christian culture created more wrongs than anything. What hogwash!

Many people argue that Rome was not a Christian nation until the end. That prior to that time it reached a very high point. During the early First Century, Rome reached perhaps the highest point of any civilization in history. It was a pagan culture. But you know what paganism did for Rome, Greece, and Cartage? It gave the people a sense of moral values. People believed that there was a Divinity which was observing how they lived. They were faithful to that code. It was only when they turned away from their own code of morality that their society began to collapse. When Americans adhered to the Christian code of ethics, America was a much better nation. When many Americans began turning away from Christianity, turning away from their moral code,

America's problems began in earnest.

With cultural decline comes the loss of economic discipline. People begin living for the moment, caring nothing of the future. Instead of working and saving for the things most people desire, most people choose to run up massive debts for instantaneous gratification. "Charge it," becomes the catch word of the day.

As a result of this loss of economic discipline, people set in motion events which make possible the rise of a bureaucracy to oversee this loss of discipline. When the economic and moral systems are no longer functioning correctly, the leadership of the country decides that what they need is more people to administer. But the people who administer are not really looking at the important issues the society or culture is involved in; the administrators are looking at their own welfare; they are looking at how they can get a bigger job, more prestige, more money. How they can skim a little off the edge, which is not to say that all bureaucrats in our country do that, but the temptation is surely there.

As the bureaucracy continues to grow it undermines individual rights and responsibilities. People become more dependent on more bureaucracy to help control all events which the people seem unable to control on a personal level. In 1932, after the Great Depression started, we had six hundred thousand people working for the government. It was a very large number because we were trying to rebuild an economy that was in dire straits. But today, just sixty years later, we have eighteen and one-half million people on the government payroll. Are we run better today than we were in 1932? No!

In our culture, the idea of change just for the sake of change has become a very accepted belief. This is a very dangerous thing, yet we act as if it is something to be wanted. We have reached the point where we simply cannot afford to change things the way we have been. Look at what we've done to our educational system. We've come so far from teaching the basics, the majority of teachers have forgotten what they are. Yet we keep hearing this move for change, change, change. Ironically, most people recoil in horror at the thought of simply going back to the point where things worked.

I think it's a process of deliberate de-education. If you look back at what John Dewey taught at Columbia Teachers College in New York, around 1916, you see that it was a deliberate process of multi generational de-education. Dewey, and other communist leaning liberal educators like him, believed that American culture was degraded; that faith in God was dangerous and that the traditional values of our country were not noble, but actually quite insidious. So Dewey and others like him wanted to get rid of the traditions, to de-construct them, and they set about doing precisely this.

Naturally, this process could not be accomplished in one generation, or even in two. So what we see happening in our schools today, the de-education of our children, is a deliberate process, that's why most American children don't even know the names of the oceans on either side of our continent.

What is important to understand in this process is that Generation One may be at five on a scale of one to ten in their understanding the basics. Under Dewey's de-education process, Generation One moves to the left and down one level to say four. Then Generation One's kids, Generation Two, start up at four, and are moved to three. Generation Three now looks at five as if it is somewhat extreme right when in reality, two generations earlier, number five was right in the middle. This is why, when Christians try to do things like home schooling, or to have private schools or to challenge the local public schools to be more responsible in teaching history, they are called censors, bigots, right-wing fanatics. This is why it is a very dangerous system that we've developed.

ALSO, what we have done is to create a new culture, where everything is done by sloganeering now, rather than by rational debate. Ironically, the letters to the editor, are sometimes some of the more cogent debates on either side of an issue. We now have a society that not only seems to be incapable of reasoning its way through anything requiring logical thought, but lacks a foundation upon which to base that reasoning.

Think back to the Reagan years. The Secretary of Education did a study called, "A Nation At Risk," because our educational standards had fallen so far. They did such things as asking high school students to make a conclusion that a list of facts would give them. We're talking two facts. Now what conclusion would you draw from that? Only five per cent of students tested could come to the logical conclusion from two facts by a series of analysis that any responsible adult should be able to do.

When Black talks about the loss of economic discipline, he looks back in history to see what the record has been. How much did economics contribute to the decline of Rome, or to the decay of Cartage? As the dictators or kings or emperors of these various empires began to slide away from the basic values that had once sustained the empires, the dictators began to want more of the wealth for themselves. They began to give the wealth of the common people, the products produced by the working people, to their friends, their favorites, their generals. The people then had to work very hard to sustain a wealthy class that was basically doing nothing.

Rome was eventually totally degraded. At one point prior to the collapse of the Roman empire, more people were taking money from the government, doing nothing to earn it, than there were people to pay into the treasury. More than fifty per cent of Romans were taking something for nothing and giving nothing back. Doesn't this sound hauntingly familiar? When you begin to consider that we have forty million people on welfare in America, most of whom are not employed in any way, you see symptoms of the same type of crisis creeping into this country.

There is no such thing as a free lunch. What has to be done is to double the work load of the people who are producing, that are trying to support those who do nothing. This is why it takes till the middle of July before working people can keep even a nickel of what they earn. That other half is going off to the government to use at its discretion without asking permission of the working class.

Another factor that seems to come into play, clear back to the Roman empire, is the debauching of the currency, either through clipping or inflation. Look at the Nazi regime of World War II when it took a wheelbarrow of Deutsche Marks to buy a loaf of bread! This same story can be told of Rome. As the currency was eventually de-graded, the Emperors kept revaluing the money. A coin that at one point had been worth the equivalent of twenty of our dollars today within a hundred years was down to a penny or less in value. Like the Deutsche Mark example, it took thousands of these coins to buy a loaf of bread.

To debase their currency, the Romans did the same things that we have seen done in third world countries, and also in the United States today. They debased the content of silver or gold in their coins. They also debased their coins through the application of what they used the money for.

Another factor signaling the decline of a nation is the loss of the sense of duty. In the early years of this country, most citizens had a sense of duty. Look back at the Great Depression of the 1930s. Even when times were tough we didn't have rioting; people pitched in and did what they could, helped each other when they could. When the full impact of this Great Depression hits, we will probably have full scale rioting. Right now, politicians are telling all Americans that, out of economic necessity, we are going to have to cut a lot of welfare programs, Medicare, and Social Security spending. Most people today cannot live without these programs. What will the people do that have come to depend on these programs? They will riot. To control the rioters, the government will step in and exert more control.

This loss of the sense of duty not only permeates the lower segments of our society, but is very evident in the upper levels off government. While I hate to keep harping on the GATT Treaty and the World Trade Organization that is attached to it. As I have said repeatedly, it is perhaps one of the most dangerous things that could have happened. It's almost as if after the November, 1994, elections, we won the card game and then gave the pot to the other players. We voted for conservative values and then turned over our portion of the world to a one world government.

The Washington Post (better known as The Washington Pravda) is a good example of this loss of the sense of duty by members of the media. During the GATT debate, the *Post* wrote glowing editorials about the benefits of GATT. Why did the *Post* do this? The *Post* did it not because of a belief in GATT, but because the *Post* stood to make out handsomely once GATT was passed. Since GATT was indeed passed, the *Post* will be given two million dollars a year from the WTO to do with whatever it sees fit. As I pointed out in a previous chapter, owners of most United States major media conglomerates receive one billion dollars under the terms of the GATT Treaty. The media praised the benefits of GATT because it was in the economic interest of the media to do so even though GATT was not in the interests the average working class American people.

The main question is, "What can the American people do to take back their country; to return America to greatness?" First, let's not hold out false hope that people on the other side, people who are strongly to the left, are ever going to agree with us. We simply have to do what we have to do. We have to get involved at every level of the community, at our schools, and certainly at our homes. Many of the people who are arguing for school prayer aren't even praying with their children at home. We have to get back and do the things we know how to do and let those people who disagree with us come to us by observing our lifestyle and by our success. We have to let our elected representatives know how we feel about all forms of legislation. We have to let our elected representatives know that we are, as a group, united and strong enough to vote them out of office should they turn their backs on us. Naturally we have to vote.

For far too long, our churches have tended to say that debate is not healthy and it doesn't sound Christian; that we should get out of the public arena before we are attacked. Unfortunately, what has been solely needed in the cultural debates is for churches and those who uphold traditional Christian values to be a part of the process. We have turned over the arena to the other side and now we are fighting to get back in the ring when it is almost too late.

Remember this! Even if the system falls apart, we will not! Even in the middle of a system falling apart, God has a role for each of us. Individuals are what really count. There is really no United States. The U.S. is just people, for the most part. People who used to share much of the same values. Unfortunately, as this nation has drifted toward liberalism, (which is Socialism) many of our shared values have disappeared. Many people believe the shift to Socialism was planned by our governmental, financial, spiritual, and educational leaders, hundreds of years ago, and that our current leaders are continuing to push us along the same path, using many deceptive means to do so. To many Americans, those people, who believe there is a conspiracy by our leaders for the planned destruction of America are fanatical maniacs. However, most Americans know that somewhere, somehow, something has gone terribly wrong which has caused the traditional values and beliefs that form the cornerstone of our country to begin to crumble.

When the subject of the cause of American's problems comes up in conversation, most Americans agree the source of all problems is the federal government. People who believe in conspiracy theories believe the main conspirators reside in Washington, D.C., and that they are using the (often illegally gained) powers of the federal government to destroy America as a part of creating a one world government to enslave all people. Whether this is true or not, I believe we have to look at all evidence and derive our own conclusions. For this reason, we will be examining the conspiracy theories and most other seemingly random events which seem to be cumulating in chaos.

Today, there is a movement to restore traditional values in America. The question is whether enough people can come together to restore these values. Most people believe the only way enough people can come together to restore traditional values is to dismantle the federal government. I agree. The question is whether we can muster enough backbone to tear apart and trash a federal bureaucracy which is destroying America. Perhaps I am naive, but I believe if we keep our eyes fixed on the goal of the reunification of America, we can take back America. We can restore America to greatness. We can overcome the corruptness of the politicians in Washington, D.C., by exercising that most powerful right off all, the vote. We must be vigilant. We must never let politicians detract us from our goal, and they are doing everything they can to detract us every minute of every day. Don't let them do it. This is still our country! Most of us still have a dream. Go for your dream.

Let the revolution begin!

2 A Case for Conspiracy

"Since I entered politics, I have chiefly had men's views confided to me privately. Some of the biggest men in the United States, in the field of commerce and manufacture, are afraid of somebody, are afraid of something. They know that there is a power somewhere so organized, so subtle, so watchful, so interlocked, so complete, so pervasive, that they had better not speak above their breath when they speak in condemnation of it."

- President Woodrow Wilson
The New Freedom (1913)

I am an optimist. I believe that being an American citizen makes me one of the most fortunate people in the world. I live in a country blessed with an abundance of resources, boundless human talent, and that I have the freedom to pursue (for the most part) my dreams.

I am also a realist. In my short time on this earth, I have witnessed many, and often detrimental, changes sweep across the American landscape. There has been a marked decline in morality coupled with an explosive upsurge in what has come to be called victimization where everyone blames everyone else for everything. I find myself living with a generation of hopeless illiterates created by a welfare system that was once envisioned to be the salvation of the needy. I listen to different politicians come up with different plans to

fix the ever growing list of domestic and international ills. I
try to vote for people I believe will help steer our ship of state
away from what appears a to be a rocky coastline coming ever
closer on the horizon. Like countless other Americans, I have
the nagging feeling that many things are not what they seem,
especially in the area of world trade.

A lot of times in public, a lot of things just don't seem
to make sense. We often ask why is this happening if our
leaders say they are trying to do that. If they are trying to do
that then why is it resulting in something totally different?
Why did NAFTA suddenly appear on the horizon? Who
thought up NAFTA? Where did it come from? One day,
NAFTA just sort of appeared in the media, *and yet it is a
thousand-plus page treaty.* Who thought it up? The same
thing for GATT.

*Is it any accident that the Club of Rome, back in the
1950s, was talking about ten regional trade areas of the world
that would be required as the first big step into global
government?* Is it any coincidence that ten trade regions are
now being outlined by the various trade agreements that are
being set up around the world? Is there any reason why, back
in 1913 President Roosevelt Wilson, writing in <u>The New
Freedom</u> said: "Since I entered politics, I have chiefly had
men's views confided to me privately."

Some of the most powerful men in the area of world
commerce and manufacturing *seem* to be afraid of somebody
or something. Do they know that there is a power somewhere
so organized, so subtle, so watchful, so interlocked, so
complete, so pervasive, that they had better not speak above
their breath when they speak in condemnation of it? Why is
it since 1913 that various people in various organizations keep
talking about global government? Is there a loose conspiracy
going on? Why is it that H.G. Wells wrote a book called *The
Open Conspiracy, Blueprints for a World Revolution.* Why in

the early 1980s did Marilyn Fergison come out with another book, *The Aquarian Conspiracy*, in which she said there is a whole host of insiders controlling future events? These are insider books, people saying yes there have been and continue to be people conspiring to control the world and that these conspirators are not meeting in back rooms, they are men and women of influence and they are all working together to achieve a common goal, global government.

There are theories involving conspiracies, which most of us feel are nothing more than the paranoid delusions of the uninformed because they are not grounded on fact. There are other theories which have a tremendous amount of documentation. It is, perhaps, no accident that virtually everything the John Birch Society was saying about Communism, after the collapse of the Soviet Union, was proved to be true despite all the negative publicity the organization has been receiving from some of the very globalist organizations who have controlled the media since the 1960s and especially since David Rockefeller's speech at the Democratic Convention in 1964.

As one considers the possibility of a loose conspiracy, one begins to ask questions, keeping in mind the bottom line to any question should be: is it true? Is there ample documentation to support that point of view? And if there is, who are the people? What are their goals? And what is it going to do to me?

Today we have an argument about the GATT Treaty. Is GATT going to cause us to give up sovereignty as a nation? Many people are saying, yes, it is. A member of Parliament in England has written a book called *The Trap* in which he is warning: *beware!* This is a trap and you are being suckered into it. The NAFTA agreement. What will it ultimately do? Are there different levels of conspirators? Are there people who control and others who simply collaborate without even knowing, half the time, that they are collaborating with a conspiracy? Although some theories are delusional, it's also just as much of a mistake to brand all theories about any conspiracy as being delusional. For example: The Federal Reserve Banking System was created at a secret meeting among Congressmen and bankers at Jekyll Island, Georgia, in 1913. It wasn't a plan to save the United States banking system, it was a plan to consolidate power, monetary power, in the hands of a few bankers. They did it secretly. It was a conspiracy. And it affects us to this very day.

So why is it that people are always against believing in conspiracies when history is just chocked full of them? Speaking for myself, I am not comfortable with conspiracy theories, because I believe it is impossible to *ultimately* control all governments representing billions of people around the world. In my opinion, there are too many people, cultures, and self interests involved. I am, however, willing to consider the possibility of various power groups *attempting* to form alliances which ultimately prove beneficial to the alleged groups involved.

Common sense tells us our leaders do not always make decisions which seem rational. For instance, why didn't we rid the world of Saddam Hussein when we not only had the chance but the means? Why were the recent U.N. bombings of Serbian rebels done with such precision that no Serb planes were destroyed? Why didn't we rid the world of Castro when the Soviet Empire collapsed? Why do we allow Castro to continue to make menacing threats even though such threats are meaningless? Why is the U.S. in Haiti? What is the ultimate goal of the U.N.? Why does the U.S. government foster the flood of illegal immigration into the U.S. by mandating U.S. citizen tax dollars be used to feed, clothe, and educate illegal immigrants at a time when U.S. citizens can't always get the same benefits?

Is it just that we are living in a world seemingly gone mad, or is there something more involved? Are powerful and hidden interests manipulating our leaders to make seemingly irrational decisions in pursuit of an overall plan which is very rational when looked at in totality? I don't know the answer. But I have read much of what has been written by three credible men, Dr. Dennis Cuddy, Robert Henry Goldsborough, and Dr. Jim Wardner who not only believe in the conspiracy theory, but document much of their findings. While I remain skeptical, their writings certainly provide the necessary documentation.

Dr. Cuddy received his Doctorate Degree in American History and Political Science from the University of North Carolina at Chapel Hill. He's taught at the University level and in public school systems. Dr. Cuddy was also a political risk analyst for an international consulting firm. He has also been a Senior Associate with the U.S. Department of Education in Washington, and his editorials have appeared in quite a number of newspapers around the country, including USA Today. He's the author of *Now is The Dawning of the New Age New World Order*, also *New World Order Chronology and Critique, The New World Order Chronology and Commentary,* and *The History of Education.*

Robert Henry Goldsborough has written about the dangers of Communism, secret societies, and subversive movements since his Cum Laude graduation from Mt. St. Mary's College in 1954. He was a Staff Investigator for the House Committee on UN-American activities.   In 1975, Goldsborough developed a friendship with Norman Dodd, the former Research Director of the very special Congressional Committee ordered in 1954-55 to investigate tax exempt foundations and similar organizations - The Reese Committee, chaired by the late Congressman Carol Reese a Republican from Tennessee.   Ironically, the Reese Committee was disbanded in 1955, precisely when the Republicans lost (until 1994) control of the House of Representatives. He regularly visited Mr. Dodd at his home, recorded Dodd's experiences during the investigations of the Rockefeller, Ford, and Guggenheim Foundations, the Carnegie Foundation for International Peace. Bob publishes a frequent newsletter called The Washington Dateline. Bob is also President of the American Research Foundation.

Dr. James Wardner has authored a book called *The Planned Destruction of America* which is written in a very documentary type style to show clearly, exactly where much of the material for a case about things such as where The Council on Foreign Relations (CFR), The Trilateral Commission, and the Federal Reserve came from, trying to show this in the words of the alleged conspiratists rather than in his own.

In researching many of his books, Dr. Cuddy came across interesting statements by many major politicians like the one made in 1913 by Woodrow Wilson who said, "There is a power elite behind everything going on in the government." According to Dr. Cuddy, there have been other, later, quotes just like it. In 1933 President Franklin Delano Roosevelt's (FDR) chief advisor, Colonel Mandell House, received a letter from FDR, after FDR had talked with Jack Morgan, J.P. Morgan's son, which said FDR and Morgan knew, "The government of the United States had been owned by this power elite ever since the days of Andrew Jackson."

Carol Quigly, who was the mentor of Bill Clinton when Clinton was at Georgetown University, also spelled this out. Quigly was not an enemy of these 'people,' he said, he liked what they were doing, for the most part. He'd looked at their secret records for a couple of years in the early 1960s and he thought they should be out in the open. Quigly used such language as "front organizations" for these various groups like the Council of Foreign Relations which was originally a "front organization" for J.P. Morgan and international bankers and others.

Even recently, an editor for Time Magazine, Walter Iasscson, wrote a book entitled *The Wise Men* which is about six of these leaders. In this book, Iasscson, who is a member of the CFR and a friend of the six men, said the Carnegie Foundation, The Rockefeller Foundation, and the CFR are all "front organizations" for this "power elite."

In 1913, Frank Vanderlip, President of Rockefeller's National City Bank of New York, described his role at the conference at Jekyll Island to set up the Federal Reserve, "There was an occasion near the close of 1910 when I was as secretive, indeed as furtive, as any conspirator. I do not feel it any exaggeration to speak of our secret expedition to Jekyll Island as the occasion of the actual conception of what eventually became The Federal Reserve System."

Once the plan for The Federal Reserve had been drawn up, the plan had to be shoved through Congress. The stage had to be set. Events had to be set in motion long before the actual plan was drawn up. According to the conspiracy theorists, as early as 1907, members of the "power elite" began discussing the need for a central banking system. One of these members, Paul Wolberg, when lecturing the New York Chamber of Commerce in 1907, said that unless, "The U.S. set up a central bank, there would be a financial collapse." Later that year, there was a financial collapse in the U.S.

The question is whether the collapse was simply the result of excessive credit expansion, or whether it was planned and engineered by the "power elite" in order to set in motion all the events necessary to set up the Federal Reserve System. The conspiratists believe the collapse was engineered by the international bankers, like J.P. Morgan, who wanted to bring about a monopoly so they wouldn't have competition in the banking industry.

According to the conspiratists, the "power elite" created this planned economic collapse, through the sudden withdrawal of money from the U.S. banking system, to tell the American people Paul Wolberg predicted this would happen and happen again in the future if a central bank was not created and given ever increasing power to control the entire banking system.

Enter the politicians. Suddenly there was both a Democrat plan and a Republican plan for the establishment of a central bank in the U.S. The conspiratists say both plans were necessary in case the American public didn't like one plan, the other plan could be implemented.

The conspiratists feel the next step came when Colonel Mandell House engineered the picking of Woodrow Wilson as the Democratic candidate for President of the U.S. Mandel searched for a person he felt could be manipulated, after arranging for the election of three governors in Texas, including Governor Hogg. After looking around, Mandell picked a New Jersey Governor who had been president of Princeton, nurtured him, fed him ideas, and then went around writing and talking to Democrats and other political big wigs, telling them Woodrow Wilson was the man they should elect President. Already, Mandell had spelled out his plans for a Socialist America in a novel. So he hand picked Woodrow Wilson to help bring about a total conspiracy. If you read the intimate papers of Colonel House, you can see how he went about setting up Woodrow Wilson as President of the United States so he could manipulate him.

After Woodrow Wilson was elected President, Colonel House then set about becoming Wilson's alter ego. In 1910, House often attended secret meetings with the trustees of the Carnegie Endowment for International Peace, to discuss how best to change the morays of the American people *from a patriotic Christian free enterprise nation to a Socialist, internationalist secular humanist nation*, outside of war. After a year of these meetings, they determined the only way to change America was through war. American then became enmeshed in World War I.

Minutes of these secret trustees meetings were later uncovered by the Reece Committee of the House of Representatives in 1953-54. The Reece Committee also uncovered old minutes of meetings of the trustees of the Carnegie Foundation back when the president of the Carnegie Foundation was Elia Root, a very powerful U.S. Senator and lawyer who also represented J.P. Morgan. Root also had access to the President and Colonel Mandell House. After the War started, Root got a message to Wilson, telling Wilson to get the U.S. out of the War.

The whole plan for The League of Nations was a Socialist plan of which Col. Mandell House played a very important part. When the U.S. Senate did not initially ratify the League of Nations, thus (according to the conspiratists) taking the first step in getting the U.S. into a world government, Colonel Mandell House, working with the Fabian Socialists, had a meeting at the Majestic Hotel in Paris in 1919 to set up the plans based on Cecil Rhodes and Lord Rothschild's plan to set up international control of the world's resources for the Secret Society of the Round Table.

At this meeting Colonel Mandell House, with a few of his hand picked young intellectuals, Christian Herder, (who later became Secretary of State) John Foster Dulles, (who later became Secretary of State under Eisenhower), Allen Dulles, (who later became the head of the CIA under Eisenhower) began planning for the creation of an organization that would (behind the scenes) change the thinking of the American people and the U.S. Senate, regarding the direction of U.S.

Foreign policy. The organization that ultimately evolved was/is The Council on Foreign Relations, established in 1921, incorporated in 1922 with the funding and backing of a network of powerful people like Wolberg.

The purpose of the Council on Foreign Relations (CFR) was to change the direction of America so that it became part of the internationalist plan to bring the U.S. into world government. According to the Reece Committee findings, the CFR sufficiently infiltrated and influenced FDR's Administration so that by 1939 the CFR was determining foreign policy. At this juncture, the CFR helped establish the United Nations (U.N.) and the U.S. became a big player. According to the Reece Committee Hearings, by 1939, the CFR had supplied position papers and everything else for the FDR Administration; and, also, White Papers for Foreign policy.

The Reece Committee was disbanded when the Democrats gained control of the House of Representatives in 1955. Interesting enough, minutes of the meetings of the Carnegie Endowment for International peace, which were subpoenaed and obtained by the Reece Committee, disappeared. Minutes of the Reece Committee hearings, testimony, reports, and conclusions were once in many libraries around the country. Strangely enough, all but two copies (one owned by Robert Goldsborough) have disappeared. Many people, when requesting The Reece Reports from various libraries, are told data shows the libraries own the reports, but they can never be found - in essence, the reports were stolen from various libraries.

Reading through the Reece reports is very interesting. According to the reports, the Committee found out how the Communists and U.S. tax exempt organizations like The Carnegie Endowment for International Peace, The Rockefeller Foundation, The Guggenheim Foundation, and the Ford

Foundation all interacted. They set up a network of power. They would give bright young college students scholarships to go on and get Masters Degrees and Phd's, and then fund them in the writing of new history books. This way they directed the thinking of the intellectuals that they picked (after brainwashing them to believe in their cause). Obviously, many of these intellectuals have influenced the (downhill) direction of the American education system. For example, John Dewy, who came out of John's Hopkins University in Baltimore, was influenced by Daniel Coyt Gillman (the first president of John's Hopkins) who earlier had brought to John's Hopkins in 1899, Sidney & Beatrice Webb, two of the co-founders of the Fabian Socialist Society in England. The Webb's were to inundate the professors of John's Hopkins with Fabian Socialism, so the professors would, in-turn, do the same to their students.

One of the Students so influenced was John Dewy. After leaving John's Hopkins, John Dewy went on to become a professor teaching at Columbia Teachers College and then later at the University of Chicago, where he infected several generations of teachers who went through Columbia and then spread out across the country to teach the advantages of Socialism. The egalitarian philosophy was inculcated in the teaching. Then the foundations would fund more bright students who eagerly embraced the Socialist philosophy to attain higher degrees and write more books and teach more incoming students.

Through these teachers, the whole thing just sort of snowballed. If you weren't of their thinking, you did not get a grant from one of the major foundations. If you thought the way they wanted you to think, then you could go on and get fellowships, be underwritten if you wrote a history book, etc.

I have a copy of the 83rd Congress Second Session House Report Number 2681 on Tax Exempt Foundations,

printed December 16, 1954. One of the references they found
was to the Council on Foreign Relations. What they
discovered about the Council on Foreign Relations is that its
main priority is selling the American people what they deem
Internationalism which is nothing more than totalitarianism
(the education of people towards a globalist Socialist mindset)
with a very nice name. The 83rd Congress documents this on
page 176 of this Tax Exempt Foundation Report of the Special
Committee to Investigate Tax Exempt Foundations and
Comparable Organizations.

The next question is, who are members of the CFR
today? Are they still attempting to pursue their goal? Do
they have interlocking directorates with major companies and
news organizations? Take a look at the Clinton
Administration. The whole thing is made up of members of
the Council on Foreign Relations. Bill Clinton, CFR,
Trilateral Commission; Vernon Jordan, Transition Team, CFR,
Trilateral Commission; Jeanetta Cole, Transition Team, CFR;
Warren Christopher, Secretary of State, CFR (he was vice-
chairman of the CFR), Trilateral Commission; Les Aspin (bad
pick, former Secretary of Defense), CFR; Lloyd Bensen,
Secretary of Treasury, CFR; Henry Cisneros, Secretary of
Housing and Urban Development (who is under a cloud for
paying off a girfriend), CFR; Donna Shalala, Secretary of
Health and Human Services, CFR, Trilateral Commission,
Committee on Economic Development; Bruce Babbit,
Secretary of the Interior, CFR; James Woolsey, Director of the
CIA, CFR, Rhodes Scholar; Madeline Albright, U.N.
Ambassabor for the U.S., CFR; Roger Altman, Deputy
Secretary of the Treasury (he's out under a cloud), CFR;
William Crow, Joint Chief of Staff in the early Reagan years,
became a big pusher of Bill Clinton, Chairman of Foreign
Intelligence Advisory Board, CFR; Lynn Davis, Under
Secretary of State International Security Affairs, CFR.

The CFR has a publication called *Foreign Affairs*. In this publication they tell us much of what is going to happen ahead of time; it's almost like a predictor if you know how to read their Cryptic language, the Hegelian Dialectic which is a play on words, calls things what they are not. For example, sixteen years before the founding of the Federal Reserve, the concept was being developed by Colonel Garrison (who wrote a book about it) who met Wolberg after Wolberg had come to the U.S. in 1902 from Germany, they were modeling the Federal Reserve after what had been developed in Europe. J.P. Morgan gave Wolberg the assignment to come up with the concept. We've already discussed what happened in 1907. Later on, Harrison, a friend of Teddy Roosevelt, Woodrow Wilson, and Wolberg, was meeting with Garrison deciding how they would develop the plan. Garrison was also meeting with William Jennings Bryant, describing the plan when Bryant said, "We can't do that, that's a Central Bank." Garrison agreed but said it would be called something else - the Federal Reserve. Bryant latched onto the idea, put it into the platform and this is what Woodrow Wilson ran on.

Colonel House was a facilitator using the Hegelian Dialectic. On one hand House is playing with the international bankers, on the other hand he's got this book out that's speaking of Socialism as dreamed by Karl Marx. House continues as the lead facilitator until the mid 1930s, then after him comes John J. McCloy. On the one hand McCloy is sitting in Hitler's box at the 1936 Olympics, later on he's swimming and smiling with Kruschev on the other side. McCloy is a member of the CFR, head of the World Bank, head of the Ford Foundation. In the early 1950s he's getting a young protegee, Henry Kissinger, into a Soviet American studies team. Later, Kissinger becomes a big member of the CFR. On one hand, Kissinger is prosecuting the Vietnamese War while on the other hand he's opening the door to China for Richard Nixon.

One must keep in mind the CFR has in its ranks people that are *temporarily* useful. For example, why did George Bush, a member of the CFR lose and Bill Clinton, also a member of the CFR, win the 1992 Presidential election? Two reasons. There was a *domestic* agenda. Out of the many appeals court Judges in the U.S., only three are CFR members, and the CFR wanted two of them Ruth Ginsberg and Steven Bryer, to become Supreme Court members, so Clinton had to appoint them. If Bush had appointed either Ginsberg or Bryer (even though both are very liberally oriented) the Democratically controlled Congress and House of Representatives would have fought Bush. There was also an *international* agenda. The CFR had to have Clinton elected to get NAFTA passed, because only a Democrat asking for party loyalty (remember the Democrats controlled both Congress and The House of Representatives - and even though Bush was all for NAFTA, the CFR knew the Democrats would never pass anything Bush wanted). Ironically, even Clinton could only get about forty percent of the Democrats to go along with NAFTA, but it was enough to squeak it through.

Clinton's actions, though, were becoming troublesome for the CFR. Hillary's commodity trades, Vince Foster's alleged suicide, Whitewater, rumors of drugs, allegations by various women of sexual trysts, etc., were becoming too commonplace. Since Clinton had completed his CFR agenda, he was no longer needed. Perhaps this is why, in 1993, Henry Kissinger began putting Clinton down. But was there more? Was Clinton put in the office of the President to also divert attention from other, even more sinister plans of the CFR? While no one will ever know, it is interesting that Clinton was elected, accomplished his agenda, then brought the wrath of public opinion down on the Democratic party just prior to the 1994 Congressional elections. Was this also part of the

Clinton agenda? Over the last 40 years, American citizens had grown cynical of Democratic control of the Congress and House of Representatives, where it seemed all reason had evaporated from legislation continually passed; legislation requiring higher taxes, more entitlement spending, (part of the humanist/Socialist bend of the CFR), the rapid rise of crime, the decay of the educational system, and so on. Something had to give, sometime. Thanks to Bill and Hillary, the Republicans re-gained control of not only the Congress but the House of Representatives. Americans rejoiced. The back of liberalism was broken. But was it? Did Americans just elect new faces eager to implement the same agenda - just a little more cleverly? Who knows. Only time will tell. It   is interesting, however, to find that Newt Gingrich is a member of the CFR, World Future Society, Congressional Clearing House. It is Newt Gingrich, CFR, whose voting index is 68 per cent for bringing in a New America, a pretty liberal voting record for an alleged conservative. If it hadn't been for Newt Gingrich, Clinton would never have been able to pass the NAFTA regional government accord. Gingrich rallied 'conservatives' to vote for NAFTA.

Quigly, writing in his book, *Tragedy and Hope*, in 1966, says, "They expect they will be able to control, both political parties equally. Indeed some of them intend to contribute to both and to allow an alternation of the two parties in public office in order to conceal their own influence, inhibit any exhibition of independence by politicians, and allow the electorate to believe that they were exercising their own free choice."

Is this what really happened in the 'historic' 1994 Congressional elections where the Democrats lost overwhelmingly to the Republicans? Only time will tell. But isn't also odd that President Bush didn't put up more of a fight in the 1992 Presidential elections? There were many, myself included, who feel Bush acted like a man who wanted to lose. Was Bush merely playing out his role? Again, who knows. Certainly, politics makes for strange bedfellows.

Tod Foley, outgoing Democratic Speaker of the House is a member of the CFR. Newt Gingrich, incoming Republican Speaker of the House is also a member of the CFR. Gingrich pushed for the World Trade Organization, under GATT. Gingrich helped push GATT through the House of Representatives.

After the 1994 elections, Pat Robertson, in his publication *Christian America* came out and said, "the pro-family surge swayed the election." Then on page 4, Robertson has a picture of Foley and under the picture is a caption that says, "Tom Foley, the first Speaker of The House to be voted out of office since Lincoln was President." The concept that's being given to readers who do not understand American politics is that there has been a great shift. But informed people, like Pat Robertson, know that nothing has changed at all, just the faces. The deception continues. A deception perhaps aided by what some of us feel are false prophets like Pat Robertson.

To understand why I question Pat Robertson, one only has to pick up a copy of his book entitled *The Millennium*. True Christians believe many of the New Age, New Order cultists dabble in the occult and in astrology. Pat Robinson professes to be a Christian of the highest order, yet on every page of *The Millennium* is a point with a circle around it, an occult sign. Was this planned? I don't know, but a true Christian would not allow something like this to just happen. It is also interesting that Pat Robertson published another book entitled, *The New World Order, It Will Change The Way You Live*, which outlined much of what is happening in politics, education, and morality today.

The Council on Foreign Relations is very much in

power. There has been no change since George Bush left the White House. Both George Bush and Bill Clinton know one another through The Institute for Policy Studies. As a matter of fact, it was a member of Skull and Bones, George Bush's secret society, which started what became known as The Research Institute which became The Institute for Policy Studies.

Most members of the CFR are also members of the Institute for Policy Studies, which is a Marxist/terrorist organization worldwide. Some members are heavily indoctrinated into the occult as well.

In looking back, Congressman Reece said, "There is ample evidence to show there is a diabolical conspiracy in back of all of this."

Is there really a conspiracy by the power elite to ultimately control the world? Have there been select societies who keep recruiting new individuals through the decades to continue and thus ultimately achieve complete control? I don't know. A lot of what is written here makes one wonder. But is there more? Yes! Much more.

A good example of just one of the interlocks of the overall conspiracy is Alger Hiss. Alger Hiss was the chief foreign policy advisor President Franklin Roosevelt at Yalta, the great give away to the Soviets. Alger Hiss was later found guilty of perjury when he denied he was a Soviet agent. But, before that happened he was the chief foreign policy advisor at Yalta. He later was the co-author of the United Nations Charter, written in San Francisco. He was the first acting Secretary General of the U.N. at the first meeting in San Francisco. He traveled to the meeting with Nelson Rockefeller, who helped fund the U.N., as well as the CFR. Hiss was a CFR member. When Hiss left the government he became President of the Carnegie Endowment for International Peace. All these interlocks were funded by Rockefeller money. This is just one example of the interlocking control of our whole foreign policy - an interlock that continues to this day.

Basically, politics is a good old boys' club with very high stakes involved. Unfortunately, citizens think they are electing people who suddenly decide to run for public office, when in reality most politicians have been put up, groomed, financed, and are totally indoctrinated and owned.

Another good example is the Rhodes Scholar. Cecil Rhodes (who was discussed earlier) who had a plan for world control had a secret society. Rhodes was to be considered like the general, there was an executive committee around him with people like Lord Esher who (prior to World War I) would meet with Henry Morganthal and they would say they both agreed, "We need to shed American blood as quickly as possible to get the U.S. into the War." Alfred Milner was another member of the executive Committee who picked up after Rhodes death around 1902. Outside of these members was a circle of initiates whose job was to permeate the upper levels of politics, education, economics, journalism, to get in high places and subtly change public opinion over to the belief that a humanist one world government is superior to fragmented nations of differing religious beliefs.

This is where, according to Cuddy, Goldsborough, and Wardner, a person needs to understand what a conspiracy does. When you had such things like the Illuminate and so forth many years ago, it was not necessary there be some sort of initiation at midnight and so on. We have a clear record of people like Babuf and the French Revolution and after him Warnaradi, and after him Marks and Engles, all deliberately referring to their successors, and they are forming these secret societies all along. They may not be meeting at 2:00 A.M. with some kind of handshake, but in their own words they are following a pattern, a world view. And so, the conspiracy that should be considered is not someone in a black hat sneaking around to dark, smoke filled rooms. In the case of the Rhodes Scholars, for example, these scholars were part of Cecil Rhodes plan, and they would fit under what is known as an association of helpers. They are outside the circle if initiates. Nobody is necessarily calling them up and saying, "Hello, you are part of a conspiracy to take over the world." What they do is they monitor people in politics, economics, education, and journalism. They select people with their viewpoint, they groom them and then see to it that they get into positions of authority in banks, public office, universities, etc. Take universities, for example, here's an example in the U.S. Carol Quigly says that the American branch of what was called the Milner group, became the Round Table and so on, until it became known as The Institute for Advance Study at Princeton. The head of this group was Flexter who was also with the Carnegie Foundation, also with Rockefeller's General Education Board, also with The Educational Trust, and if you look at their minutes, these people were deliberately plotting to take over education. George Strayer who became head of the NEA in the year in which it was founded, 1915, said, "Give them the axe if they don't do what we want them to." This was a deliberate plan through the Rhodes Scholars and the CFR to take control of various aspects of private life.

Let's look at the relationship between Bill Clinton and Carol Quigly. Clinton was encouraged to go to Georgetown. While at Georgetown, he mentioned it was run by Jesuits who encouraged him to apply for a Rhodes Scholarship and model himself after Fulbright, but he took a Western Civilization course under Quigly and Quigly's mentor Crane Brenton (who was a Rhodes Scholar himself). Quigly thought these people were wonderful and Clinton was extremely impressed and mentioned Quigly at his acceptance speech at the Democratic Convention. During Clinton's last year at Georgetown, John

Foster Dulles' son Avery, who was a high level Jesuit at the time became a member of the board of Georgetown, when Clinton along with his roommate Strob Talbott (who believes national sovereignty is not such a hot idea) went on to become Rhodes Scholars at Oxford.

Keep in mind, while Clinton was a Rhodes Scholar at Oxford, he led the demonstration against the United States Embassy in London, during the Vietnam War. He was not a participant, he was a leader. Then he took a vacation to Moscow at a time when college students from America weren't allowed in Moscow, unless they were very friendly with the Soviet Union.

Conspiracies are not confined just to politicians, bankers, journalists, and educators. Let's look at what may one day be viewed as conspiracies by several other well known people Starting with Ross Perot.

Ross Perot was building a $200 million dollar airport in Dallas, Texas, during the very time he was coming out against NAFTA. Given the powers that be in the federal government today, a person could never get FAA clearance to build an international airport unless that person was part of the scenario the power structure is trying to implement. And the NAFTA scenario is so well knit, so tight, at this point in time, that many people are talking about very serious consequences to the United States. There has also been talk about George Bush nominating Ross Perot to the Council on Foreign Relations. If this is true, then Bush and Perot should be nominated for an Oscar based on their performance in the 1992 elections.

Perot made the bulk of his billion dollar fortune through governmental contracts, so he must be an insider. This makes the deception all the more probable. Especially since Perot was coming out against the very thing he was embracing. That is what makes for good political soap opera.

If a person can come out and talk vehemently against the liberals and yet be one by virtue of the fact he or she knows where we are all going, then that person is a part of the problem.

In the days of old, there were sins of commission and sins of omission. Today, there are many people holding themselves out as being conservative Christians, pastors, evangelists, etc., who are committing the sin of omission because they are not talking about anything that is going on today - enlightening their followers - at probably the most strategic and urgent time in all of American History,

During the 1992 campaign, any time Bush began to lead anywhere in the polls, Ross Perot jerked his knee and the polls went the opposite direction. Looking back, I and so many others should have been able to see that Perot was nothing more than a detractor. Perot had to keep Bush from winning so Clinton could get the Democrats to pass NAFTA.

In a special issue of *Foreign Affairs* (the publication of the CFR) the winter before the election, it was said that Pat Buchanan had set back the New World Order timetable by about ten years. Then the attack dogs, including William F. Buckley, and Rush's good friends Bennett and Kemp, went after Pat Buchanan because he really represented old American values and ideals and virtues. So they had to go after Buchanan, they had to get him. The CFR crowd had already decided, at that point, according to their writings in *Foreign Affairs* that Bush was not moving ahead with the new world order timetable as quickly as they wanted. So they settled on Clinton. Clinton was not going to win. Enter Perot to take away part of the Bush vote to ensure a Clinton win. As we know, Perot succeeded because of fools like me.

Remember the debate between Perot and Gore? Gore is perhaps the world's worst debater. Gore a moving mannequin wearing nice clothes. Nobody could really lose a debate to Gore. Ross Perot not only lost the debate, but he made NAFTA look good in the eyes of the American public. Talk about superb acting. Perot, with his quirky style and beady little eyes, should be given a special place in the Oscar Hall of Fame.

In addition, there are people in the main-line media walking and talking like conservatives, but at critical junctures they zig to the left for unexplained reasons. These people can best be called Judas goats; a Judas goat is someone who leads the innocent, the unknowing, or the blind, over the cliff to a certain death. A person who supports NAFTA and GATT is really a person who supports loss of sovereignty for the U.S. To promote NAFTA and GATT and The World Trade Organization, is to promote regional government and world government. How can any conservative who believes in less government support a World Trade Organization that promotes more government worldwide? They can't!

Who are the so called conservative talk show hosts who: (1. deny there is a conspiracy; (2. Won't talk about it on their talk shows; (3. Support NAFTA and GATT? One name certainly comes to mind. *Rush Limbaugh!* Here's a guy building up a tremendous following who unknowingly or unwittingly are being led right up to the cliff where, right at the critical time, they will, like the lemmings they are, go sailing right out into oblivion finding they suddenly have no rights, no income, no hope.

Don't get me wrong. I listen to Rush on a regular basis. In the beginning, I thought the guy was a saint (but then again I almost fell for Perot). In the beginning, perhaps Rush really stood for the things he spoke so passionately about. Then along came all that money and we know what always happens when money's involved. Rush still talks the talk of the common man, but I believe Rush is now out for Rush alone. Has he become part of the conspiracy, or is he just a pawn as well? At times, I think he's just not bright enough to do more than just scratch the surface, and he gets most of his 'inside information' from the likes of Bennett and Kemp who probably laugh all the way to the next meeting of the CFR. But Rush is so good at entertaining his audience he doesn't have to dig beneath the surface. Only time will tell if I am right. Unfortunately, for many it may well be too late - much too late.

As I said before, I believe Pat Robertson is another Judas goat. On foreign affairs, Pat was recently asked a question about some sort of economic punishment metered out by the U.N. against Yugoslavia. Pat responded that Yugoslavia was being reprimanded because it hadn't complied with its U. N. Mandates. As said earlier, the U.N. is a Communist organization. It was founded by high ranking members of the CFR and the Communist party together which are really one in the same. The politicians in control are well aware of this. *The only people who do not realize what the U.N. is all about seem to be the American people.* Pat Robertson has also sponsored people like Jeremy Rifkin on the 700 Club. Rifkin is a blatant new ager. Robertson is also a friend of Matt Hatfield who is a Mason and a cultist who supports depopulation. Robertson is another conservative who never comes out with any "facts" about what is really going on. Pat simply dresses well, answers questions well and does some good things for people.

Isn't it interesting that today a person has no problem in convincing people that Pope John Paul is bad, but God forbid you should say something bad about Pat Robertson or Billy Graham. If we are able to debunk the Catholic Church, at least at the level of the Vatican, why can't we see what might lie behind Pat Robertson?

Let's look at another great conservative Judas goat, Bill Bennett, author of *The Book of Virtues* and guest and friend of

Focus On The Family, who also helped usher in Outcome Based Education and was against Proposition 187 in California. Will the real Bill Bennett please stand up? Here's a man who professes to be a conservative Christian but who promotes new age new world ideas. Bill Bennett was brought in to do away with the Department of Education. He didn't do it. The real Bill Bennett stumped against Proposition 187, saying it would cause a great bureaucracy. He had a huge bureaucracy in the Department of Education and he could have whittled it down and done away with it. He did not.

Most of the major media outlets are owned and/or controlled by members of the CFR. Elizabeth Grant who owns Newsweek Magazine, The Washington Post, and several major television stations is not only a member of the CFR but a major financial contributor to the CFR. Karen Elliott House, one of the editorial page editors of the Wall Street Journal, along with several other members of the editorial staff, is a member of the CFR. The list of names just goes go on and on.

The anchor people of the major television stations are members of the CFR. Catherine Graham, of the New York Times is a member of the CFR. When people ask "why don't I hear about the CFR on television," the answer is simple, members of the CFR control the media. Ask yourself why the three major nightly television newscasts cover the same stories at almost the same time. Do some channel surfing to see what I mean.

Felix Rodan, senior managing partner of the international mortgage banking firm of Lazar Frahar went to the Senate Commerce Committee and said "unless GATT is passed and the World Trade Organization is implemented, there will be serious consequences." Rodan is one of a handful of men so powerful, he controls America. Rodan is a member of the inner circle of the CFR. White House Chief of Staff, Leon Panetta, also said the same thing. Panetta is a member of the CFR.

In the coming months and years, keep the concept of the Judas goat in mind. While there are many people wearing the coat of conservative colors, they are not conservatives, they are liberals in disguise. They are part of something much bigger than you and I, but if we combine forces then we can overcome their interlocking network of power and return this country back to the Republic it once was.

Is the GATT Treaty a Trojan Horse? I don't know. Only time will tell. The powerful forces behind it, however, certainly provide food for thought. Are powerful forces attempting to sell-out America and all Americans? To listen to members of the media, including Rush Limbaugh, one would have to say no. Then again, are we privy to the real truth from the media? You can answer that one for yourself. Buried in the very small print of the 22,500 page GATT Treaty is a clause that authorizes payment of $1 billion dollars to several prominent people who also own several major media organizations.

Since passage of GATT, most of the politicians who voted for it have admitted they never read the Treaty. The only thing we ever heard them harp on was that they just had to pass GATT because it was going to help our ability to trade. Most are now admitting a lot of U.S. jobs will be moving off shore. Basically, GATT was a sell-out to the big boys and the daily worker will pay the price. I believe the Republicans will pay for this sell-out in the next election. Most Americans are angry that the Republicans ran on the issue of change (reminiscent of Bill Clinton) only to stand by and allow deceptive legislation to be passed when they could have blocked it. Passage of the GATT treaty was not something that had to be done quickly. We could have gotten it out of the way sometime after the new Congress came in.

Predictably, after the Treaty passed, Bob Dole (while at the White House) came out and said, "It is not a matter of sovereignty. It's not a matter of the new world order. It's a matter of tariffs and trade."

If the conspiracy theory is true, American citizens had better wake-up and smell the roses. I still believe no group, no matter how powerful, can *ultimately* control everyone. Perhaps the skeptics need to begin, in unison, presenting hard factual evidence to the American public before it is too late. If we do not act, if we do nothing, then perhaps we are doomed. When you hear a politician flip-flop on the issues, zig from right to left, remember it and vote accordingly.

If enough of us band together, we can break the strangle hold of the Judas goats, we can come together and form a true third party, nominating and electing uncorrupted politicians. I suspect fissures are developing in both the Democratic and Republican parties that could help end the reign of power. Recently, conservatives from across the nation met in Florida to discuss "getting back to the basics of less government," ending welfare, etc. Interestingly, many of today's powerful Republicans boycotted the meeting including, Dan Quayle, CFR; Bill Bennett, CFR; Jack Kemp; CFR, and so on. Then again, these are just a *few* of the Judas goats.

When one looks at our political system from this standpoint, many of the seemingly confusing and contradictory actions and pieces of legislation certainly seem to make very good sense. If there is indeed a power elite behind every stinking thing going on in Babylon, everything makes perfect sense. When one side of the equation angers the majority of Americans, bring the other side in power. Anger the public and they vote the Republicans out. Bring in the Democrats. When the Democrats anger the public, give the public the appearance of choice and they will vote the Republicans back in. In the interim, during the shift in power from one party to the other, pass outrageous legislation like GATT, postal rate increases, political pension increases, etc. The incoming party can then say, "What could we do? Nothing, right? At least we won't do this to you!" Of course, when their time is up, they do the same, and we keep losing more of our rights, more of our country in the process.

If one believes in the conspiracy theory, as the CFR has evolved, its members have seen to it that for at least two generations, that they are involved in *both* parties and control the foreign policy, the internal policy, the debt and the deficit of America. If you believe in the conspiracy theory, of which I did not, until recently - but which I still have trouble with - until we can break up the Federal Reserve System, and elect people outside the power elite, the future of a *free* America is doubtful indeed.

3 Our Country Under Siege

By M. Kenneth Creamer

The fact that there exist extra political international organizations such as the Trilateral Commission, World Bank, the IMF, the Council for Foreign Relations, etc. is well documented. The fact that many of our very influential political, media, and industrial leaders belong to various of these organizations is also well documented. Not having ever attended any of their gatherings it would be impossible for me to provide any insight whatsoever into what is actually discussed in any of these fraternal meetings. However, I can point to various nefarious happenings which have been both sponsored and supported by those (members) in attendance and the consequential effects on our liberty and economic well being.

Every social structure that man has put together since the beginning of time has been composed of two basic types, producers and non-producers. It is the goal of the non-producer to live off of the producer at a higher standard of living than the producer. Today, the United States, a country founded to preserve and cultivate productivity in mankind, is no exception. How our own non producing population accomplished this is quite interesting.

In the very beginning of the Republic, our Founding Fathers established an umbrella Government through the United States Constitution. This new Government body was to act as the interface to all external Governments and to provide a forum for the redress of grievances for wrong doings by the State and Local Governments. Great care was taken in the creation of the Constitution to prevent the Federal Government from acting as a central government with unlimited control over the States and individuals living within the several States. The concept of Nationalism (the concept of one central government with supreme authority through out the land) and its implementation was rejected at every juncture. Thomas Jefferson, one of the key authors of the Constitution, intended to maintain individual sovereignty and prevent this new layer of government from encroaching on any of the inalienable rights of the individual. See (and study) the white paper on Federal Jurisdiction contained in the Appendix.

The underlying principle of that day was that individuals left to their own devices, so long as they did not interfere with the rights of others, would best serve the interest of the individual and the rest of society, a society being made up of individuals. Jefferson and other statesman of the time had read much of the theories and thinking of John Locke, a social and political philosopher who wrote in the late 17th and early 18th century. It was from these writings (and reasoning) that those who structured our republic based much of the concepts found in words in our own Constitution. Locke's thinking (reasoning) was instrumental in establishing these underlying principles and is credited with forbearing the concept of the separation of Church and State which is embodied in our own Second Amendment to the Federal Constitution.

Look around. Do you think that we still live by this simple underlying principle. I think not. Our liberties have been steadily declining and the invasion of a bigger and bigger central government of our private lives has been going on since the turn of the 20th century. To help illustrate how this has taken place we can look to a fable about "The Sensitivities of a Frog." It purports that if you put a frog in a pan of boiling water he will immediately jump out but if you put him in a pan of cold water and gradually heat the water over a considerable period of time the frog will remain in the water until he is cooked.   I see the citizens of the United States sitting in a pan of boiling water that in 1913 was a pan of cold water.   Very few people understand the temperature of the water, the size of the fire under the pan, or who is providing the fuel for the fire.

One of the primary functions of government beyond protecting the rights of individuals is to protect the free market or a free economy.   Actually, one can argue that the two, rights of the individual and the free market are one in the same.   Economics is the study of the production, distribution, and the consumption of goods and services.   It is the foundation of human existence as we know it.   But what is the root foundation of economics or an economy?   To answer this we must go back to the cave man to a time when man did not interchange with man to further his well being.   To a point in time when no market existed.   In the beginning of human existence, man provided food, shelter, and clothing for his family and in many instances fought others for theirs if his provisions were short.   At some point through his own ingenuity he was able to produce more food, clothing, and/or tools than was necessary for his family's survival.   That is he over produced.   At this point he has a surplus which he is able to trade with another family provider, who also over produced, for his over production.   The over production could have been more berries than his family could consume, mores skins than his family needed to keep warm, or more spears and arrows than necessary for hunting for his family needs.   One family's overproduction may have been another family's shortage.   By trading this over production each family had more of each commodity than they had before, either from their own over production or by trading their over production for that of another.   This over production and their trading has now provided each of them with a new "standard of living." This rise in the standard of living due to over production is the foundation of economics and the free market.

It wasn't until a third party joins the equation that money comes in to the picture. A situation develops when provider A who has overproduced skins would like to trade for arrows. Provider B who has over produced berries has no arrows but is interested in trading for skins. To complete the triangle, Provider C who over produces arrows is interested in berries. Now they could all get together and do a three way trade or they could develop a value media which they all agree would provide a value substitute for trading. This value substitute is money. To begin to establish the market, Provider A meets with Provider C and trades his skins for the arrows. The skins are now money for the time being because Provider C is now going to trade the skins he took in trade from Provider A to trade for berries with Provider B. For this latter trade, the skins are the value substitute.

Now a fourth party comes onto the scene. We'll call him the Warehouseman D. Provider A has so many surplus skins that he needs a save place to store them. He does not want to take the time or effort to make a save place of his own so he contracts with Warehouseman D to store his pelts for him. Warehouseman D agrees to do so for one (1) pelt a month. That's twelve (12) pelts a year just to store the surplus overproduction of Provider A. This means that Provider A needs to over produce twelve (12) pelts a year just to break even. If he over produces only eleven (11) beyond his own consumption his economic well being has decreased. Now with a little imagination and the help of a couple of thugs Warehouseman D can increase his business if only a few providers are robbed of their excess productivity. Not only Provider A will contract with Warehouseman D but everyone else who is worried about the thugs relieving him of his overproduction.

Very few people today have this simplistic view of the root of economics. It is the KISS (Keep It Simple Stupid) approach that should be taught in the schools today. Every citizen should have this view of economics ingrained in his every day thinking. It would contribute to his ability to sense the temperature rise in the water. It should be the under pinning of every economic theory espoused for it to have any credibility.. Too many theories start with capital as the root of economic activity. Capital is the effect not the cause of economic activity. Over production is the cause. Capital when created out of thin air such as happens today has a negative affect on the economic activity of a society, that is it ultimately begets the effects of under production.

The study of economic activity is like trying to study the leaves on all the trees in all the forests in the United States. What size are they, how many are on each tree, where will each leaf fall, how many will fall each day, which will have insect bites, which will be deceased, etc. There isn't enough computer power or enough sensors (nor will there ever be) to accurately study the leaves down to each individual leaf/branch in order to predict what will happen in the future to each leaf on a particular branch. Likewise, we can never know from an academic or political sense what will be the economic factors affecting each individual citizen in the United States. To think that such is possible is to think that we can control each individual's economic activity in an attempt to control his destiny. However, it would appear that this is the precise thinking of the master politician of the day.

This country was founded by statesmen. At its inception, the citizens of this country were represented in all levels of Government by statesman. Today we have only politicians as our representatives. A politician is a person who seeks public office for his own well being and his desire to be elevated to the stature of master (or King) over his constituents. He offers them a "free lunch" for their vote. A statesman is a person who seeks public office for the well being of his constituents and future generations and is humble and proud enough to serve as a public servant for the term. He promises them nothing but sincere efforts to act in their best interest and protect the environment for them to work for their own lunch. A politician, a non-producer, connives and conspires to rob people of their productivity. A statesman, a producer, stands alone, if necessary, to protect the inalienable rights of the individual and his property.

There can be no doubt that the market is the ultimate dictator of all human activity. Statesman protect the market and let it integrate any economic perturbations on its own while politicians invade the market and use economic perturbations as an excuse to inflict more control and more invasion. If the participants in the market are astute, they elect statesman to protect the market and the market improves human life; if they are not, they elect politicians who invade the market and human life degenerates. Today few people know or even care what mechanisms control their own lives. They measure their standard of living by how many toys they have at their disposal to play with not by their own economic well being. We are all suckers for the "free lunch."

There are four (4) basic instruments of the non-producer to usurp the production of the producer; taxes, interest, inflation, and insurance premiums. Each is sold under the guise of a free lunch and each has a direct negative affect on the economic well being of the producers.

Taxes are sold to us that they will only affect the rich and that we could also gain some benefit "free" from the tax. As time progresses, more and more people become "rich" and the tax burden grows and grows and grows. With respect to taxes there are two things to remember. One, no matter how poor you think you are there are a lot of people who think you are rich and should bear the brunt of all taxes. It is fundamental that there are fewer people who are rich than there are that are poor. Therefore, there are more people who think you are rich and should be taxed than you wish to be taxed because they are richer than you. Second, even if only the rich are taxed, the amount of the tax is the exact amount that they would have spent on consuming services from the poor and is therefore funds taken from the poor. The first law of taxation: "Only the poor suffer from taxes." The second law of taxation: "The number of people who will become poor is directly related to the severity of the tax."

Interest, it is believed provides us wealth without work. Since this is the motive of the non-producer, it is also used as the trap for the producer. Warehouseman D (from above) says that if you will let me store a great amount of your over production, I will not only not charge you a fee for the storage I will pay you a small amount for your guarantee that you will leave your over production with me so that I can lend some of to others in need charging them a fee also. Wow, protection and return. Double barrel benefit (free lunch)! Beware of Greeks bearing gifts! As we will see latter, inflation eats up what is stored and the scheme devised in modern times literally saps the life blood out of the economy.

Insurance gains its popularity based on the notions that "if I contribute a little amount of money periodically into a pool I will get back more later than I contributed" and/or "if I contribute a little amount of money periodically into a pool I will be protected against natural disasters." The first is based on greed and the second on fear. Each uses the free lunch as its carrot. Think of it this way. The insurance man is betting that you will live a long time, drive your car in a very responsible cautious manner, that your house will not burn, etc. while you on the other hand are betting that you will die early, wreck your car, and burn your house down. Lets get real! Nature is Nature and we are all part of it. Why do we allow such a con.

However, nothing can compare with the monster that appeared on the horizon in 1913. That monster was Nationalism. Our founding fathers had to spent a great deal of time in forming our State and Federal Constitutions to guarantee that Nationalism (a central all powerful government) would never exist in the United States. In 1913 three events took place which were to set the stage to gradually and deliberately provide a growth path for Nationalism in this country. Those three events were: the Federal Reserve Act, the 16th Amendment establishing an income tax, and the 17th Amendment which removed the States voice in Congress and made Congress a one body legislature with all seats filed under popular vote. That this is significant will become evident later.

The 16th Amendment was rendered nearly meaningless when the Supreme Court ruled that it conferred no new power of taxation, but simply prohibited the previous complete and plenary power of income taxation possessed by Congress from the beginning from being taken out of the category of an indirect excise tax which it inherently belonged. I do not think that the supporters of the 16th amendment expected this response from the Supreme Court. I believe they fully intended to tax the productivity of the producers without further ado.

The Federal Reserve Act being the most devious and diabolical scheme ever devised and perpetrated by the money changers to circumvent the usury laws in recorded time fared much better. Again, few people have any idea how the Federal Reserve Act has affected their lives. It was sold to, I believe, unsuspecting legislators by its supporters as an insurance (there's that word again) against bank failures. The

Federal Reserve is a group of private international banks which ultimately control the political and economic activities of the United States. Its creation has created massive debt both public and private. It is based on fractional reserve banking.

Most people are under the impression that when they deposit one thousand (1000) dollars into their savings account under fractional reserve banking at a Federal Reserve Bank (FRB), the bank deposits one hundred (100) dollars (for a ten (10) percent reserve requirement) with the Federal Deposit Insurance Corporation (FDIC). This leaves nine hundred (900) dollars to loan out for cars, refrigerators, TV's, etc. Assuming an average of twelve (12) percent interest, the bank could make a cool hundred and eight (108) dollars in interest ON that one thousand (1000) dollar savings deposit. Wrong!!! What really happens is that the bank deposits the entire one thousand (1000) dollars with the FDIC as the ten (10) percent reserve requirement and then loans out ten thousand (10,000) dollars (1000/.10) for cars, refrigerators, TV's, etc. Again assuming an average interest rate of twelve (12) percent, that puts one thousand two hundred (1,200) dollars into the banks coffers as pure profit. That is also one hundred and twenty (120) percent return on the original deposit annually. Of course we must subtract the paltry six (6) percent (60 dollars) paid the depositor for the use of his hard earned productivity. With today's five (5) percent reserve requirement, the percentage return jumps to two hundred and forty (240) percent.

By any stretch of the imagination two hundred and forty (240) percent interest is usury. But no one individual pays the two hundred and forty (240) percent so there can be no cause for action in the courts complaining of usury. However, it is a two hundred and forty (240) percent drain on the economy and therefore a two hundred and forty (240) percent drain on the producers. Stated another way; for every dollar deposited in a Federal Reserve Bank, the United States economy coughs up two dollars and forty cents ($2.40) to the owners of the Federal Reserve. That says that for every dollar of surplus productivity on deposit in a Federal Reserve Bank the economy loses that dollar plus another dollar and forty (40) cents and that doesn't include what the tax man has confiscated. Looking at this still another way, that says that the producers must OVER produce another two dollars and forty cents ($2.40) just to break even on the one (1) dollar on deposit in a Federal Reserve Bank. Any questions about why I don't deal with FRB's?

That's the private debt. The Federal public debt created by the Federal Reserve Act is another matter and is just as ingenious and devious as the method to create the private debt. Title 31 of the United States Code is called the Banking Statutes. It is where the Federal Reserve Act of 1913 is codified. It is where the mechanism is defined for monetizing the debt for interest bearing notes to be circulated to the public while the Federal Government pays interest to the Federal Reserve a private consortium of international banks. Basically, when the Federal Government desires to spend more than it takes in it simply prints Federal Reserve Notes on its own printing presses and by law pays interest on these notes as if the money was actually lent to the Treasury by the Federal Reserve. Its not enough that the Federal Reserve does not actually loan any money to the United States but the interest on this bogus money (monetized debt) is to be paid in gold! I wonder just how much of the Fort Knox gold actually belongs to the United States? It may also not be too surprising to discover that the only two presidents that I am aware of that issued non interest bearing notes on the United States Treasury never finished their term of office, Lincoln and Kennedy.

But, before we look at what I consider to be the most pernicious attack on liberty and inalienable rights we most look at a particular clause in the Constitution and its real significance is. (See also the article on Federal Jurisdiction appearing in the Appendix.)   Article I, Section 8, Clause 17 of the Federal Constitution grants Congress Exclusive Legislative Jurisdiction in territories ceded by the States and accepted by Congress.   From the beginning of the Union Federal Legislative Jurisdiction within a State Boundary was limited to the grant of power through this Clause of the Federal Constitution. In Fort Leavenworth R. R. v. Lowe, 114 U.S. 525 (1885) the United States Supreme Court set down for all time the particular processes upon which the Federal Government could acquire Legislative Jurisdiction within a State Boundary; Federal Acquisition (by purchase) with consent, State Cession and Federal Reservation.   The Legislature of a State may by an act or convention cede certain areas of its jurisdiction to the Federal Government with the latter's assent.   Not until both the cession by a State Legislature and the assent of the Federal Government does Legislative Jurisdiction transfer from the State to the General Federal Government. In 1943 the Supreme Court threw out a murder conviction which was committed on an Army base and tried in a Federal Court because the Supreme Court found that the Federal Government had not accepted the transfer of legislative jurisdiction from the State to the Federal Government.   See Adams v. United States, 319 U.S. 312 (1943). Federal Reservation relates to the reserving of certain jurisdictions upon a territory's acquisition of statehood to the Union.

On December the 15, 1954, the United States Attorney General formed an Interdepartmental Committee for the Study of Jurisdiction over Federal Areas within the States with full approval of the President of the United States and the Cabinet.

The Study was published in two volumes and Part II, which shall be referred to here, was transmitted to the President of the United States on June 28, 1957.

On page 45 of Part II of this report, the committee stated the following:

> No Federal legislative jurisdiction without consent, cession, or reservation. - It scarcely needs to be said that unless there has been a transfer of jurisdiction (1) pursuant to clause 17 by a Federal acquisition of land with State consent, or (2) by cession from the State to the Federal Government, or unless the Federal Government has reserved jurisdiction upon the admission of the State, **the Federal Government possesses no legislative jurisdiction over any area with in the State, such jurisdiction being for the exercise entirely by the State,** (emphasis added) subject to the free exercise by the Federal Government of the rights with respect to the use, protection, and disposition of its property.

(Remember this reference to property.)

This says that all the laws enacted by Congress apply to areas under Federal Government control but NOT to areas within the States control. Such areas under Federal Control include the District of Columbia, Possessions, National Parks, and Military Compounds (if the States Ceded jurisdiction). The power to tax is a legislative power. The Legislature needs jurisdiction over the area or activities within the area in order to tax the activities or property. The Legislative body most first have legislative jurisdiction before it can lay and collect taxes. The Constitution gives Congress the power to lay and collect taxes in the form of Duties, Imposts, and Excises (Article I, Section 8, Clause 1). Congress was also given the power to regulate commerce with foreign nations, and among the several States, and with Indian Tribes. Duties and impost are laid upon goods flowing to and from foreign nations. Excises, therefore, can be laid on privileges anywhere where Congress has legislative jurisdiction such as the District of Columbia, National Parks, Possessions, and Military Compounds, and on interstate commerce and commerce with Indian Tribes. (This issue is covered in much greater detail in the Appendix in a treatise on Federal Jurisdiction.)

This may be a surprise to most readers but I am convinced this limitation of power in the Federal Government was well known to those attempting to gain control of the United States and its people through Nationalism. You see, the creators of the Constitution had created a layer of insulation between the people and the Federal Government. The Federal Government could make all the laws and sign all the Treaties it wanted but they had no impact on the States or the people themselves. It was to serve as a unified voice for the States but in no way replace their scope of power.

Events occurring after 1913 would also have a great impact on the movement toward Nationalism. Just before the turn of the century, the United States became increasing more enthralled in international affairs. After 1913 the tempo of our involvement would accelerate at an alarming rate. In 1914 we would enter a World War. After the War we would get involved in a coalition of nations in an attempt to form a World Government through the League of Nations. Due primarily to the lack of support of the people of the United States, the League of Nations petered out. The people of the United States were not yet ready to be the "Roman Empire" of the 20th Century.

After the war the Federal Reserve turned on the money spigot. Prosperity through debt (a contradiction in terms) appeared to have the nation on a standard of living spiral that promised to go through the stratosphere. However, in 1929, this artificial economic bubble burst. People were scrambling again to cover the basic necessities of life, not too much different from the cave man.

In 1933, the Federal Government passed a joint resolution (not a law) that it was "against public policy to own gold" and requested the citizens of the States to turn their gold in at their local Federal Reserve Bank. Now remember, the Federal Reserve is a private institution with special arrangements with the Federal Government, but it is NOT the Federal Government! So we obediently turned over our material assets in specie to a private consortium on the mere suggestion of our government. This appears to have been a "trial balloon" to test just how gullible the U.S. citizens really were.

Article I, Section 10, Clause 1 of the Constitution states in part that "No State shall ...; make any Thing but gold and silver Coin a Tender in Payment of Debts;..." Now we start to see the significance of the 17th Amendment to eliminate State Representation in Congress. If one were to read the debates that arose over the issue of State representation at the first Constitutional Convention, one would know that the States house (the Senate) was no causal matter. It was a well thought out deliberate attempt to maintain an equal vote in Congress for the other Sovereign, the State (the chief sovereign, of course, being the people). Since the States were prohibited from making anything but gold or silver coin a tender in payment of debt, I think there is little doubt that a State represented Senate would not have gone along with such a Joint House Resolution. It took away the ability of the States to function in accordance with the Constitutional mandate.

One can only speculate as to whether or not the request for gold was a trial balloon to see just how gullible the people were at that juncture. Irregardless, in 1935, the grand daddy of all politicians, FDR (Franklin D. Roosevelt) sold the people of the United States what was and is the most pernicious attack on individual liberty and states rights ever devised by man. It was to be the ultimate weapon to penetrate that layer of insulation referred to above between the people and the Federal Government established by the Constitution. The mechanism was the Federal Insurance (there's that word again!) Contribution Act (FICA) also known as Social Security (sic). Remember, the Federal Reserve was sold as an insurance against fluctuating economies and what did it produce? Only the greatest depression this country had seen to date! So what did the FICA do that would allow it to achieve such an infamous reputation? Well, I'll tell you what it did!

It would be very surprising if the average reader at this point had an in depth grasp on the concept portrayed by the facts the courts see. To better understand the concept let's look at a contractual relationship between two human beings and draw an analogy to the relationship between the Federal Government and individual citizens.

Two persons, Tom and Harry desire to enter into a contractual agreement. Tom wants Harry to provide him and certain of his heirs with sums of money at regular intervals and in proportion to his productivity at a later date, say age 62. Now Harry needs some guarantees that he will have the money to pay Tom. Therefore, Harry requires Tom to abide by rules and regulations that he, Harry, will prescribe from time to time to require Tom to surrender certain percentages of his productivity to Harry. As a consequence and as an absolute point of fact, Tom becomes an indentured servant to Harry. Harry has a contractual right to review the affairs of Tom and Tom has a contractual obligation to allow Harry to review them. Moreover, Tom is contractually obligated to perform any and all duties Harry deems necessary to protect his, Tom's, welfare. Harry must protect his only source of money, Tom's productivity, and therefore must have the latitude to decide what is best for Tom. Now no moneys will have been paid to Tom by Harry during his productive life but Tom will be presumed to exercise his contractual right to receive them when they become available. As long as that presumption is valid the contract is in force.

Before this contractual arrangement, Tom had all of his rights and immunities guaranteed by the Constitution including his unlimited right to contract. He, Tom forfeits certain of his rights to labor and the fruits stemming therefrom when he exercises his unlimited right to contract with Harry. Harry becomes the Master and Tom becomes the Servant. There exists an absolute master/servant relationship.

Now reread the previous two paragraphs substituting yourself as Tom and the Federal Government as Harry. Remember, you the SSN holder, requested the contract. You forfeited your right to labor and the fruits stemming therefrom in exchange for perpetual care. You appear to history to have lacked the faith in yourself to rely on your own ability to exist in a Constitutionally protected environment and maintain your own life without the assistance of the other members of society. You will NOT find a law or a legal concept any where in the universe that requires you to request such a contract or Social Security number. We have done it to ourselves, pure and simple. Certainly by ignorance, but nonetheless self inflicted.

Ironically most religions forbid their followers to serve another master yet every holder of a Social Security card is serving a secular master. Also, ironically, some have even turned over their children to bondage for a mere five (5) dollar deduction on the form 1040.

The Federal Insurance Contribution Act of 1935 for

those that were to sign up (and nearly everyone has) created a Federal Legislative jurisdiction which theretofore was non existent.   In 1939 the Supreme Court ruled that the Contribution part was a tax and not the insurance premium it was sold as.   This decision, if you can believe it, got very little publicity.   However, be that as it may, every penny contributed to Social Security (sic) is a tax.   Furthermore for employees including the 'self employed' the tax is defined by statute as an "Income Tax."

The whole of the individual Federal Income Tax is based on one's participation in the FICA program (Social Security Contract).   It is this contract that creates the benefit by which the Federal Government can impose an indirect excise tax measured by the amount of wages attributable to that benefit.   To better understand this we need to review Section 3101 of the IRC (Internal Revenue Code) below.

The pertinent part of 3101 which is the FICA tax reads as follows:

In addition to other taxes, there is hereby imposed on the INCOME of every individual a TAX equal TO   the following percentages of WAGES (as defined in section 3121(a)) received by him with respect to employment (as defined in section 3121(b))-- (emphasis added)

This is to say that the voluntary allowance of the FICA deduction defines for all time that the total sum of all wages so used as a measure becomes taxable income.   Sometime after 1957 the Social Security card has a declaration that the Card is the property of the Social Security Administration which is an instrumentality of the Federal Government. Remember, the Federal Government has a right to the use, protection, and disposition of its property within a State. Everyone who possess a Social Security Card is presumed to have it on his person and is therefore subject to Federal Legislative Jurisdiction as a matter of fact.   Anyone who is enrolled in the Social Security (sic) program is now within the equity jurisdiction of the Federal Government in personam. So much for the level of insulation between us and the federal Government created by the forward thinking of our forefathers.

The Federal Government launched a very successful propaganda campaign to entice more participation into the Social Security (sic) program. The Second World War captured droves of participants. (Perhaps the real purpose for it.) People with no contract theretofore with the Federal Government were enticed into FICA participation by enlistment or other "services" to their country. By the 1950's the FICA program was nearly universally accepted by the general population of the United States. Those who did not chose to participate were obviously wacky. No one, absolutely no one was remotely aware of the newly acquired Federal Jurisdiction over individuals. All forms and documents were carefully worded to hide the concept and guard the secret. However, the Federal Courts were aware of it and rulings were starting to appear which reflect their knowledge that it existed. Unfortunately and probably intentionally, the written opinions were not stating what they, the courts, had judicially noticed, i.e.. the facts creating Federal legislative jurisdiction to control the affairs of an individual within a state boundary and thereby impose an excise tax on these affairs as they relate to benefits received.

Having been conditioned to believe that the only certainties of life are death and taxes and that we are, after all, subjects to obey every edict that our government wishes to proclaim, the differentiation between rights and privileges has become very blurred. We talk about the privilege of living in this country, the privilege of a good job, or nice home, etc. The concept of rights comes from the Declaration of Independence. We ALL have a right to Life, Liberty, and the pursuit of happiness and the right to protect them by whatever means necessary. The law in this country is whatever the Supreme Court says it is. We may from time to time disagree with their rulings but nevertheless their rulings are the law. With that in mind lets take a stroll through some of its rulings to see how it applies to rights, privileges, excises, and obligations. The first quote is from a case where a corporation is attempting to maintain that its books and records are not open to scrutiny by the Government. Here is what the Supreme Court had to say about that:

> We are of the opinion that there is a clear distinction in this particular area between an individual and a corporation, and that the latter has no right to refuse to submit its books and papers for an examination at the suite of the state. The individual may stand on his Constitutional rights as a citizen. He is entitled to carry on his private business in his own way. His power to contract is unlimited. He owes no duty to the state or to his neighbors to divulge his business, or to open his doors to an investigation, so far as it may tend to incriminate him. He owes no such duty to the state, since he receives nothing therefrom, beyond the protection of his life and property. His rights are such as existed by the law of the land long antecedent to the organization of the state, and can only be taken from him by due process of law, and in accordance with the [C]onstitution. Among his rights are a refusal to incriminate himself, and the immunity of himself and his property from arrest or seizure except under warrant of the law. He owes nothing to the public so long as he does not trespass upon their rights... An individual may lawfully refuse to answer incriminating questions unless

protected by an immunity statute... " <u>Hale v. Henkel</u>,
201 U.S. 43, 74

Notice the difference between a corporation and an
individual. A corporation is a creature of the state. That is to
say it was created by the state. Its rights and privileges are
only what the state grants it. Any right or privilege so granted
may also be withdrawn. Don't forget, we combined are the
state. A corporation is duty bound by any and all edicts from
the state. However, the individual has no such duty for he
owes nothing to the State because he derives nothing
therefrom. That of course changes under the Social Security
contract. He (the individual) now expects perpetual care and
must therefore be expected to pay his fair share. The Social
Security participant owes his fair share to the State because he
derives perpetual care therefrom.

Another authority on legal interpretations in this
country is the American Jurisprudence, Second Edition. It has
this to say about labor:

The right to labor and to its protection from
unlawful interference is a constitutional as well as a
common-law right. Every man has a natural right to
the fruits of his own industry. 48 <u>Am Jur 2d</u>, Section
2 Page 80.

Notice we have a NATURAL right to the fruits of our own
labor. Does that sound like anything you'd find in any IRS
bulletin?

Similarly, with respect to rights and taxation the
Supreme Court states succinctly:

A state may not impose a charge for the
enjoyment of a right granted by the Federal

Constitution. <u>Murdock v. Pennsylvania</u>, 319 U.S. 105, at 113 (1943)

Very early in our history the Supreme Court stated:

"The power to tax involves the power to destroy."
<u>McCullock v. Maryland</u>, 4 Wheat. 316; <u>Crandall v. Nevada</u>, 6 Wall 35, 46

Is there anyone who would suggest that we the people created a government whereupon we gave them the power to destroy us? But isn't that exactly what the income tax is doing to us or in many cases already has done to us? If we have a right to the fruits of our labor or industry do we then not have a right to keep those well earned fruits from the tax man? The answer is quite obviously YES, but don't forget that we have an unlimited power to contract. We contracted that very important right away by the Social Security (sic) contract.

Even Congress knows what they were doing with the income tax. The following is taken from the Congressional record:

The income tax is, therefore, not a tax on income as such. It is an excise tax with respect to certain activities and privileges which is measured by reference to the income which they produce. The income is not the subject of the tax: it is the basis for determining the tax. (4) <u>House Congressional Record</u>, March 27, 1943, page 2580.

WOW! I bet you didn't know that. The income tax is a tax on privileges. What is the privilege that average citizen has been granted in order to obligated to pay an income tax? Again and again it is the privilege of perpetual care.

There is a series of quotes from the Tennessee Supreme Court which bring the issue of right and privileges in as sharp a focus as possibly can be documented.

It cannot be denied that the Legislature can name any privilege a taxable privilege and tax it by means other than an income tax, but the <u>Legislature cannot name something to be a taxable privilege unless it is first a privilege.</u>

"A Privilege is whatever business, pursuit, occupation, or vocation, affecting the public, the Legislature chooses to declare and tax as such." <u>Corn et al. v. Fort</u>, 170 Tenn. 377, 385, 95 S.W. 2d 620, 623, 106 A.L.R. 647.

Privileges are special rights, belonging to the individual or class, and not to the mass; properly, an exemption from some general burden, obligation or duty; a right peculiar to some individual or body." <u>Lonas v. State,</u> 50 Tenn. 287, 307

Since the <u>right</u> to receive income or earnings is a right belonging to every person, this <u>right cannot be taxed</u> as a privilege.
<u>Jack Cole Co. v. MacFarland</u>, 337 S.W. 2d 453, 455-456 (Tenn. 1960) (Emphasis added)

For decades now we have fallen for the political rhetoric that the next tax act will be a tax on the rich. Two things. First, there is no tax on the rich. All taxes are really in fact taken from the mouths of the poor. The rich can absorb any tax that the state can levy upon them. That may ultimately be the definition of being rich. The amount of the tax is simply an amount turned over the state instead of being spent for items and services that can be supplied by the lower classes. As the lower classes have less and less money to spend the last class to suffer is the lowest class who now have no jobs because their services can no longer be afforded by the class above them.

Second, we tend to focus on the people who have more than we and fall for the "tax the rich" concept as a leveling mechanism. However, we fail to notice the people who look at us in this manner. We then become the rich who should be taxed. It doesn't take a genius to perceive that as you ascend the economic ladder there are fewer people on the next rung than there are on the one below it. Therefore, for any individual who votes for the state to tax the rich there are greater numbers below him on the economic ladder that see him as the target of that same tax which he thinks only applies to those above him. A sad corollary to this is that our natural instinct to covet seems to make us want to tear others down to our level rather than work a harder or smarter to reach their level. With this concept of leveling the ultimate conclusion is that our whole society will end up in the ditch. The incentive to prosper stand up to the tax man are waning.

There are two quotes that I have read in my adult life that stick in my head like a bad tune. The first quotation took place at the turn of this century when one of the bankers from the House of Rothschild stated at a private gathering that "if I can control the banks of a country I care not who makes their laws." The second was uttered by our own FDR (Franklin D. Roosevelt), when he stated that "nothing in politics happens by accident."

However, the Constitutional restriction on Federal

Legislative Jurisdiction created a problem to the bankers because the Federal Reserve Act did not provide them the control they sought. It took FDR's FICA scam to put the icing on the cake. The Federal Reserve created the mass of hungry folks with the Great Depression and the FDR Congress without the States interference (remember the 17th amendment) promised the hungry folks a free lunch for permission to institute individual Nationalism.

The "bottom line" is that it is the Social Security program (contract) that creates Federal Legislative jurisdiction over individual citizens residing in the states. There is absolutely no individual liberties to a Social Security card holder.

The Social Security program (contract) was deliberately enacted by the Roosevelt administration to give the Federal Government control over the citizens. (Nothing in politics happens by accident. Roosevelt)

The Social Security program (contract) binds us to the wishes and desires of the international cartel of power brokers (the IMF through the Federal Reserve) who control of the Federal Government. ("if I can control a country's banks, I care not who makes its laws." Rothschild)

The Social Security program (contract) enticed us all into bondage. We are no longer a free society. The Constitution is still there. It is still intact. However, most have contracted away certain protections and rights guaranteed by it. We are currently being set up to accept a replacement. Few appreciate what is happening, few will actively resist any replacement, and few will even care. We are being told that the European continent should be our model and we should all rush to imitate that society in order to form a "new world order for peace'." This is the very society that we escaped from and defeated two hundred (200) years ago for our freedom. Should we now throw away our Constitution and accept what we left 200 years ago?

The Social Security program (contract) allows the Federal Government to require our sons to leave the home land and fight on foreign soil. Without it the Federal Government is powerless to turn us into the "New Roman Empire."

It is the Social Security program (contract) that no court in the land will break or deem inoperative especially since no one knows enough to plead ignorance of the facts. (Readers with any legal understanding at all should dwell on the last sentence.)

The Social Security program (contract) strips us of our wealth and savings through the income tax and requires us all to go into debt to provide for ourselves and our families and prevents us from acquiring enough wealth to assist our offsprings with a financial beginning to shield them form the loan shark. This debt plays into the hands of the bankers by siphoning even more productivity from us through its diabolical reserve banking scam.

The "Grand Plan" has been implemented. The majority of the citizens are now reduced to the status of indentured servants to the Federal Government. They are citizens of the Federal Government. They are not "the People" referred to in the 9th and 10th Amendments to the Constitution.. They reside in the state as a matter of privilege not as a matter of right and taxed on the privilege.

The main questions remaining now are who will educate the public. Who will break the contract by forfeiting the benefit. That's all it takes. Who will force the Government to inform the public and how.

It takes more than an organization. Organizations exist to protect the status of the leaders. To expect an organization organized for a purpose to redirect itself to focus on another issue is tantamount to the expectation that the laws of nature will be repealed.

Don't expect the Republicans or Democrats to come to your aid. They're the puppets who are responsible for the erosion of our liberties. Why should they do an about face?

Don't expect the media to let the cat out of the bag and publicize how to break the chains of bondage. They're the ones who provided the propaganda blitz extolling the benefits of Federal bondage. Why should they now publish the truth.

Don't expect the large corporate employer to take up your cause. They're the ones who ultimately benefit from slave labor. Why should they help you escape.

It takes a massive underground movement to awaken the public. We must circulate the information through uncontrolled media. We must talk to our friends about it. We must begin to force our local and state representatives to protect our rights within the States. There is absolutely no law or regulation existing anywhere that requires one to be enrolled in the Social Security (sic) program. We must elect statesmen that will pass legislation prohibiting employers from implying that there is such a requirement.

Not till then do we have a shred of hope of regaining (not preserving) or liberties.

It is the hope of the author that the readers will at least begin to see the big picture and question the motives of their Federal representatives and to think about where their real freedoms went and how to get them back. To know where they went is to know where to go find them. History will show us as a dumb slave society so greedy for perpetual care that we forfeited the most advanced political system ever devised by man in favor of international serfdom and another trip back through the "dark ages" if we do not en mass insist that our indenture servant contracts with the Federal Government be declared null and void form this date forward.

Empires rise on the creative productivity of the masses operating in a free market. They fall by suppressing the free market largely through oppressive taxes. Each built its monuments and temples with slave labor. In the United States involuntary servitude or involuntary slave labor has been abolished. However, voluntary servitude or voluntary slave labor is legal. Throughout history Empires had maintained approximately fifty percent of their population as slaves. In the United States we maintain one hundred percent of the productive population in public servitude fifty percent of the time. See any big difference?

It is my view that the Social Security is our own juggernaut to freedom. As for our frog, the international banking cartel is the fuel for the fire, the Federal Reserve is the fire, FICA is the pan, and debt is the water. Do you think the frog is now cooked?

We are conditioned by our various institutions that "I" is the least significant letter in the alphabet. Society is the supreme value. "I", "me", or the individual are insignificant. This makes us easy marks for anyone wishing to strip our productivity from us in the name of some "worthy cause." It is interesting to note that the primary mechanisms used for the "stripping" are concepts which each start with the letter "I". They are Income taxation, Interest (at usury levels), Insurance and Inflation. It doesn't take a rocket scientist to calculate what these four mechanisms strip from the average producer. The Income tax alone, including , FICA (7.65%), the employers share of FICA (7.65%), the remaining portion of income tax (35-40%) plus state and local income taxes is well over 50 percent in the waning years of the 20th century. Such a bite forces the population to solicit loans for the basic necessities to produce, i.e.. automobiles for transportation to work, food storage devices for purchasing leverage, home mortgages, etc. The interest on these loans probably takes another 4 or 5 % on the average. Inflation takes an additional 10% and then we have all the insurance we are compelled to fund which probably consumes another 5 to 10%. All tolled, we are forfeiting in the neighborhood of 75 percent of our productivity to the modern scams of the non producers for their consumption without a fight. We get to keep 25% to cover the basic necessities of life.

My Father died in July, 1994. His father had purchased a twenty five hundred (2500) dollar Life Insurance policy on my father's life in 1929 when he loaned my father the funds to purchase a new 1929 Ford Coupe. The only new car my father ever purchased, by the way. The premium on this policy was fifty one (51) dollars and change a year. My father kept this policy active all these years.. The total amount paid into this policy was about thirty three hundred (3300) dollars. Remember, when he died the policy was worth only $2500. However, the issue of the eight hundred (800) dollars is not the real issue. The real issue is the relative worth of the number $2500 in 1929 versus its value in 1994. A good measure of average relative cost of commodities form time to time seems to be gas and cigarettes. In 1929 each sold for around ten (10) cents. Today each sells for over a dollar. That's a ten (10) fold increase in 65 years. Assuming a linear rate of inflation over these 65 years one can normalize the actual relative cost of this policy in today's dollars. This means that In today's dollars, the actual paid in was five (5) times the $3300 or sixteen thousand five hundred (16,500) dollars. My father paid $16,500 of his hard earned productivity to leave his heirs $2500. That is he paid six dollars and sixty cents ($6.60) for every dollar passed on. Think that's a good deal?

The income tax begets debt which begets interest payments which together begets fear of survival which begets various insurance "protection" scams all the while the money changers are cutting the value of the currency by pumping capital created out of thin air into the economy.

There are three basic necessities to human existence; food, clothing, and shelter. A quick glance at the institutions supporting these basics will give you a pretty good gauge to measure the overall well being of a society. In the United States, we import a large majority of our perishable food goods, a great majority of our clothing is manufactured offshore with slave labor in mainland China, and most of out homes are mortgaged through the productive years of their owners. At the turn of the century none of this was true!

There is no free market when it must endure usury rates of two hundred and forty (240) percent for every dollar on deposit in its banking system. There is no free market when the tax man takes 50 percent off of the top from the local economies and sends them to foreign lands to perpetuate the debt and the need to borrow money. There is no free market when politicians legislate insurance premiums. If there is no free market there are no basic freedoms and no access to inalienable rights. If there are no basic freedoms and no inalienable rights our country is under siege.

In this country we have three votes. We are only told about one, the one man one vote concept. The one that is used world wide to promote democracy. The one vote is counted against one hundred (100) million to determine the out come. The other two are far more powerful. The second vote we have is the vote on a grand jury. This vote is one vote in about 25 to determine the outcome. The grand jury is that forum which was given to us as an instrument to prevent the government from hauling whomever it wished into court to stand trial. This is a place where your vote counts. It sends a stringing message to your representative about what you think of their acts or appointments. The third, and most important vote comes on the petit jury. It is one vote against one vote. It stands alone. It is the one voice heard over the multitudes. It is our veto of oppression. One person can stop the government in its tracks. Not only do you have the power to determine the guilt or innocence of the defendant, you have the power to determine the validity of the law. It is our ultimate weapon. Ben Franklin said that the pen was mightier that the sword. You vote on the petit jury is mightier than the two combined. It can counteract the propaganda, the tax man, the gun grabbers, or any of the other offenses against the liberties of man.

There is currently a proposed "Informed Jury" amendment to the Federal Constitution which states that the judge must inform the jury that they have the right to judge the law as well as the facts in determining the guilt or innocence of the defendant. This proposed amendment currently (1994) lacks only two states to qualify for ratification.

Persons sitting on a jury have the right to ask questions the same as any defendant, plaintiff, or counsel. In a tax case, ask the defendant if his parents acquired his SSN for him. Ask him if he knows the SSN was evidence of a contract into bondage. Ask him if he understood that he was an indentured servant would he wish to maintain that status. Ask him if anyone ever informed him that he was an indentured servant to the Federal Government as evidence by his SSN. Wouldn't it be fraud by the Federal Government if any of this is true? Wouldn't he be innocent of any wrong doing since all tax crimes are based on willfulness? If we want our liberties back this is where the power is. This is how we break the chains of bondage. We remove them first from our fellow man and in so doing we remove them from ourselves.

Many lawyers are currently deriving a large measure of their income from preparing and filing taxes for individuals and applaud the complex nature of the tax laws as being good for business. Some are even enrolled agents with the IRS and have no interest in seeing liberties return to the population. However, as more and more people fail to enlist the services of the legal profession for their tax return preparation due to the lack of funds, the legal profession will need to pause and take stock of their real purpose in life. Any lawyer with an eye toward helping the general population restore their personal liberties could become wealthy by simply helping people drop out of Social Security. Who wouldn't be willing to pay a lawyer ten (10) percent of what would have been his tax bite for five years for the legal assistance to eliminate it.

The great majority of the economic health or standard of living of each individual comes from the health of the local economies. The federal income tax is money which is drained directly out of each and every local economy and never comes back. Granted, there are a few "bones" offered to create the facade of assistance but minuscule compared to what is taken. Given that the average take is fifty percent of each and every individual that says that the local economy exits on the remaining fifty percent. However, it is a little more obscure than that. This tax has a cascading affect on local economies. Let's suppose that there was no personal income tax and each natural person was willing to work for his current "take home" pay. Let's also suppose that the employers paid no FICA tax for the privilege of having FICA participants working for him. His labor cost just got cut by fifty percent. Let's again suppose that the employer's labor cost amount to fifty percent of his operating cost and that he will maintain his same level of profit. The price for his goods or services are now seventy five percent of what they previously were. However, we're not finished. Each employer buys from other employers which now also have reduced labor costs of fifty percent and are selling the products at seventy five percent of their original cost. Now with labor cost down fifty percent and material cost down twenty five percent the employer can now sell his wares at sixty two and a half percent of his original price. Remember, the employee has his original "take home" pay. That same money is now worth one point six (1.6) times what it was worth when he paid income tax. Now families can begin to envision the return of the economic security of one provider. The other spouse can now stay home and accept responsibility for the siblings. This is before we discuss any of the positive impacts which precipitate from abandoning many of the useless mandates currently laid upon the employers or the interest and insurance each of s falls for. The reader is invited to allow his or her own thinking and deductive reasoning to investigate further the benefits to the health and stability this creates to the local environments under this scenario. We should be able to envision the return of healthy family farms where the great majority of the food stuff is produced in this country. We should be able to envision the return of a healthy textile and clothing industry where the great majority of the clothing is produced in this country. We should be able to envision the erosion of private debt and the return of mortgage free housing.

Humans trap monkeys by cutting a hole in a coconut large enough for the monkey to fit his empty hand into but too small to allow him to extract his hand containing coconut or any other bait. By chaining the coconut shell to a tree or other large object the trap is set waiting for the monkey to take the free handout. The monkey will not let go of the bait even under the threat of capture. He will forfeit his liberty before he will forfeit the bait. Humans trap other humans by offering a "free lunch." By chaining the "free lunch" to bondage, the trap is set. The human will forfeit his liberty before he will forfeit the "free lunch."   We need only convince the producers that the "free lunch" costs them a great deal more in bondage than the same commodity produced by them in liberty would cost in the free market.

The foregoing is Copyrighted at the Common Law by the author. Permission is hereby   granted to publish any or all of the foregoing under the condition that all credit for the concepts and text contained herein is given to the author.

About the Author
-          I was born in 1935 (the year of the FDR Trap) on a farm in Southern New Jersey. My father worked the farm in the summer and drove an oil truck delivering home heating oils in the winter. My mother, besides being a housewife, taught sewing in grade school, studied art, music, baroque instruments, sculpturing and marble carving and spends most of her time practicing in each. I was the first of 2 children. My sister is a graduate musician and is a music director at an Episcopal Cathedral in Minnesota. She also sells real estate to make up for the confiscation of her over production by taxes, interest, and insurance.
-          I spent my spring, summer, and fall working on the farm from the time I was 6 or 7 years old until I graduated from high school.   I dreamed of building mechanical contrivances to take the place of manual harvesting. I later graduated from Lehigh University as a Mechanical Engineer but got side tracked by the computer industry; I worked for IBM designing computers and computer systems for 23 years. I left IBM in 1985 and started my own software development business developing turnkey applications for local municipal Governments. IBM became a bureaucratic microcosm of the Federal Government and currently shows no signs of or interest in reversing its course. I am standing up to the tax

man.

As for the future, I see little hope of the dream of our forefathers (liberty for the producers) surviving if the people in this country do not wake up (and jump out of the pan). There is much work to be done, people to be informed of the truth, crisp concepts and procedures to be taught. If we don't get this under way soon, there is little doubt in my mind that we are headed world wide for a return to the Dark Ages where a scant few will hold all of the gold and will meter out only enough to the remaining slaves to sustain their king like existence. The New Roman Empire will have risen and fallen. At that point the power elite will not care a twit if the people have any bread or circus.

The Appendix contains copy of the United States Constitution along with a copy of the Communist Manifesto. Which do you think better represents what we see in the United States today, these Ten Planks or the Bill of Rights? The answer breaks me out in a cold sweat.

4

The Report From Iron Mountain
The Blueprint for Absolute Tyranny
by Thomas McConnell
Economic and Monetary Consultant, FAMC

With mankind rushing headlong into world government through a process of seemingly chaotic and unrelated events, it is enlightening to find published, concrete evidence of a calculated "world order plan" which not only ties these events together, but also reveals the cold and methodical heart of the tyranny behind it. One such piece of evidence is the "Report from Iron Mountain - The Possibility and Desirability of Peace," a report commissioned in 1963 by John F. Kennedy through the Department of Defense to (1) *consider the problems involved in the "contingency of a transition to a general condition of peace, and (2) recommended procedures for dealing with this contingency."*

The study, which cumulated in the "Iron Mountain" report, was done over a two and a half year period in absolute secrecy by an anonymous group of fifteen American men representing a wide range of disciplines. The group included a lawyer, businessman, professional war planner, economist, psychiatrist, biochemist, astronomer, anthropologist, and sociologist, among others. Because of the shocking conclusions presented in this report, it was the intention of its authors that *the report never be made public.* In fact, the group chose not to justify its work to *"the lay reader, unexposed to the exigencies of higher political or military responsibility."* The report was purposely addressed to *"unnamed government administrators of high rank having considerable political sophistication."*

One of the group (identified only as John Doe), under pain of conscience, and at risk of professional jeopardy to himself, submitted the report to Dial Press for publication in 1967. It was quickly dismissed as a "hoax" by the government. However, one of its authors, John Kenneth Galbraith (a renowned historian and professor at Harvard) revealed his participation in it and has spoken quite openly about its authenticity. Indeed, the authenticity of the report becomes clearer with the passage of time and with world events unfolding in frightening congruency with the recommendations in the report. Today, the seemingly preposterous recommendations made in this report begin to take on a cold clarity as we relate them to the events of the past 30 years. The report appears to explain aspects of American policy which, by ordinary standards of common sense, have seemed completely incomprehensible.

The entire two and a half year study, as well as the conclusions and recommendations reached, was based on the axiom, a consensus shared unanimously by all 15 members of the group, that, *"War itself is the basic social system, within which other secondary modes of social organization conflict or conspire."* It is also important to note that the group concluded, finally, that, *"lasting peace . . . even if it could be achieved . . . would almost certainly not be in the interests of a stable society."*

The IM study was predicated on the belief that some kind of general peace might soon be negotiated, however, and that the transition to general world peace would lead to changes in the social structures of the nations of unparalleled and revolutionary magnitude. That scenario would require the construction of a feasible system of "substitutes" for those *functions of war* (below), which the IM study identified as "necessary to the stability and survival of human societies."

Economic: "War has provided . . . a dependable system for stabilizing and controlling national economies."

Political: "It (war) has ensured the subordination of the citizen to the state."

Sociological: "War has served . . . as an indispensable controller of dangerous social dissidence."

Ecological: "War has been the principal evolutionary device for maintaining a satisfactory ecological balance between gross . . . population and supplies."

Scientific: "War is the principal motivational force for the development of science."

Having identified the major functions of war, the IM group quickly surmised that complete disarmament would pose enormous problems. The end of war means the end of national sovereignty, or nationhood. This raises political problems: How to govern relations between nations after disarmament? What about the need for an external enemy as a unifying force? IM proposes institutions more or less like a World Court, or United Nations, but *vested with real authority - a well-armed international police force, operating under the authority of a supranational court* could serve that function. They even go on to suggest that "external threats" may have to be invented!

* * * * * * * *

*The authenticity of the report
becomes clearer with the
passage of time.*

* * * * * * * *

Sociological problems that crop up in the IM peace scenario include the postwar problem of controlling the socially alienated; this might require some variant of the Peace Corps of so-called Job Corps. But IM goes much further: "Another possible surrogate for the control of potential enemies of society is the reintroduction, in some form consistent with modern technology and political processes, of *slavery* . . . It is entirely possible that the development of a sophisticated form of slavery may be an absolute prerequisite for social control in a world at peace."

And even further: "The motivational function of war requires the existence of a genuinely menacing social enemy . . . It must justify the need for taking and paying a 'blood price' in wide areas of human concern . . . games theorists have suggested . . . the development of 'blood games' for the effective control of individual impulses." (The Romans threw Christians to the lions and relished gladiator "death games.") Proceeding with this grisly hypothesis, IM proposes that such a ritual might be "socialized" in the manner of the Spanish Inquisition and witch trials of other eras.

The "problems of peace" in the IM peace scenario continue. In a peaceful world, the mechanism of war as population control would disappear. IM suggests that the "universal requirement that procreation be limited to the products of artificial insemination would provide a fully adequate substitute control for population levels." They suggest an immediate step be birth control via water supplies or certain essential foods.

The establishment of world peace by, and under the authority of, a world government, serves the unequivocally noble purpose of "saving the species" (mankind). What we found troubling about their emphasis on "saving the species" is that the Iron Mountain planners deliberately discarded the "baggage" of cultural, religious, and moral values in their study of the feasibility and desirability of world peace. In their own words, *"Previous studies have taken the desirability of peace, the importance of human life, the superiority of democratic institutions, the greatest 'good' for the greatest number, the 'dignity' of the individual, the desirability of maximum health and longevity, and other such wishful premises as axiomatic values necessary for the justification of a study of peace issues. We have not found them so."*

This cold and calculated, military-style "objectivity" manifests itself in the series of recommendations that disregarded the individual worth and sanctity of a human life. In one bold statement the IM planners have declared that any value that speaks of compassion or "good" has no value when it comes to solving the problems of mankind. The truth is, we are conscience-driven, moral beings by design (creation) not by accident (evolution). In attempting to function otherwise, we ultimately bring great harm to ourselves and others. In dismissing "wishful premises," the authors have ultimately dismissed God and have therefore subjected themselves to satanic deception and eventual destruction. This ought to remind us of the dangers of ignoring morality when electing our leaders. (Psalm 16:4: *"The sorrows of those who have bartered for another god will be multiplied; I shall not pour out their libations of blood, nor shall I take their names upon my lips."*)

Simple words found in the Iron Mountain report, such as *society, peace, war, good,* and *bad* take on ominous meanings when understood in the context of the writings and actions of the NWO. However, if we understand that Satan is ultimately behind this, it should not surprise us that so-called "men of peace" conspire to plunder and destroy us through government. In Ephesians 6:12 we read: *:For our struggle is not against flesh and blood, but against the rulers, against the powers, against world forces of this darkness, against the spiritual forces of wickedness in the heavenly places."* We need to understand that these principalities, authorities, and world rulers are manifested here on earth through human agency - through godless men who speak of "peace" while planning destruction.

Good and *bad* are defined in the context of how they serve the purposes of evolution and population control. Actions that we would perceive as *good,* such as medical advances to save the sick or weak, are defined as short sighted and ultimately *bad.* Following this "logic," plagues, wars, natural and economic disasters and other devastating events are defined as necessary population control measures, and therefore, *good.* Now whose logic is this? In John 10:10 the Word tells us *"The thief does come except to steal, and kill, and to destroy. I have come that they may have life, and that they may have it more abundantly."* (NKJV)

Surrogates for War

Since war, as defined in the Iron Mountain document, is the glue that keeps a nation together politically, economically, sociologically, and ecologically, it follows by their logic that replacements for war would have to be found, so that "useful purposes" of war could be maintained.

In a chilling and methodical manner, the economic, political, sociological, and ecological surrogates for war are set out in the "recommendations" section of the report. All of them are now in different stages of fulfillment, but are fast approaching the point of completion. As you read the following recommendations by the Iron Mountain group, keep in mind that these recommendations were made no later than 1966.

Economic Surrogates: *(a) Massive social-welfare programs, directed towards "maximum improvement of general conditions of human life"; (b) giant open-ended space research program aimed at unreachable targets; (c) permanent, elaborate disarmament inspection systems.*

What we have seen:
* Starting in the '60s we saw the Great Society of

LBJ, a massive welfare program which has continued to grow, resulting in a sub-culture of economically dependent millions who, but for the fact that they have the privilege of exercising their vote, are virtually in bondage. Now, we have seen the Clintons' proposed health reform - 585,0000 pages of documentation for a plan formulated in secret for the complete, sweeping restructure of the entire health care industry in this nation - the greatest social welfare scheme in history.

     * During the Reagan administration we were introduced to the concept of "Star Wars" technology - a giant, high-tech space network which would be designed to provide a line of defense for the United States against hostile incoming missiles.

     * Nuclear test ban treaties; SALT 1, SALT 2; ongoing negotiations with North Korea; and now, the necessity to deal with the potential for terrorist acquisition of nuclear arsenals of the now collapsed USSR. Monitoring and regulating such activity is probably an insurmountable task.

     Political surrogates: *(a) an omnipresent, international police force; (b) an established and recognized extraterrestrial menace; and (c)) fictitious alternate enemies.*

     What we have seen:

     * A strengthening of the United Nations, concurrent with the downsizing strength of U.S. military; recent presidential executive orders that convert U.S. troops into U.N. police; U.N. troops deployed as "peacekeepers" all over the world; troop "maneuvers" on American soil; American troops deployed under U.N. command at various points around the globe.

     *Concurrent with build-up of U.N. forces, we are seeing discrediting of our fundamental American points of orientation, such as the U.S. Constitution, Declaration of

Independence, Bill of Rights, and law and order; undermining national sovereignty in favor of "global" order; collapse of communism fueling the drive for disarmament; drive for merger of super powers Russia and U.S. in implementing world government.

* * * * * * * *

Keep in mind that these
recommendations were made
no later than 1966.

* * * * * * * *

* Accelerated interest in UFOs; millions of dollars allocated to SETI programs to contact extraterrestrials; wide spread interest in books and articles that purportedly detail the kidnapping of human beings by "aliens"
* Waco massacre in Texas, 1993; orchestrated major-media coverage presented Branch Davidians as the enemy; unsubstantiated reports of drug use and child abuse were calculated to give the impression of a dangerous armed subculture - a public enemy possessing a threat of such magnitude as to require armed government intervention.

Sociological Surrogates: *(a) programs based on Peace Corps model; (b) modern, sophisticated form of slavery; (c) socialistically oriented "blood games" . . . "for purposes of social purification, state security, or other rationale"; (d) new religions or mythologies.*

What we have seen:

* President Clinton's proposal for "Americorps" work program for 20,000 youth of America, kicked off in September 1994.

* Millions ensnared by ignorance, unemployment, and addictions, wholly dependent on the social-welfare system

(Could these slaves of the social-welfare system conceivably be forced to earn their "benefits" through some form of "unarmed" service in an Iron Mountain scenario?)

*Waco massacre in Texas, 1993; Bureau of Alcohol, Tobacco & Firearms personnel utilized in a virtual bloodbath; government "mouthpiece" media justify the deaths of BATF personnel and the immolation of Davidians, including their women and children, as the necessary eradication of a dangerous arsenal of illegal weapons in the hands of a fanatical, misguided "cult."

* Proliferation of "New Age" religions; "Mother Earth" obsession; fascination with pagan, American Indian religions; Al Gore's book, *Earth in the Balance,* the politically correct handbook of zealous environmentalism.

Ecological Surrogates: *(a) massive global environmental pollution which would constitute a huge threat to the survival of the species; would have to be dealt with through social organization and political power (i.e., world government); (b) comprehensive program of applied eugenics ("better babies") with conception and embryonic growth taking place wholly under laboratory conditions. Procreation limited, government controlled.*

What we have seen:
* Ozone depletion hysteria; global warming panic; zealous, almost religious emphasis on environmental issues being promoted in our schools; ruthless power manipulation by EPA; staggering numbers of environmental laws; politically correct environmentalism now overriding individual human rights.

* Increasing emphasis on "limited world resources" and propaganda programs worldwide that emphasize the necessity for abortion as a population control method (Cairo Conference, September, 1994); fetal tissue research now

becoming "politically acceptable" as Clinton reverses the ban on funding which had existed under two previous administrations; condom distribution to children in our schools; breakup of traditional family; emphasis on homosexuality as a socially accepted "alternative lifestyle" which does not contribute to "problems" of population growth.

As the reader has perceived by now, the benign title of the Iron Mountain report is misleading; its conclusions and recommendations are, in fact, the blueprints for total global slavery under a world government system commonly referred to as the "New World Order." This push for world government through "peace" has been quietly building up over the last 90 years. It started with the League of Nations, was later resurrected as the United Nations, and is now centralizing into world government. By a carefully calculated process of redefining key words, the elite planners of the New World Order have convinced the world of their "good" intentions while building their power base, virtually unopposed.

It is apparent that the explosion of events and changes we are witnessing today shows an amazing correlation with *"The Report from Iron Mountain."* All of its recommendations have been, or are being, implemented in one fashion or another.

For those of you who still deny the existence of a conspiracy for a New World Order: *"Will these events overtake you as a thief in the night?"* In 1 Thessalonians 5:4-6 God's word states: *"Bout you, brethren, are not in darkness, so that this Day should overtake you as a thief. You are all sons of light and sons of the day. We are not of the night nor of darkness. Therefore let us not sleep, as others do, but let us watch and be sober."* (NKJV)

When men forsake God's law and create their own salvation they end up in torment. Isaiah 50:11 says, *"Behold, all you {enemies of your own selves} who attempt to kindle your own fire {and work out your own plan of salvation}, who surround and gird yourself with momentary sparks, darts and firebrands you set aflame! Walk by the light of your own self-made fire, and in sparks you will have kindled {for yourself if you will}! But this ye shall have from my hand: you shall lie down in grief and torment." (AMP)*

Don't let bold plans (sparks) of Godless men put you in fear. Remember that our Heavenly Father is infinitely greater than all the grand schemes of Satan or man. *"For I am persuaded that neither death nor life, nor angels nor principalities nor powers, nor things present nor things to come, nor height nor depth, nor any other created thing, shall be able to separate us from the love of God which is in Christ Jesus our Lord."* (Romans 8:38-39, NKJV)1

5

The Global Economy
Toward a One-World Government

"In a list of questions and answers that the publisher of *The Keys of This Blood*, Simon and Schuster, sent out as part of a press kit, Malachi Martin relates: *"Willing or not, ready or not, Pope John Paul II says that by the end of this decade, we will all live in the first one-world government that has existed in the society of nations . . . a government with absolute authority to decide the basic issues of human survival and human prosperity . . . our food supply . . . war, population control . . ."* And when the questioner asks, *"Suppose Gorbachev or John Paul or some of the really powerful Western leaders leave the scene in one way or another? Would the Pope's prediction of a one-world government still stand?"* Martin replies: *"John Paul says that the forces that have propelled these people to the top - himself included - are exactly the forces that are propelling us toward a one-world government. And he says that those forces won't change, just because our leaders come and go. One-world government is inevitable in his view."*

- Dennis Laurence Cuddy, Ph.D.
NOW IS THE DAWNING OF THE NEW AGE NEW WORLD ORDER

"As we stated in 'The Truth About NAFTA' (Monetary & Economic Review, July 1994), the true purpose for NAFTA was to create a supra-national government that merges the U.S., Canada, and Mexico. Further proof of this comes from

the new '1995 Federal Tax Deposits Requirements' bulletin that FAMC received from the IRS.
"It states that, 'PROVISIONS OF THE NORTH AMERICAN FREE TRADE AGREEMENT (NAFTA) LEGISLATION REQUIRE DEPOSITS TO BE MADE BY ELECTRONIC FUNDS TRANSFER (EFT).' The question here is what does NAFTA legislation concerning U.S. Federal Employment Tax Deposits have to do with free trade? The answer is nothing! It has to do with the merging of governments and their federal employment tax deposit money into a cashless system (EFT) One-world government is upon us.

- Monetary & Economic Review, January 1995.

Those who favored passage of the GATT Treaty were correct when they said American workers must compete in an economy that is dependent on global trade. To attempt to erect a protectionist wall around the U.S., in all probability, would trigger another Great Depression, just as passage of the protectionist Smoot-Hawley Tariff in 1930 helped deepen the suffering of the Great Depression of the 1930s. What supporters of GATT did not emphasize, is that GATT bears no resemblance to the Smoot-Hawley Tariff. Even if our politicians delayed implementation of the GATT Treaty that would not have sent a message to the rest of the world that America was considering the implementation of tariffs.

Our politicians sold us out. They told us that had they failed to immediately pass the GATT Treaty we would face serious consequences. They told the American people that failure to pass GATT would cause the stock market to crash overnight, triggering a rash of unthinkable events cumulating in another Great Depression. That was a lie. An outright lie.

Influential people like Henry Kissinger, Strobe Talbot, and Pat Buchanan say GATT is a movement toward world socialism. What most American citizens probably do not realize is that the GATT controversy was not something unique to the U.S. Around the world, politicians have been frantically attempting to pass similar legislation using the same scare tactics used in America to pass GATT. Not everyone is falling for the scam.

One week prior to the passage of GATT in the U.S., the citizens of Norway voted against becoming members of the European Union despite the efforts of the Norwegian Prime Minister, one of the world's leading campaigners for global socialism, to sell Norwegians on the benefits of joining the E.U. Some of the arguments used to try to sell the Norwegian people on the benefits of the E.U. sound hauntingly familiar to the tactics used by U.S. politicians to pass GATT.

For many years, the prime ministers of Scandinavia (Sweden, Norway, and Finland) had been working together to bring these three countries into the E.U. Because people wanted to vote on the issue, the prime ministers decided to start with Finland, then go to Sweden, and then to Norway. The prime ministers knew Finland was for it, Sweden was more or less sure and ready to join the E.U., but in Norway there was intense opposition against the European Community because Norwegians feel Europe is on the way to becoming a Union, a State. Norwegians, on the other hand, want to be free. Norway has everything it needs. It is not dependent on other countries. It is one of the richest countries in Europe. It has everything it needs in the way of water, forests, energy, oil, gas, and fish.

By waiting to bring Norway in last, the government felt Norwegians would be influenced by the votes of the neighboring countries. That is why the government had

Norway vote last. The prime ministers reasoned that first we will do Finland, then we will do Sweden, and after the Norwegians have seen the light, which in Norway is hard to see this time of year, they will vote for it, too.

Norway's Prime minister pressed very hard to get Norwegians to vote for entry into the E.U. As part of a massive sales campaign, the Prime Minister spread false information about trading deals with Europe and with the European Economical Cooperation, and GATT. Norwegians were told that failure to become part of the E.U. would jeopardize existing favorable tax and trade deals to a degree that many could be canceled, and that the Norwegian economy could be thrown into an economic depression. (Weren't we fed the same line in the U.S. in relation to GATT? Didn't our politicians tell us that if we don't do this, somebody else is going to do something and we've got to do it first to protect our trading interests?)

After Finland and Sweden voted to join the E.U., Norway's prime Minister, realizing most Norwegians still indicated they would not vote to join the Union, tried one final scare tactic by telling Norwegians that failure to join the E.U. would result in Norway being isolated from the rest of the trading world. Hearing this, many people became frightened and changed their votes. It was quite a campaign.

The "No" movement won in the end and the reactions were quite the opposite of what the "Yes" movement predicted. Interest rates are moving *down* in Norway not up (as they are in the U.S. and Europe). Norwegian money is increasing in value. No factory is going to move to another E.U. country as the "Yes" voters said would happen if Norway did not join the E.U. All the agreements on trade with Europe, the E.U. and GATT are the same now as before and have been reconfirmed by the countries of Europe. AND the Norwegians have even gotten new trade agreements with

Japan through GATT. Norway is not isolated at all. The contrary has happened.

The Norwegian people had the intelligence to stand up to their politicians. Maybe Norwegians have the intelligence because they live on a diet rich in fish instead of greasy Big Mac's (I hope you read this, Bill Clinton.)

Many people in the U.S. feel American politicians wanted to push the GATT Treaty through very quickly, so the American people would not have ample time to come back and demand a general vote on the entire issue. Unfortunately, I have to agree. It's merely another sign of the arrogance of some elected officials and the ignorance of the rest.

I believe we would have witnessed much of the same scenario in the U.S., had our politicians simply voted to delay passage of GATT. The truth is that we are being sold out to a World Trade Organization which will dictate trade. I foresee the WTO favoring developing countries in trade issues, and hindering developed countries like the U.S. It seems you just don't get much for $31 billion taxpayer dollars these days, unless you are a politician entitled to perks.

We must understand that what is taking place worldwide is a giant push to global socialism. On the record, in many of their publications, such as the Cairo Treaty and the Rio Treaty meetings on population and in one case on the environment, the politicians are making no bones about what it is they intend to do. It is just when it comes down to the public debate, and people rely on such publications like the Washington Pravda, AKA The Washington Post, to report things, it ain't going to happen.

In refusing to join the E.U., Norway is not isolated at all. The contrary is happening. In England, travel agencies go all out to offer tours to the European Free Country of Norway. Bookings of overseas tourists increased overnight. The government suddenly had money to support industry and offered the same food prices as in Europe. No wonder, the Norwegians saved tens of millions of Norwegian Crowns to belong to the E.U. Before the vote, one of the arguments the politicians used to attempt to sell Norwegians on the idea of joining the E.U. was that people would get lower food prices. *Weren't Americans told this same lie when the selling of GATT was underway in the U.S.? You bet!* Norwegians get lower food prices without belonging to the E.U.

The whole argument for bringing Norway into the E.U. was a plot, a conspiracy, which the leaders lost against the people of Norway. The European Commission continues to hold secret meetings in Brussels, and many politicians in Denmark had told already a long time before that they get no information on what is being decided and what the arguments for decision are. This is exactly what is going to happen in GATT at the World Trade Organization in Geneva. Everything is top secret in the inner sanctum of the E.U. The same thing will happen in the WTO.

While Bob Dole says GATT has nothing to do with sovereignty, others disagree. As far back as July 18, 1993, Henry Kissinger said in the *Los Angeles Times,* when talking about NAFTA, "What Congress will have before it is not a conventional trade agreement, but the architecture of a new international system. A first step to a new world order." Somebody should inform Bob Dole of this. On September 29, 1992, at a town hall meeting in Los Angeles, Winston Lord, whose a member of the Trilateral Commission and former president of the Council on Foreign Relations, delivered a speech called Changing Our Ways, America and The New World. In the speech he said, "To a certain extent we are going to have to yield some of our sovereignty, which will be controversial at home, under the North American Free Trade Agreement, NAFTA. Some Americans are going to be hurt as low wage jobs are being taken away." Lord later became

Assistant Secretary of State in the Clinton Administration. Strobe Talbot says world government is coming, in fact it is inevitable.

Perhaps the main reason most Americans do not understand what is happening in America is due to the often intentional dereliction of the press. We are never really told the truth about anything by the main stream media.

Former Presidential Assistant Lynn Nofsinger recently said the press wants absolute freedom for itself but it often sides with the actions of the government and the proposals of presidents that take freedoms away from individuals, from colleges and universities, from businesses and industries, and from the states. Nofsinger says the press are zealous defenders of their first Amendment Rights, but they ignore the Tenth Amendment which reserves to the states and to the people those powers not specifically granted to the federal government. How true it is.

We have a generation of journalists who are either too arrogant or too stupid to really investigate anything. Like Rush Limbaugh, many journalists simply cuddle up to those in power and bask in the limelight of acceptance, losing all objectivity and credibility in the process. But, they can always say, they got their information from pure sources.

The United States has been a part of the world economy from the time America was founded. The argument that we are becoming increasingly more dependent on this world economy, though, is flawed (except for our increased reliance on foreign money to fund our debt structure because our government and its people do not live within our means).

To compete effectively in today's economy, we must continue to deregulate, lower marginal income tax rates, and lessen the capital gains tax to allow U.S. business to hang onto the capital necessary to continue to invest in new technology. Naturally, this will cause a continuation of job dislocations in mature industries - layoffs, especially at the middle management and blue collar levels. Hopefully, though, there will continue to be creations of new jobs in the new industries based on new technologies.

America's trade problem lies in the failure of Americans to become educated in the new technologies. Middle aged people, accustomed to decades of post-war industries based on the old technology, suddenly find they have no work as these older industries move to other countries where production costs are lower.

To understand why education is crucial in today's new technology, I recommend you read Charles Murray's book, *The Bell Curve; Intelligence and Class Structure in American Life.* The thrust of the argument of *The Bell Curve* is that the persons who are the most educated are the ones who understand the new technologies, who have the ability to communicate in the new technology. They get the good jobs. They are very productive people, and they are sending their children to private schools where they meet other children of high intellect, intermarry and are producing a class Murray calls the "Cognitive Elite."

These cognitive elite are now rising above the blue collar workers who rode high in the post war U.S. when our manufacturing industry was relied on to help rebuild much of the world's industry destroyed during World War II. The industries of Germany and Japan were rebuilt with the latest technology and when this process was complete, American industry was suddenly disadvantaged, operating on the older technology that could not compete. For a while, our leaders, depended on anti-competitive regulatory means to compete but we were the losers until we began the long process of deregulation and implementation of the new technologies. Unfortunately, the people who did not continue to pursue more education to understand the new technologies were swept aside.

The remedy is to increase education in both quantity and quality. Today those who do not pursue higher education are doomed to lesser lives. They simply cannot function at today's higher technology levels. There is a distribution of intelligence throughout all races in the population. Unfortunately, without an education that provides people the capability to understand the new technology, a generation will be left behind. In addition there are those who simply do not possess the intellect necessary to grasp the new technologies, even if they have the education. These people will never achieve the best the job market has to offer. But these people are not doomed.

We have to dispel the myth that everyone has to go to college to make it in the new system. There are people who simply do not have the intellect necessary to go to college, unless we fully implement an outcome based educational system, which would be a tragic mistake. If you think it is tragic that we graduate high school students who can neither read nor write, imagine a generation of college students (our future leaders) who can't read or write either. Kiss America Goodbye!

We will always have need of carpenters, electricians, welders, brick layers, etc. These are good jobs, jobs that non-college trained people could excel at.

America is still the world's superpower. Or should I say America was the world's superpower before the passage of GATT. We have got to come together and demand the repeal of the GATT Treaty before our politicians sell America down the river.

6

The Tax Man Taketh

"A conservative is someone who tries to earn what he/she makes. A liberal is someone who wants to be given what a conservative has worked for."

"Upper income people are net tax payers. Lower income people are net tax receivers."

"The politics of envy is great for getting politicians elected but it is poison for the economy."

- Mike Haga

Back around 1911 or 1912, when the Congress was first debating whether or not they could get away with having an income tax in this country, somebody proposed that they set the maximum rate of tax at six and one-half per cent of income. They laughed it out of Congress, saying, "The American people will never pay that rate of tax." So they backed it off, saying they had to have something smaller, maybe five per cent or five and one-half percent in the beginning. Of course, we've seen what's happened since that time. Tax rates have escalated continuously. When you bundle together all the taxes the American people now have to pay, and I'm talking about Federal, State, Social Security, Sales, and Property taxes, each of us is now working until about the middle of July before all the taxes are paid. In essence taxes in total now take over fifty per cent of everything the average person makes.

To look at it another way, each of us working class men and women are working for Uncle Sam and our local governments until the middle of the year before we get to keep that first nickel of our own. It's shocking. Its tearing our country apart, and our elected officials know it.

That's why tax reform will be one of the top items on the agenda of the 104th Congress when it convenes in January, 1995. The new Republican Congress promises to enact sweeping tax legislation which will either cut or eliminate the capital gains tax and give most Americans a tax *rate* cut.

Liberals are furious. Hillary Clinton has come out spitting venom at the very notion of a tax rate cut for middle and upper class American citizens. Hillary feels tax rate cuts will undermine all entitlement programs and she paints a vivid picture of homeless women and children being thrown out into the streets as a result.

Hey, Hillary! Instead of lashing out at people who work for a living; ordinary people who are trying to make ends meet on whatever your liberal friends don't take away in taxes, why don't you get out and get a real job and pitch in the same way you think everyone else should? And when I say a real job, I'm not talking about sweetheart commodity trades that turn one thousand dollars into one hundred thousand dollars practically overnight. I'm not talking about pseudo high priced legal work for a few well placed friends; I'm talking about making it on your own. Oh Yea! I almost forgot! Please try to remember to pay your fair share of taxes in the future, something you conveniently forgot to do in the past.

Liberals tolerate capitalism but they cannot stand capitalists. They don't mind the economy growing, but the thought that investors are actually going to make some money really troubles them. They actually believe that if investors have to make money, then the least we can do is to apply onerous taxes on profits to take away gains.

Leon Panetta is living proof of the hatred liberals not only have for business, but for the men and women who own businesses. According to Panetta, anyone who is really successful has to be punished. Panetta has said on numerous occasions that if welfare benefits are cut back, corporate welfare should be cut back, too.

Most off us who work for a living are still trying to figure out what Panetta meant by the term corporate welfare. Even giving Panetta the benefit of the doubt - since he's never had to make a living in the private sector - his belief that corporations are on the public dole is nuts! The red tape and tax burdens faced by all businesses is staggering. If there were truly proper punishment for ignorant people in high places, Panetta's punishment would be that he has to start his own company and then live on what the Panetta's of the world don't take in taxes.

The liberals want to make sure that if the 104th Congress passes a middle class tax cut that the tax cut applies only to the middle class. Liberals also want us to remember what happened in the 1980s. Their assertion is that this nation cannot afford to reenact the "great give away of 1981." The liberal definition of a give away is simple; when people make money, if they are allowed to keep it, that is giving them something.

According to fools like Panetta, the "great give away of 1981" occurred when Congress and the Reagan Administration outbid each other on tax *rate* cuts. The result, according to Liberals? The tax burden on the rich was slashed nearly a third while the burden on the middle class fell slightly but then increased while the Federal Debt ballooned by three trillion dollars in twelve years.

First, the liberals assertion that the tax burden on

the rich was slashed by nearly a third is preposterous. *Tax rates* were cut a third *across the board*, for rich and poor alike. That is a fact. As a result of that reduction in tax *rates*, tax revenues increased, especially tax revenues from rich people. The underlying philosophy was that incentives matter. If you want to stimulate investment and savings you make the rewards for saving and investment greater. If you want to realize more tax revenues from capital gains you encourage people to turn over capital assets. If somebody sits on a capital asset, no one derives revenue from it.

The liberals always revert to the worn out argument that we should soak the rich to help the poor. Well, soaking the rich for thirty years hasn't helped the poor even though we've transferred three trillion dollars from the rich to the poor through entitlement programs.

Who are the rich anyway? According to most Americans, the filthy rich are those with adjusted gross incomes in excess of one million dollars. In 1981, the total income tax bill for the filthy rich was $4.9 billion dollars. By 1988, after what the liberals maintain was "the great give away," the total income tax bill for the filthy rich went from $4.9 billion dollars to $42.3 billion dollars. It multiplied by a factor of ten. On the other hand, if you look at people who made $15,000.00 or less, their total income tax bill in 1981 was $26 billion dollars; in 1988 it was $13 billion dollars. It was cut in half. That was the result of the income tax reforms of the Reagan years. The rich paid much more, even though their tax rates were much less and the poor paid much less.

But these figures reflect only the total amount of dollars paid in taxes. Let's take a look at the share of the income tax burden on the rich in the 1980s. First let's look at the filthy rich again; those with an adjusted gross income in excess of $1 million dollars. In 1981, the filthy rich paid 1.7 per cent of the total income tax bill. In 1988, the filthy rich paid 10.3 per cent of the total income tax bill. An increase again of almost a factor of ten. At the other end of the scale, those with incomes of under $15,000, their total share of the income tax bill in 1981 was 9 per cent. By 1988, that had fallen to 3.4 per cent. They were relieved of the income tax burden because it shifted to upper income people.

Regardless of what you hear from Tom Brokaw or Peter Jennings about the tax cuts of the 1980s, there were no tax cuts. There were, however, tax *rate* cuts and massive increases in tax dollar collections. Unfortunately those massive increases in tax dollar collections were exceeded by massive increases in spending *especially for entitlement programs.*

The liberals say that defense spending went up during the Reagan years. That is true. But non defense spending went up four times the amount of defense spending. You have to just keep setting the record straight on this because the liberals will continually try to distort the facts.

Liberals also like to lump Social Security Taxes together with income taxes. Statistically, that helps the liberals make their case for taxing the rich even more. Keep the two separate. The Social Security program is a totally separate program that inordinately benefits lower income Social Security taxpayers as compared to upper income Social Security taxpayers. It is true that Social Security taxes increased during the 1980s and that the Social Security tax burden increased more on lower income people because Social Security taxes are capped. But Social Security taxes should be capped. Upper income people do not utilize Social Security benefits to the extent lower income people do. Upper income people have the means to *plan* for their retirement income and thus are not dependent on Social Security during retirement.

One-third of the rich never utilize the Social Security Benefits they paid for. You will never hear a liberal talk about this fact. In essence, the rich simply add money to the Social Security system that the lower income people get to take advantage of. It's like having a rich uncle give you something for nothing.

I suppose the ignorant liberals will always berate the Reagan years. The bottom line is that when Reagan reduced tax rates, not only was economic growth stimulated, the Federal government took in more in taxes. We would have had a balanced budget in the 1980s if the Democratically controlled and very liberally oriented Congress had not kept increasing entitlement programs.

The Clinton Administration would do well to return to Reaganomics. Reagan ran the country more like one would run a business. It is a simple law of business that any time a retailer wants to increase revenues, the retailer has a sale. In marking down prices, sales increase and the retailer actually profits. Why can't liberals understand this? I believe it goes back to the quote I used at the beginning of this chapter; "A conservative is someone who tries to earn what he/she makes. A liberal is someone who wants to be given what a conservative has worked for."

According to the Laffer Curve, you can have a tax rate that is so low that increases in tax rates will still produce more revenues but beyond a certain point, you will have tax rates that are so high that increasing the rates even more reduces revenue. A great example of this is New York City. It is a place that is massively overtaxed. In addition to the federal income tax, there is a New York State income tax, a New York City income tax, very high property taxes, and very high sales taxes. In fact, the taxes were so onerous in New York that, as their budget deficit grew worse and they raised tax rates, a lot of businesses left New York; they went to Connecticut and New Jersey. The budgeteers in New York simply assumed they would always have the same level of economic activity and raised taxes figuring they would get more revenue. The fallacy of their assumption was that tax rates got so high people simply left, causing economic activity to decline. The economic dead heads in New York then raised taxes even higher to make up for declining revenues only to watch more businesses leave and revenues fall even further, bringing New York to the Brink of fiscal collapse. I wish the liberals would remember this.

In 1981, we raised $286 billion dollars in individual taxes, $182 billion dollars in Social Security taxes, $61 billion in corporate income taxes, and $69 billion in other taxes. Thanks to the "great give away," in 1989, we raised $446 billion dollars in individual income taxes, $359 billion dollars in Social Security taxes, $103 billion dollars in corporate income taxes, and $82 billion dollars in other taxes. These statistics prove that Reagan, in cutting tax *rates*, knew what to do to stimulate economic growth.

The deficit problem has never been about insufficient revenues. The problem is excessive spending. We will never balance the budget until we bring spending down to our tax capacity. To do this, our politicians have to cut entitlement spending. Since politicians, out of fear of not being re-elected, have never been able to stomach making hard decisions, I doubt we will ever cut entitlement spending until we reach the point where the entire economic structure comes crashing down around us. If present spending trends continue, can that point be far off? I don't think so.

Not only do we have to cut entitlement spending, we have to get our entire tax code back to the point of neutrality. The tax code should be as un-invasive as possible. It shouldn't discourage prudent economic activity. To liberals, the current tax code is nothing more than a cleverly constructed scheme to redistribute income. This is Robin Hood economics; taking from the rich and giving to the poor.

With the incoming Republicans proposing a tax

rate cut, the liberals are screaming about what they feel is a return to the failed policies of the Reagan years where the rich got richer and the poor suffered. Their arguments are not only unfounded but outright wrong. All one has to do to understand the liberal lie is to look at what happened to tax revenues during the Reagan years which I set out above.

Since the Democrats won't acknowledge the benefits of the Reagan tax rate cut, does it mean that Democrats are just plain stupid? It could. But I believe most Democrats do understand, they just work backwards from their bias and their objectives which is to do everything they can to help government grow and, also, to use the tax code at every opportunity to redistribute income from people who make more to people who make less. Most Democratic politicians are, in my opinion, Socialists. They do not want people, other than themselves, to succeed. To level the playing field, Democrats penalize people that save and reward people that spend. The Democrats love to take what people save and give it to people who spend.

Democrats spend too much time and resources worrying about the problems of the poor and not enough time worrying about the middle and upper income people. The future of our society lies with middle and upper income people. It doesn't mean you throw all the poor overboard or that you cut a huge hole in the safety net. It does mean, however, that you don't become obsessed with their problems and you don't ham string the achievers of society in order to subsidize the people who need help. This is exactly what the Democrats have been doing for thirty years. We've been fighting the war on poverty for thirty years and we are losing. And it has cost us trillions of dollars in the process.

If the incoming members of the 104th Congress do not make the hard and politically unpalatable choice of cutting all forms of entitlement spending then America will be in for some very tough sledding in the coming years. I don't have a good feeling about the incoming Congress doing what needs to be done, based strictly on what the Republicans failed to do in relation to passage of the GATT Treaty. The Republicans could have dug in their heels and held up passage of the GATT Treaty until next year, allowing full discussions of the treaty to be held, which is what I believe the silent majority wanted. By allowing GATT to pass, the Republicans added the Treaty's thirty-one billion dollar price tag to be added to the deficit they pledged to cut. The American people will remember this! The Republicans have already technically violated their Contract With America in which they promised to stop increasing deficit spending and I believe the Republicans will be held accountable by the American people.

If the Republicans do begin to cut entitlement spending, as they promised in their Contract With America, conservative politicians will be attacked as never before by the liberal press. We can look forward to more mud slinging, more allegations of how the hard hearted rich Republicans don't care about the less fortunate members of society. We will witness a nightly parade of tears on the national news that will make even the most diabolical soap opera look tame in comparison.

The simple fact of the matter is that this new group of elected officials has got to make the hard choices we have talked about for years. The incoming 104th Congress has to cut income tax *rates* to stimulate economic growth *and* cut back welfare benefits, Social Security benefits and so forth, if this Nation is to survive. Nineteen-ninety-five promises to be a watershed year of economic and political intrigue.

In addition to cutting income tax rates, the incoming Congress would do well by the American people to completely overhaul or abolish the Internal Revenue Service. The IRS is the most outmoded, probably unconstitutional and power hungry organization known to man. The petty bureaucrats running the Service are not only inept, but could be compared to pit bulls waiting to pounce on the weak and innocent among us.

Over the years, we the American people, have been continually duped by the IRS. Duped and threatened in order to get us to pay taxes that in many instances were not owed. The bureaucratic pit bulls know we will pay when we get a bill. It just costs too much time, energy, and money to fight the IRS. Even though we've been told how consumer friendly the IRS has become over the years, none of us really believes it.

Over the years, the IRS computers have had the nasty habit of kicking out tax notices left and right. In the 1980s, while Reagan was cutting tax rates, the IRS was operating under a different agenda. In the 1980s, one-third of the notices the IRS sent out were fraudulent - just to get people to pay taxes. And you know what? Fifty per cent off the people just paid the tax without challenging it.

When you get a notice from the IRS that you owe more tax, if you believe you are correct in not owing any money, you probably sit down and fire off a challenging response, often with proof attached, that you do not owe the money. A period of time will go by, and just when you think the matter is closed, you will get another notice. In anger, you sit down and respond to this notice, often attaching a copy of your first response. More time goes by and you forget the matter. Then one day, another notice comes in the mail. Anger turns to frustration as you respond to this notice, attaching copies of your first and second responses. This time, you even go so far as to write a separate letter explaining your complete frustration. A short time later another notice comes, only this notice sounds somewhat threatening, accusing you of failing to respond to prior notices properly sent to you. In each of the notices, you can't help but notice how the IRS keeps adding on additional interest and penalties to the amount the IRS alleges you owe.

By the time you get the sixth notice, the IRS is threatening to send the multi-jurisdictional task force to your front door to take everything you own. Meanwhile you are still writing letters and sending proof you do not owe anything.

When you get one off these notices, what you must file back with the IRS, is a Notice of Demand For Abatement of Tax. Under the IRS system, you assess the tax. The IRS does not really have any heavy handed authority to access more tax. They can only audit what you have assessed, and then agree or disagree with it, or try to assess what they feel you haven't reported, which is a different issue.

When you file this Notice of Demand for Abatement of Tax, it forces them to abate the tax. Now you are back at square one again. It stops that little computer in Ogden, Utah, or wherever, from running, compounding interest and penalties, spitting out notices, etc., which often cumulates in the IRS showing up at your doorstep, seizing your bank account and all the property you own, and all the wonderfully unconstitutional things this organization has been empowered to do by our politicians.

If you ever get into a disagreement with the IRS, only proceed when you are properly informed of the proper procedures. Dan Pilla is perhaps the most knowledgeable man in America on how to challenge the IRS. I recommend you read Pilla's book, *Forty-One Ways To Lick The IRS With A Postage Stamp*. This book deals with the ordinary conversations you can have with the IRS about all the little forms they send to you and how you can respond to them.

Another one of Pilla's books everyone should read is entitled *Tax Amnesty*. A lot of people don't know about this program. A lot of people have been paying tax upon penalty upon interest upon tax upon penalty upon interest, etc., for all sorts of back taxes when they know there is not a chance in a million they will catch up. But they don't know about the tax amnesty program because the IRS doesn't tell you about it.

What this means is that you can actually make application where all your past tax debt is forgiven. Then you start clean and you agree to keep yourself current for the next four or five years or so.

If you cannot find Pilla's books in bookstores, call 1-800-348-6829.

Of course, the easiest way to get the IRS out of your hair is to go on welfare. I suppose nothing gripes me more than knowing welfare recipients, people who get for free the money I have to work for, don't have to spend countless anguished hours pouring over IRS tax forms each March and April, worrying if they've dotted every I and crossed every T. Oh! no. While I slave over the most confusingly designed forms in the history of the world, people on welfare get to settle back and watch the Monday Night Movie, etc. It isn't fair.

Hillary and Leon, please remember this: you can lecture all you want about the heartlessness of the upper middle class, but I am willing to bet most Americans have more genuine compassion in their little toe than both of you combined have in totality. You continually talk about the duty of people to help the downtrodden, while you live in elegant rooms in luxurious buildings paid for by middle class Americans. Would you dirty your hands for anything other than money? Would you have your chauffeur pull over to give a homeless person a ride into town? I wouldn't bet the farm on it.

Wake up, America. Isn't it time we banded together to stop the insanity? We can do it. We can do it if we band together!   We must begin the long process of restoring America to greatness.   We must begin electing real Americans to positions of power.   We can only do this by selecting and electing the people we believe in.   We must not continue to be hamstrung by politicians chosen by the elite. As long as we just continue to vote one of the choices someone else gives us, we will never end the hidden corruption destroying our lives.

7

The Dumbing of America
GOALS 2000
Outcome Based Education

"If our children are our hope for America's future, why are we allowing our public school systems to de-educate our children? None of us can deny this is happening. Most children graduating from public schools in America today cannot read, write, add, or subtract. Most children cannot name all fifty states in the United States. Most children cannot, when looking at a map of the United States, point to the state in which they live, nor even hope to find their city."

"Educators in our public school systems no longer teach history or logic. Is it any wonder American public schools graduate children with no appreciation for their country or themselves? Is it any wonder our children grow up feeling alienated and alone and full of rage over their inability to achieve success? Sadly, these children become adults who turn to violence rather than to reason; crime rather than work."

"In 1989, President George Bush worked with then Arkansas Governor Bill Clinton to draft the preliminary legislation necessary for the federal government to take over our educational system in the name of "national education reform." This legislation was enacted by Congress in the HR6 Bill, better known as "GOALS 2000", which allows our federal government to create national educational standards designed to de-educate all American children."

"The 104th Congress must completely scrap the GOALS 2000

legislation. The thing that frightens me the most about the Goals 20000 legislation is the "Opportunity To Learn Standards" which <u>gives the federal government total power to decide how all kids are to be educated</u>. Parents of all children must come together to stop the madness."

The majority of Americans have never agreed with the Supreme Court's decision to ban prayer in the classroom, yet our educators ban prayer. The majority of parents do not want their children to attend sex education classes but these classes are taught. If parents object to sex education, they can opt their children out of sex education classes. If parents can opt children out of sex education, why can't the Supreme Court uphold prayer in the classroom but allow parents not wishing their children to participate to opt the children out of prayer?

- Mike Haga

I don't think anyone with children in today's public school system would *strongly* disagree when I say *the current system is defunct*. We graduate children who can neither read nor write and expect them to make it in the business world. Naturally, they can't, so they turn to a life of crime or get on the welfare rolls, becoming dependent, cynical, bitter, envious, often violently angry people in the process.

Is it my belief that children who fail have to shoulder some of the responsibility for their perceived misfortunes. Success requires a certain amount of ambition, determination, and education. Unfortunately, children who succeed today do so in spite of an educational system designed to punish the achievers.

How have we ever come to the place where

teachers do not teach and cannot discipline? It is a known fact discipline is the very cornerstone of learning. How have we reached the point where students can terrorize, with impunity, not only teachers but other students trying to make something of their lives? How? Through the same bleeding heart approach we take toward those on welfare and those in prison. We look upon those who fail as victims. But then again, most liberals view everyone as being a victim of something at sometime or other. *The failed policies of liberalism have created a generation of "victims" who are in turn victimizing all Americans.*

Thanks to legislation passed by corrupt politicians and legitimized by corrupt judges, our public school systems no longer allow teachers to teach. Teachers in today's public school systems are nothing more than glorified baby sitters simply trying to maintain order in the classroom in a non-threatening way, often being threatened in the process. *Our schools have become day care centers for hopeless children of dysfunctional families.* Parents no longer care what their children are taught, as long as the children are out of sight and mind most of the day. With free rein to indoctrinate children in the lessons of superficial social values of constant change, children begin to accept as truth the belief everything is situational; that there is no right or wrong, black or white, only shades of gray. By fostering situational ethics and promoting social skills over historical precedent and rock solid logic, our school administrators, our courts, and our federal government are creating a tragedy that could destroy America as all Americans stand on the threshold of a new millennium where even basic educational skills are no longer adequate.

A perfect example of the failed disciplinary policies off our public school systems recently occurred in Denver, Colorado, when Ruben Perez, Vice Principal of the Horace Mann Middle School, attempted a mass suspension of

97 unruly students when the school's principal was on vacation. Word of Perez' plan was leaked to the media. The story received nationwide attention. Perez was hailed a hero by many who felt discipline was totally lacking at Horace Mann. Denver became a city divided over the issue. The liberals felt Perez was in violation of the students' rights of due process. The conservatives felt the kids should be thrown out permanently. In the end the school board quashed the suspensions and Perez was counseled for not following procedure (i.e., trying to suspend students without his Principal's approval). Of the 97 students, it is reported most are now totally arrogant and completely disruptive, knowing they can get away with anything.

Denver is not an isolated example. Discipline is totally lacking in all public schools. Can we stop this insanity and return education to the classroom? Anything is possible. To begin taking back America, we have to get the federal government out of education, and dismantle school boards and school administration systems in every city and state. Until we can dismantle the administration systems of all public school systems, Charter Schools may be a wise alternative for all children. It is the failed policies of the U.S. Department of Education coupled with the corrupt hierarchies of all school administration systems that has brought us to this sad juncture.

Just as parents are beginning to wake up, to come together to figure out how take back our public school systems, our Congress quietly passed legislation designed to completely turn our public education system over to the federal government, perhaps in an attempt to prevent parents from taking back control of our defunct educational system. Recently, members of the 103rd Congress saw fit to pass onerous federal legislation in the form of the HR6 Bill, called "GOALS 2000." Under the guise of creating national educational standards, our politicians have created a perfect vehicle for the continued de-education of our children; our future.

Wake up, America! Wake up before it is too late! Concerned citizens must band together to overturn HR6, and then concentrate on finding ways to get the corrupt politicians and judges out of education. To do less will prove a travesty that will ensure the future destruction of American children and America.

We have allowed the federal government to take prayer out of the classroom. We have allowed federal politicians to pass laws prohibiting the recitation of the Pledge of Allegiance in school. We have allowed our federal government to make it illegal for teachers to teach and to maintain discipline in the classroom. We have allowed local school boards to create top heavy bureaucracy's filled with arrogant individuals whose sole purpose is to create layer upon layer of insane regulation having nothing to do with enhancing the quality of education. Today, we are witnessing the results. Children do not learn anything anymore. Teachers are held hostage by their students. If a child is disciplined, the teacher is suspended while the over-bloated bureaucrats decide whether the teacher violated the student's rights of due process. If HR6 is not repealed the federal government will control all aspects of public education. I cannot imagine a more ominous threat to this great nation.

We can start taking back our America by flooding the halls of Congress with letters, by calling the Congressional switchboard, demanding HR6 be repealed. Let this new crop of politicians know that in 1996 there will be another massive house cleaning if HR6 is not repealed well in advance of the elections.

To help you understand the magnitude of the deception of HR6, I have included an article on HR6 written by Marilyn Brannan, Associate Editor of Monetary &

Economic Review, a monthly publication of FAMC, Inc., a
conservative Christian think-tank located in Fort Collins,
Colorado.

The Dumbing Factor:
Goals 2000
by Marilyn Brannan, Associate Editor, FAMC

Another giant step in the implementation of the
New World Order occurred with the passage of "GOALS
2000," the education bill ratified in Congress recently. This
bill will spell out what 40 million children must be taught and
tested on in public schools, thereby serving as a powerful
engine for molding public opinion to accept America's entry
into the New World Order.

The following quotes from a story that appeared in
The Washington Post give some idea of the impact this
legislation will have on our educational system, and as a
consequence, on the very basis of our society.

*"Education Secretary Richard Riley calls the
legislation the 'North Star' because it would guide so
many other classroom changes, from new text books
and exams to the retraining of teachers. Mike Cohen,
senior adviser to Riley, says, 'It's a big deal, because
it changes the federal government's role."

*"For this Congress and this administration, this is the
single most important piece of educational legislation.
No question about it." (Gordon Ambach, Executive
Director of the Council of Chief State School Offices.)

*"Thomas Sobol, New York State's education
commissioner, said the time for a national consensus
on what every child needs to learn has come. 'The
standard setting process simply can't be left to the
discretion of thousands of local boards of education,'

he said. "We've outlived that time. The national interest is at stake.'"

The effort that culminated in the GOALS 2000 bill began with an extraordinary 1989 education summit in Charlottesville, Virginia, wherein then President Bush and the nation's governors, led by Arkansas' Bill Clinton, agreed to create a national baseline of knowledge setting forth what students should know in math, science, history, geography, and other subjects (in preparation for world government)?

Local Control Disappearing

Since Colonial times, the American educational system has been characterized by the fact that most major decisions are local. That is going to change now, with the intrusion of the federal government into the educational equation nationwide.

Reaction to the GOALS 2000 plan ranges from unbridled optimism to caution. Those who are optimistic have trained their rose-colored spectacles on the hope for greater funding and "academic standards" for every child. Others, at the opposite end of the spectrum, fear the program will amount to a "national curriculum," something that has never been perceived as practical - or desirable - in such a diverse nation.

Why Don't We Teach the Kids to Read?

A question that has puzzled Americans for years now is, "Why don't we teach the kids to read?" Interestingly, Samuel Blumenfeld, in his *Education Letter*, says that John Dewey, "the father of Modern Education," identified high literacy as the culprit in traditional education, the sustaining force behind individualism.

Individualism was anathema to Dewey, just as it is to his followers, our so-called "leaders" in education today. Why? *Individualism opposes Socialism.* It is through

Socialism that the educational establishment plans to "blend" (coerce?) our citizenry into a New World Order. Dewey was convinced that Socialism was the wave of the future and that individualism was passé. However, individualism would not fade as long as it was sustained by the education American children were getting in their schools. Dewey realized that radical reform would not be accepted by the American people. Therefore, he recommended, "Change must come gradually. To force it unduly would compromise its final success by favoring a violent reaction."

Social Change to Move Us Toward Socialism

Dewey's whole program was *social change*, not academic excellence. He was committed to bringing about Socialism in America, and the schools were merely the vehicle that he, and other radical social planners envisioned for accomplishing that goal.

Question: How do the Socialist planners program a nation for Socialism? *Answer*: They "dumb down" the electorate, beginning with the children who will be the electorate in the not-too-distant-future. They de-emphasize the virtues of literacy and downplay the importance of critical thinking. Any sense of responsibility for ordered, reasoned thought on the part of the individual will naturally begin to disappear. At some point, the electorate will no longer be equipped to engage in an educated, intelligent process for selecting its leaders, no longer able to weigh alternatives for political or social action in the light of past history.

Literacy Breakdown is No Accident

Dewey's program advocated that literacy skills be drastically de-emphasized in favor of social skills. The phonetic method for teaching reading was dumped in favor of the "sight" method whereby students never learn to sound out the words phonetically. Interestingly, the sight method of teaching reading was devised in the 1830s by Thomas Gallaudet, a famous *teacher of the deaf and dumb*. Obviously, deaf students would have no concept of phonetics, or sound symbols, and the sight method was introduced specifically *for the benefit of these handicapped students!* Amazingly, the nation's leading educational reformers managed to successfully foist the system on our school systems.

In response to the resulting wave of poor and non-readers, Rudolph Flesch's book, *"Why Johnny Can't Read"* appeared on the scene. The educators were furious with Flesch. In his book, he had made them appear stupid and incompetent. Later, in 1970, Karl Shapiro, the eminent poet-professor who had taught creative writing for over 20 years, told his audience: "What is really distressing is that this generation cannot and does not read. I am speaking of university students in what are supposed to be our best universities. Their illiteracy is staggering . . . We are experiencing a literacy breakdown which is unlike anything I know in the history of letters!"

This literacy breakdown is no accident. It is not the result of ignorance or incompetence. It has been deliberately fostered by our progressive-humanist-behaviorist educators whose social agenda is far more important to them than anything connected with academic excellence.

* * * * * *

Those who think they are
exempt from the goals set
forth in this bill because their
children are not attending
the public schools are
badly mistaken

* * * * * *

Tightening the Controls on Homeschoolers

Because the Homeschoolers of this nation comprise one of the last bastions of educational freedom in America, attempts were made within the framework of the HR6 Bill to tighten the clamps on parents that choose to educate their children in the privacy of their own homes. There was such an outcry from people all across the nation that the section of the bill that would have put stringent limitations on Homeschoolers was struck from the bill at the last minute. Most pro-Homeschoolers saw this as a major victory, but the proponents of "GOALS 2000" continued to quietly move forward in implementing their "values based" curriculum in many public school districts.

Further, those who think they are exempt from the goals set forth in this bill because their children are not attending the public schools are badly mistaken; the sweeping restructure of the education system through GOALS 2000 has engaged even the Department of Labor, and may ultimately require a "Certificate of Initial Mastery" to enter college or the work force. Community service on the part of children could be just one of the prerequisites to obtaining such a certification, and could play a major role in the development of a national workforce.

Outcome Based Education a
Powerful Engine for Change

The tool being used to force school districts to accept federal educational standards through the curriculum is, of course, dollars. If school districts don't comply by implementing programs such as Outcome Based Education (OBE), which concentrates on teaching values rather than content, there is the threat of federal funds being withheld - an issue most school superintendents are not willing to confront.

Aside from the fact that funding is the "Half

Nelson" tactic being used to foist OBE on schools all across
the nation, there is the distressing issue of "whose values" are
being indoctrinated into our youth. These are not necessarily
the traditional, conservative, "family values" that many of us
believe to be the underlying strength of any great nation.
Rather, these values are determined solely at the discretion of
the curriculum planners. If these planners should decide, for
example, that a particular set of mores (i.e., Christian, Judaic,
etc.) is for any reason "unacceptable," then the desired
"outcome" of a particular unit of learning might be "tolerance"
and "acceptance" of *all* moral or religious views and practices.

To insure their success in inculcating said "values,"
educrats simply convey the message that, for the student,
success and achievement within the educational system will be
dependent upon assimilation of the values espoused therein.
The potential for calculated social change resident in such a
system is horrifyingly obvious.

The Less We Know,
The Less We Will Resist

The reaction from many parents when told about
the plans to restructure the educational system is often, "Why
the uproar? I don't see this happening in my school." In all
too many cases, this is probably true - we *don't* see it
happening. The New World Order planners know that the
American people will not accept radical reform, and if
progress in implementing their agenda is gradual, there is not
likely to be a lot of resistance.

* * * * * *

These are not necessarily the
traditional, conservative,
"family values" that many
of us believe to be the

*underlying strength of any
great nation. Rather, these
values are determined solely
at the discretion of the
curriculum planners.*

* * * * * *

However, some are alert to the threat, and these are the parents that are returning to home schooling in an attempt to "save the children." Don McAlvaney, a diligent analyst of the New World Order, recently commented that he believes the children being home schooled today may be not only the torchbearers of our Christian values, but may be the single largest group of people standing in the way of the New World Order government. If this is the case, the enemy will work overtime to destroy Americans' freedom to home school their children.

Now an additional alarm has been sounded. Bill Clinton's choice of Stephen G. Breyer for the Supreme Court has dangerous implications for freedom of religion in private education. Michael P. Farris, President of Home School Legal Defense Association and an experienced religious freedom litigator, has published an analysis of Breyer's stance on religious freedom in education, based on Judge Breyer's opinion rendered in *New Life Baptist Academy V. East Longmeadow School District* in 1989. Following are the essentials of Judge Breyer's philosophy on this subject, clearly manifested in his opinion in the *New Life* case:

* * * * * * * *

Children being home
schooled today may be

the torchbearers of our
Christian values.

* * * * * * * *

*Breyer endorses the concept that the government has the power to "approve" private religious education, employing standards which are entirely discretionary.
*Breyer clearly implies that it is constitutional for states to totally ban home schooling.
*Breyer holds inconsistent views of the two First Amendment clauses on religion.   When religious schools want to be free from regulation, he says such schools are "secular."   But when they want to participate in programs of government funding, he says such schools are "religious."
*Breyer believes that public school authorities have the power to decide whether private school teachers and home school teachers are "properly qualified."
A person with these views is extremely dangerous sitting on our highest court. Not only could it sound the death knell for home schooling in this nation, but it could destroy the freedom of private schools to control their curriculum, their teaching methods, their standards.1
I want to thank Marilyn for allowing the use of her well researched, well reasoned analysis of the GOALS 20000 legislation to be included in this book. For those wishing more information about FAMC,   Monetary & Economic Review, and other well researched articles by other members of FAMC, their address and phone numbers can be found on the last page of Chapter 17.
While it is imperative we make our politicians scrap the GOALS 2000 legislation, until that goal is accomplished, we must also be vigilant in prohibiting

implementation of all of the new educational standards; especially the new history standards.

Most parents probably aren't even aware that proposed new history standards have been drafted or that many schools have already begun adopting these proposed new history standards, or that a fundamentally flawed history textbook for high school students, patterned on these new standards, is already being used to teach American history to our children.

These new history standards are a watershed of multiculturalism and political correctness that every parent, every American, should demand be thrown out of all classrooms. By the time you finish this chapter, you will understand why the new history standards are nothing more than politically correct revisionism of American History in a manner that should frighten every American.

Turn back to Chapter Two. Re-read the provisions relating to education. Isn't it eerie that Non-profit organizations and governmental entities fund research grants to people of Socialist mindsets willing to write politically correct works? Is there a conspiracy? You be the judge. Don't let your children be the victims?

Like myself, Lynn Cheney, former head of The National Endowment For The Humanities, and now a Fellow of The American Enterprise Institute in Washington, D.C., takes strong exception to the proposed new history standards. Under GOALS 2000, if parents or teachers fight adopted curriculum, like the new history standards, funding can be cut off, schools shut down.

When the new history standards were first proposed, it sounded innocuous enough. There are standards for teaching different subjects in the curriculum in almost every other industrialized nation. The French have standards. The Japanese have standards. The Koreans have standards.

The Germans have standards. The result for those countries has been a good one. A parent who wakes up one morning in Southern France will know that his/her child is being taught the same thing as a student in the Northern part of France, and being held to the same high level of expectations.

In the United States, we do not have this. It has led to some unfortunate situations. A few years ago a doctor in West Virginian made the very astute observation that all states across the nation were reporting their students as being above average. Of course, not everybody can be above average. Because of the way we test; there is no common measure, it was possible for every state to report students being above average. The Lake Woebegone effect.

The idea of standards was to provide a common measure. To come up with a measurement of what kids should know and be able to do at different age levels, at different grades, so that parents would know what to expect and we could give students some idea of what excellence consists of. While this type measurement may work in some fields, science for instance, it certainly has not worked in history. The reasons are many, but the main reason is the sorry state of history in higher education - that I believe was planned. What you see in the national standards for American history is a mess. No where is there mention of George Washington's Presidency, but there is a lot of emphasis on the founding of The National Organization for Women. There is no mention of a whole range of people who have been very important figures in American history, people like Edison, The Wright Brothers, Alexander Graham Bell, but there is a lot of attention paid to The Sierra Club.

What you see in these standards is the reflection of the state of history in higher education. I have become convinced the new history standards are dangerous. The people writing these standards have, at the very least, questionable political agendas, which could severely damage the fabric, the unity of the United States. The standards are largely a history of protest, the history of groups, many predisposed. I look at the new history standards, I see a dark skeptical look at the past full of conflict, full of unfulfilled promises and deceptions. I do not see, in the history standards, threads of the fabric of truth holding this fragile nation together. I worry that if these should become the pattern for teaching history in our schools, students will be puzzled about why their parents and immigrants recent to this country feel as though living in the U.S. is one of the great blessings that could be visited upon someone. They will read this gloomy and grim story of the American past and have no idea how fortunate they are, we all are, to live in this once great and free country where the majority once ruled.

The gathering of the First Congress is not mentioned in the new history standards, but there are at least nineteen mentions of Joe McCarthy and Mccarthyism. What happens is there is a lack of balance, the good things. Crucial historical events are often omitted but when it comes to something like feminism or the Klu Klux Clan, dozens of references are made. The dark episodes in our history are paid a lot of attention to. One of the places where the national history standards become especially grim is the opening of the West, which, as a westerner, I feel indignant about. Time and again, kids are asked to discuss the difference between what the pioneers dreamed and the horrors they found. Time and again, kids are asked to study the depredations that were wreaked upon the environment and the horrors that were visited upon Native Americans. I do think that we do need to understand the sad states that Native Americans were reduced to by westward expansion, but that is not the whole story, and what this curriculum does is concentrate on that and neglect the fact a great nation was opened from coast to coast; that democratic institutions were spread far and wide as a result of that expansion.

It seems to me the motives of the people who drew up these standards were to accentuate the negative and discount the positive. The result is a document that completely distorts the truth. If we are to survive, as a nation, we must understand our history - truthfully.

Sadly, for the last forty years, our public school systems have done a very poor job of teaching history. Most Americans have no sense of their own history. That is tragic. History is the glue that binds families and nations together. One of the primary goals of the education reform movement that started in the early 1980s was to try to get more history in the schools. The outcome of that effort to get more history in schools has been this document which would put more politically correct history in the schools. It is such a sad commentary on the state of affairs of historical scholarship in this country, right now, that more history turns out to be more politically correct history. Could all this be planned? One has to wonder.

What are the new history standards? A pattern for future historical textbooks to be written by. They could become officially sanctioned. The GOALS 2000 legislation has a provision that sets up a committee to sanction these standards; to say these are good standards, they are certified and every school district should look at them quite seriously as a possible pattern for teaching. While there is nothing in the GOALS 2000 legislation (as currently structured) that mandates all school districts utilize the standards, what happens when there is something out there and states are trying to figure out what to teach in terms of history, it is very easy to turn to the one thing that has been set out as a set of standards. It is a very complicated and lengthy process to build standards. Especially since we can presume the existing educational establishment, led by the National Education Association, the Teachers Union, probably is politically sympathetic to these standards in this approach to teaching history. There was a report recently in Education Week, that these standards had been very enthusiastically received at the annual convention of the National Council for the Social Studies.

The people who wrote these standards want to use history as a vehicle for shaping young minds in the politically correct direction they would like to see those young minds shaped. For these people, history is a political platform. It is not history as an attempt to understand the past as clearly and as accurately as we can, rather history as a political tool to shape attitudes.

Who are the people writing the new history standards? The organization that put the new history standards together is in California (I don't want to give the name because I don't want to help promote their cause). The organization is currently selling the standards for between eighteen and twenty-five dollars. Every time people buy one of the standards, these people are making a profit to continue their organization.

Historians were involved in the drafting of these standards. The outcome of the new history standards makes one shudder at what historians must teach. History, as it is currently studied and taught on our campuses has become a very politically correct discipline. Two historians from the University of Pennsylvania recently said that, "In writing history, we should not be concerned with truth but what is politically useful." That is an idea that has become very important in the Feminist movement, for example. Feminists tell history in a way to emphasize the role of women, whether or not women have in the past, had a chance to shape history as much as men have had. Some have called this type of history "herstory." I am sure many men have encountered the results of herstory.

We must never distort the past in the name of present "fleeting" interests, like feminism and homosexualism. From the standpoint of national policy, parents should not put themselves in a position they have to defend. Why not start with these standards and make changes right now so these standards are not imposed? Why not have something more to the liking of most Americans, right now, at the national policy level?

As previously mentioned, there is a new textbook of history for American high school students patterned on the proposed history standards. Gary Nash, who heads up the creation of the new historical standards is the main author of the textbook. Gary Nash is a leftist/Socialist. Gary Nash is at the University of California at Los Angeles.

Prior to heading up the project to create new historical standards, Nash and a colleague, Charlotte Crabtree, had produced a very fine set of preliminary standards. It was a document that was very inclusive; it told the story of women, minorities. It told everything in a very balanced way. It was uplifting at the same time as it noted America's flaws.

Based on their preliminary standards, Nash and Crabtree prepared an application for the Endowment for The Department of Education that promised they would develop national standards for GOALS 2000, based on their preliminary document. Clearly that is not what they did. They did something very different. They re-wrote history to their own liking. Nash and Crabtree might like to give back the money they took from the Department of Education, since they did not adhere to their promise of writing factual historical standards. In addition, Nash used the Endowment money to fund the writing of his own fundamentally flawed historical textbook. Not only did he breach his contract, he has turned around and is profiting from his deceptions. Of course, his historical standards are very deceptive.

Even more deceptive is the fact most American citizens had never even heard of the new history standards, mush less being aware that a major historical textbook patterned on the standards had not only been written, but was being sold to schools around the country. Ironically, one of the first copies of Nash's history book showed up in a classroom of a school in one of the most conservative cities in the United States, Colorado Springs, Colorado. Naturally, parents were outraged and frightened when they realized what their children were being taught. Many heated school board meetings followed and over four hundred signatures were gathered to get the book thrown out.

Nash's textbook was written in 1993. The book covers (quite favorably) the Clinton Administration, the Cabinet, and the Clinton Agenda. The Reagan years were not reviewed quite so favorably. Nash says, "Ronald Reagan believed that, with courage and faith, and a little help from mankind, a belief in God, and hard work, that everyone could achieve the American Dream." The book proceeds to say, "Such a simple sturdy view of American life exists only in myth."

Nash goes so far as to cover the Battle of Yorktown merely by an anecdotal reference. The battle of Yorktown is when the British surrendered. It is quite possibly one of the most crucial battles in American history. In Nash's version of the Battle, there is no mention of Rochambeau, Cornwallace, or George Washington. In the textbook, the hero of the Battle of Yorktown is a black slave named, Jake Armistead, who was one of Lafayette's slaves. According to Nash, Armistead retrieved intelligence information that turned the tide of the battle.

In reviewing all the text in the National Parks visitor center in Yorktown, there is no mention of Armistead.

American History should be presented in a balanced fashion, it shouldn't favor any side. The goal of history, in scholarship and in teaching, has to be to get as close to the truth as we can. Naturally, we are limited and fallible and we will never be able to wrap our arms around history entirely, but we have to get as close to it as we can.

If we just tell the truth about what happened in American history, our children will have a balanced view of America. Once we start down the relativistic road, we give Gary Nash perfect justification for doing what he's doing. If it is ok to politicize history, then it becomes very difficult to say Gary Nash cannot politicize it in his way, we are only going to politicize it the other way.

National historical standards chosen for our schools (if we have to have national standards) must achieve (as best can be) an accurate rendering off the past, especially since national standards come with a federal bureaucracy, federal mandates, and ultimately total federal control of another major segment of our lives; in contravention of the Constitution.

Now, that our federal government has opened another pandora's box, achieving historical objectivity will cause much turmoil in this country in coming years. Evidence of this turmoil (which will be frightening) can already be seen in newspapers like *The Denver Post* which recently carried the following article:

Whites stole this land, and they'll reap a bitter harvest

Linda Seebach's column on "A Revisionist History of the Disunited States of America" (Nov 27) clearly points to the need for telling the truth, the whole truth, and nothing but the truth, as far as so called American history is concerned.

Here are the facts:

White's stole this land from Natives and Mexicans who inhabited it. Now they want to pass laws to keep these peoples from reclaiming what is rightfully theirs. Mexicans aren't "illegal aliens." White inhabitants of California and Texas are!

Columbus didn't "discover" America. He discovered - quite by accident - a civilization that had flourished for thousands of years before his brutish band of marauders arrived.

The "great medieval universities of Europe," as Seeback refers to them, owe a debt of gratitude to the scholars of Egypt and other parts of Africa who built mathematically precise pyramids while white Europeans still foraged for food and lived in caves. The English alphabet, which was stolen without proper citation, originated from Egyptian hieroglyphics.

Your own, so-called "scholars" will admit that the first human inhabitants of this planet were African people. "Lucy" is the mother of us all. Two people-of-color can produce, as your own geneticists will substantiate, a mutant strain of the gene for skin color called albinism - white people, colorless people. It is biologically impossible for white people - a recessive gene for skin color - to produce a person of color.

So let's really talk about revisionism. Classical thought didn't begin with Aristotle, Plato, or Socrates, they 'stole' their ideologies from their African brothers across the sea in Egypt.

Mexicans are returning to reclaim the America stolen from then centuries ago. Indians are building casinos on the land wrenched from their forefathers by European thieves - most of whom were criminals or paupers escaping prison in their own land.

Quiet as it is kept, white people weren't settlers; they were barbaric thieves. Most white people weren't grand plantation owners but indentured servants - slaves - themselves. Europeans weren't noted scholars, but rather purveyors of the truths they learned at the feet of their African brothers.

If anyone has revised history, it has been the descendants of dead European males. The chickens are coming home to roost, and white folks had better get a grip. You have deluded yourselves - and people of color - for far too long. You are not the inventors, settlers, purveyors, of all that is great on this planet. Rather, you are thieves and imperialists and profiteers of the great ideas and deeds of your brothers-o-color.

It is not we who have revised history, but you. It is not we who'll reap the bitter harvest of stolen treasurers, but you. You have deluded us and yourselves into believing the myths of your greatness and majesty. It is you - not us - who will reap the bitter harvest of your lies.2

While I believe in the freedom of speech, I shudder to think of Cynthia Barnes as a college educator, molding the minds of our children. Barnes is no better than Hitler. Hitler used the educational system to promote hatred in Germany. The Holocaust was the result of Hitler's educational campaign of hate. If Barnes is willing to promote hate in the newspaper, imagine what she must be teaching our children. Our public schools must not be used as private platforms to promote discrimination and hatred.

In fact, the Colorado legislature just passed a bill requiring all districts to implement what they call *"Standards Based Education."* I'm suspicious they are attempting to sneak in OBE by another name. What makes me suspicious is that the written materials on this include a written statement that, "The implementation of standards based education shall not require districts to adopt outcome based methods of teaching." I believe the legislature is saying this to disarm and to deceive the parents. Their is so much deception in American education that I cannot believe anything until I can see the actual statistics of what they are doing. Even OBE does not tell one anything about what our educators are up to. So many other things in the past enhance this point. We've heard things like "values Clarification" and so on which are just nice high sounding terms to prevent the parents from understanding specifically what is being done. What is being done in many cases is an attempt to brainwash the children with the latest trendy and politically correct stuff. Particularly in sex education.

What gets me about sex education is that educators want to have it from kindergarten to twelfth grade. If sex were that complicated, the human race would have died out thousands of years ago. Long before these programs came along.

The term mastery learning is another euphemism for OBE. The educational system tries to appeal to the public's desire to have some academic education in their schools, and to have some standards by which it can be measured. At the same time the actual content of the program(s) may be radically different from any of this. So it is only after you see the content that it is really possible to make any type of assessment.

Isn't it the pinnacle of deception that President Clinton would propose a $10,000 tax deduction for middle class families to send their children to colleges where educators teach hate and deception? Wake up, America! Your President helped design GOALS 2000, fostered new educational standards cleverly crafted to de-educate our children as to the basic tenets that made this country great, and is now proposing an educational college tax deduction for families that send their children to schools already teaching distortion. Clinton also said, this tax credit is part of "The New America."

Is there a conspiracy to destroy our America? One has to wonder. If so, we have to stop it.

We cannot allow a bipartisan Congress to cleverly distract our attention from important issues by openly promoting illusory and cleverly crafted appearances of tax cuts and less government while they promote the hidden agendas, like "GOALS 2000" that promise to destroy America!

Why are Americans so focused on getting something back from the government (which took it from them to begin with) that they can't understand what their government is doing to them? I suppose we are already *victims* of the great de-education of all citizens of the United States of America.

We cannot allow ourselves to be lulled into a false sense of security by embracing the superficial statements off conservative talk show hosts who would lead us to believe all Republicans are moral and upright Americans and all Democrats are liberal victimizers. When you hear Rush Limbaugh expound on this theme, remember it was President Bush who put together the latest scheme to destroy our schools, children, and future. Why doesn't Rush do some investigative reporting instead of espousing as truth everything told him by the likes of Bill Bennett, Bob Dole, Newt Gingrich? One has to wonder if Rush has crossed over, joined the other side; a side now composed of both Liberals and Democrats alike. A side intent on using the detractors, like Rush, to keep attention off the real issues real Americans must immediately begin dealing with. Why doesn't Oprah Winfrey

talk about the GOALS 2000 legislation?   Oprah loves kids.
Our kids are our future.   Why is Oprah still allowing the
human debris of our society to grace her set instead of
concerned people fighting for America?   We need Oprah!   We
need Rush!   We need to take a stand.

I have taken a stand.   I will pay the price for
telling the truth.   The Cynthia Barnes' of our nation are
evidence enough of the frightening distortion taking place in
our educational system, distortion fostered by the President
who talks of celebrating our "unity through diversity"
(Hegelian doublespeak for continued racial and class
alienation).   Our politicians who no longer serve us will
probably attack me as being a bigot and a racist for daring to
speak the truth; for telling Americans about this great
deception.   I am neither a bigot nor a racist.   I am an
American with a heavy heart, hoping to help all Americans
Take Back *our* America.

Education is the only way we can emphasize our
collective strengths rather than enhance our individual
differences.   We are all Americans.   We must remember this.
We must believe this.   We must come together to celebrate
this, and this alone.   If we continue to emphasize our
differences we *will* destroy America.

I recently listened to a tape called *The Fall of The
Ivory Tower* by George Roach of Hillsdale College.   In the
tape, Roach makes the statement that many of our large
Universities are in serious trouble because they depend so
much on government support and financing.   Hillsdale College
accepts no government support or aid in any form.   Hillsdale
is in excellent financial shape.   In addition, Hillsdale has an
excellent academic curriculum.   Unfortunately there are very
few colleges in America that do not accept governmental
support.   I only know of two others, Grove City and The
College of The Southwest.   Almost everybody wants to get

their hands on the money coming out of Washington. Roach says American colleges and universities are facing a future of unprecedented financial problems because they have become so dependent on the federal government. One of the things that happens when colleges and universities get money out of Washington is that Washington dictates teaching standards.

In addition, Roach says that recent college graduates, the future leaders of this country, are uneducated, uninformed, and ignorant because they have been "educated" according to de-educational standards fostered by the federal government. This is a frightening development. Why doesn't Rush Limbaugh discuss education, or lack thereof, in America? Why doesn't Rush discuss what the government is doing to the minds of our future leaders? For that matter, why doesn't Oprah Winfrey, Connie Chung, Rush Limbaugh, Dan Rather, Joan London, or Bryant Gumble dig into the educational crisis in America?

Bryant Gumble is so smooth talking but often so ignorant of so many of the issues he *attempts* to discuss. Perhaps Bryant is simply a tragedy of our dysfunctional educational system.

Here's another interesting tidbit. The Minnesota Department of Human Rights recently found the Eden Prairie School District guilty of discrimination against a young lady by the name of Chelsey because the district failed to take sufficient action on her sexual harassment complaint. That is, she made a sexual harassment complaint, and the school district failed to take action on that complaint. It turns out that both Chelsey and the accused harasser are both six years old.

Where are we going in our country?

To understand what our dysfunctional educational system is doing to our brightest teachers, I have included three interviews I recently did with teachers in our public school system. These interviews, along with many others of people in all walks of life appeared in another book of mine entitled; IS THE AMERICAN DREAM DYING? Voices of Americans.

The Educators

Margaret A. Locarnini
Rocky Mountains, Colorado

A beautiful ranch high up in the Rocky Mountains of Colorado. It's late afternoon; it's cool and the air is crisp. We're sitting on the front porch of a large old log home looking out at a lush green yard filled with Columbine and wild roses.

Two large barns and several outbuildings surround the house. Margaret built one of the barns, one of the outbuildings, and a massive addition to the house. Her carpentry skills are only exceeded by her cooking talents. While with her I was treated to one of the best Italian meals I've ever had.

Margaret is a very attractive, middle-aged woman who loves the outdoors and savors the beauty of nature. She could not have chosen a more beautiful site on earth in which to live. As we talk, it becomes evident that Margaret is one of those rare people who has given much to many and asked for nothing in return. In the time I spend with her, many people call or come by to visit.

Although her students probably don't realize it now, their lives have been greatly enriched by the caring concern and adherence to discipline of this multifaceted, totally wonderful woman.

I was born in 1937 in Everett, Washington. We moved to Oakland, California, when I was a few months old. My family was of lower class. My father was a shipyard worker during World War II. I had one sister a year younger who died of cancer at age twenty-one. When I was around seven, my father died of cancer forcing my mother to go back to work at her profession, a nurse. She was forced to work at a VA hospital at a low wage for she only had a valid Washington State license and needed to have a California license in order to get top nursing wages. My sister and I were always well fed and taken care of. My grandmother moved into the same apartment complex so we would always have someone to look after us.

I worked as a clerk in a drug store while attending high school and college. I received an AB degree in elementary education and had my first teaching job in 1960 at Lafayette School in the heart of the slums of Oakland, California. I then taught a couple of years in a three room school in Kansas. From there I moved to a ranch in Colorado where I still reside.

I have never married but taken many troubled children into my home and given them a chance at life.

My graduate education involved an MA in Integrating the Arts into Education and a Masters equivalent with courses in education. I now teach in Canon City, Colorado.

The welfare system in this country is killing all of us. I have seen it grow from a helping hand to a destructive handout.

For the three years I taught in the Oakland slums;

there were about one quarter of the fifteen hundred students in the school on welfare. I would figure about twenty per cent of the welfare people had no intention of ever getting away from the handouts. Most of the Blacks were proud people with a dream and worked to accomplish it.

The two years I taught in Kansas in the three room rural school, none of the students were on welfare.

In the past I feel cities were the breeding grounds for handouts but now this has spread to every facet of living whether in large cities or small towns. I personally know people who move from place to place depending on the welfare rates.

In the school I now teach, there are seventy per cent plus of all student families on some sort of handout.

I find it harder and harder to save any wages for my taxes go higher than wage increases as does the price of everything.

Those of us who work give, give, give and those who don't take, take, take in the name of the practiced production of children.

I feel that if the government continues on this free-bee-road hand out, our working few will quit working in revolt of no rewards for labor - then what?

G. B. Davis
Oakland Bay Area, California

Beautiful home in the hills overlooking the Bay area. G.B. is a slender, fine featured, black woman with an air of kindness and caring about her.

We're sitting in a large living room. A magnificent baby grand piano dominates the room. G.B. plays for me a couple of her own compositions. Her music is exceptionally moving.

I was born in 1929, an only child of Negro descent. We lived in a large city, and my father left when I was only two. My mother raised me by taking odd jobs along with some state aid assistance. We were poor but happy. After completing high school, I married Frank and we had a son, Gary. Frank left when Gary was only two and one-half months old. I never knew why Frank left for I have never heard from him or seen him from that day on.

I wanted a better life for my son and me, better than a welfare existence.

I sought state aid and received it to go to college and earn a teaching degree. I paid back the borrowed money after I got a job.

I taught in a small Black school for twenty-five years as a first grade teacher. My earnings were sufficient for Gary and I to have a good life.

A tragedy struck that every mother dreads. Gary fell into the wrong group in high school and I lost my son to substance abuse.

Ten years ago I had grown tired of living alone and when the right man came along and asked me to marry him I said yes. My husband is a lawyer and we are well-off. Even though I love teaching I quit to spend more time with my husband.

This country has been good to me and given assistance where and when I needed. I paid back my debt, and gladly, for without assistance where would I be.....probably on permanent welfare and never have had the chance to accomplish a dream of being something, which I feel I really am.

I have written three books of poems for children and had them published. I have written thirty-plus songs which have also been published...but sad to say none achieved fame.

I was given a chance to accomplish some dreams and by the grace of God I saw the opportunity when it was present and took hold and made my dreams come true.

As to the future, I feel the powers that be give much-to-much away which slows down peoples' desires to accomplish much of anything.

I see the working class stalling at the prospect of paying the bill for those that don't want to work for themselves.

Guy Davis
Seattle, Washington

It's a cold day in late fall. A bone numbing chill hangs in the humid air. It's cloudy and threatening to storm. I'm sitting in a small living room of a modest home in Seattle. A fire is burning in the fireplace, the warmth feels good.

Guy is an excellent teacher and has received many certificates of achievement over the years. Numerous awards and certificates of achievement line the walls of his study. He teaches math in the Seattle public school system.

Guy is forty-four, loves to play racquetball and is

in excellent shape. He's married and has three grown children, two of which attend Seattle State University. His third and youngest child, Joe, is a high school senior. His wife, Andrea, is a warm and beautiful woman.

I grew up in the 1950s. My Dad was a good provider and we had a great home. I have two brothers and one sister who have good marriages and wonderful children. Chris works for Boeing and Chuck is a computer technician. Mary married a real estate developer and is a housewife. All of them live in Seattle.

It was a great time to be alive when we were kids. You never had to worry about locking the house or car. No one felt unsafe in our neighborhood. Mom was terrific. She loved to cook and sew and bake. Our house always smelled like a bakery. I couldn't wait to run home from school to get a piece of fresh baked bread right out of the oven. I loved to butter the hot bread and savor the taste.

Dad was a lumberjack. The work was hard but he really liked it...said nothing smelled sweeter than the smell made by a saw as it cut into a tree. He could fell more trees in a day than most men today can fell in a week...when the government lets the men cut trees.

We lived in the outskirts of town. Our home was small but it seemed plenty big because we were a close knit family.

Even though Dad wasn't religious, he took us to church every Sunday because Mom wanted to go. I was baptized in the Lutheran Church along with my brothers and sister. We still go to church, Andrea, the kids, and I. Somehow I feel uplifted every Sunday and by Sunday I need uplifting; teaching is not easy work these days.

I went to public school and never got into any serious trouble...even though some of the pranks us kids pulled could have gotten us into trouble. Back then, we never heard anything about drugs. I didn't even know what sex was until I was in college. *Guy looks away for a moment and when he looks back at me there is such sadness in his eyes it startles me.* I wish things could be that way today....

After high school, I went right on to college. The Vietnam War was going on and I lucked out and got a high draft number so I was never called. A lot of people ask me if I'd have gone if I was called. I tell them I suppose I would have.

I was a good student...not a great student but a good student....except in math. In math I got straight A's. There's something so incredibly exciting about the ordered sequence of numbers and formulas. You can do anything if you understand mathematical processes. Even today's most complex computer systems are driven by a simple sequence of numbers 01010101......

I don't think anyone was surprised when I decided to become a math teacher. I will never grow tired of math. In my day, you couldn't graduate from high school unless you passed algebra and geometry. It's not like that today...if I don't pass my students...even the one's that should fail, I'm called on the carpet. It's sad.

Andrea and I were juniors in college when we met. We dated right up to graduation. Once I landed a teaching position we got married. She's the best thing that ever happened to me. *Guy looks and Andrea and his face lights up with a big smile. Andrea Smiles, too.* It was tough to make ends meet at first, a beginning teacher's salary isn't that great. Andrea taught English our first two years of marriage so we made out all right. Once she got pregnant, she quit work to stay home and raise our kids. We wanted our kids to be raised in the same type home environment we came from. Even now there's times the money is tight but we manage and we wouldn't have it any other way.

When I first started teaching, kids still recited the Pledge of Allegiance in the classroom and teachers could still discipline students and fail students that didn't make the grade. I used to tutor kids and took pride in watching them learn. There is nothing as humbling or as exhilarating as watching a child solve a complex problem. You can see it in the face of every kid...see the understanding dawn just like the light of day.

In my early years of teaching kids didn't talk back to teachers; they respected teachers. We were there to help them learn and they respected us for it. They feared us, too. We had knowledge and we had power. The power of that knowledge. Most kids crave knowledge because they know that with knowledge comes power.

Ten years ago, I loved teaching. I loved the kids. A lot has happened during the last ten years though...a lot of things that make me wonder if I still have what it takes to teach or even if I want to teach.

Our school systems began falling apart ten years ago and the decline gets worse each year. During the last ten years, teachers have been told they can't discipline students anymore, they can't fail students anymore, they can't control students anymore, and we have chaos in the classroom today because of it.

Today's teachers are nothing more than glorified baby-sitters. We're told to keep students occupied and out of trouble. We're told not to worry about grades. We're told to pass everyone to the next grade regardless of what has or has not been learned.

Kids aren't fools. They've watched as teachers have become prisoners in their own classrooms. They've taken advantage of the lack of power teachers now have. They rule the classrooms now and very few of them are learning anything as a result.

Do you know that if I discipline a rowdy kid today I can lose my job? Do you realize that if I fail a kid I will lose my job? It's true and it's sad. And it is going to be sadder as these kids move up in life and begin running companies. How can a kid that can't add expect to run a profitable company? How can a kid that can't read a financial statement be trusted to make decisions that will affect the lives of many people in the company he or she takes over someday?

It used to be that the school administrations stood behind the decisions their teachers made....even if those decisions were wrong sometimes. Administrators and teachers worked together and kids knew it and kids toed the line because they couldn't pit the administration against a teacher. Today administrators side with students leaving teachers wide open to the most outrageous personal and professional attacks imaginable.

I know teachers who have lost jobs over allegations or innuendos made by disgruntled students. Teachers realize that today they better give students free reign if they want a paycheck to put bread on the table at home. I believe the decline in our educational system has been caused by the National Education Association. The NEA was great in the beginning. The organization not only united teachers but helped create standards of excellence in the classroom. Today, the NEA is run by a bunch of babbling do-gooder's who don't have a clue about what an education is all about. I think a lot of today's leaders in the NEA were kids that should have failed along the way but somehow slipped through the cracks and have managed to rise up in power only to create chaos.

We get letters not only from the NEA but from our principal that have enough spelling errors in them to make a moron blush. These people are educators for God's sake. What kind of standard does their folly set for students? Not much.

Just when I thought life in the classroom couldn't get worse, along comes outcome based education where we're expected to penalize the few remaining bright students we have left in favor of the dead headed, lazy goof off's. I can't give Jeff an A, even if he deserves it because it might be detrimental to Sally whose never opened her Algebra book. When I try to discuss this with the principal, I'm told to just shut-up and pass both Jeff and Sally. I'm not only hurting Jeff when I don't recognize his excellence, I'm hurting Sally because there will come a day when she will find herself in a mess because she doesn't have a basic *understanding* of anything....other than fashion and makeup and making-out.

I've reached the point that I would give up my teaching career if I could make a decent living doing something else. I even interviewed for a position outside the educational field not long ago. When I was being interviewed by the young kid that was going to hire me and I began discussing some complicated mathematical formulas, I saw the veil of ignorance wash over his face and right then I realized one of our failures had already managed to move high-up in an organization that would pay the price for it someday. I didn't get the job because I was "overqualified." They hired a young girl instead, one of my ex-students, one of my failures. Can you imagine how that makes me feel?

If I sound discouraged, I am....I really am. If I could turn back the clock to 1950 yet still be forty-four and a teacher, I would be ecstatic. I could teach again. I could watch that bright dawn of understanding wash across my students' faces knowing I was captain of my classroom.

When you ask me what I think about the future of America I have to answer not much. It's sad to think I have so little faith in my country. What's worse, I worry what life will be like for my children if our educational systems continue to deteriorate. We'll become a Third-World country or worse.

If this decline was just in the school system it would be bad enough, but it's everywhere. I talk to my Dad quite a bit and he sees the same things. For him, it's appalling what the Environmentalists have done to the timber industry. Even though he's retired he still loves to drive out to a logging site and smell chain saws cutting into wood...when the government lets loggers cut trees. Dad says the environmentalists have gone completely wacko. They've managed to get the government to outlaw logging in most of the forests where spotted owls nest claiming the owls are an endangered species. The damn owls will nest in signs and they're not endangered. It's ruined the logging industry. Dad says that if he wasn't retired he'd be out of a job anyway. And dad says it's gotten worse lately. The environmentalists claim we're cutting too many trees and are destroying forests even though we're now replacing more trees than we cut.

Then of course there's the mess in Washington where our leaders have gone wacko, too. Is it any wonder I'm discouraged?

At least there's still a few voices of reason out there. Let's just hope they can prevail.

8

Racism

Racism: *"A belief that race is the primary determinant of human traits and capacities and that racial differences produce an inherent superiority of a particular race."*
- Webster's Ninth New Collegiate Dictionary

" The President of the United States recently told all Americans that, 'We must celebrate our unity through our diversity.' This statement was nothing more than clever doublespeak designed to heighten the differences between the various races that make up America. Our government, with the willing participation of a corrupt media establishment, is attempting to destroy the unity of all Americans along racial lines. As long as our government can secretly foster racism, the resulting racial conflicts will ensure governmental control of all Americans."
- Mike Haga

"A hyphen," Webster's Ninth New College Dictionary defines, *"is a symbol used to divide a compound word or a single word." "It seems to me that when a man calls himself an Afro-American, a Mexican-American, an Italian-American, an Irish-American, a Jewish-American, and so on, what he is saying is 'I am a divided American' living in a divided America."*
- John Wayne

All Americans came from other places, different creeds, different races, to form a nation, to become as one. *Until recently we were one.* Look at the harm a hyphen has done. A hyphen is just a simple little line and yet it's as divisive as a line can get. A crooked cross the Nazi's flew and the Russian Hammer and Sickle too. Time bombs in the lives of man. But none of these could ever fan the wings of hatred faster than the hyphen.

Unfortunately, racism is flourishing in America as all Americans stand on the threshold of the 21st Century. Tragically, racism in America is fostered by the federal government as a necessary means of controlling all races. The government (rightly) believes that as long as there is discord along racial lines, there will never be unity among all Americans. Without unity the American people will never be able to rid America of an oppressive federal government intent on destroying the freedoms of all Americans. The age old battle plan, *divide and conquer*, seems to work very well in times of peace; especially in America where members of the corrupt media work so closely with members of the corrupt government so each can share the material rewards of their continual thievery.

Today, our government leaders are leery of using the words "race" or "racism" when referring to the discord among races in America. This is because these words now connote negative images thanks to the munificent members of the media who recently began calling every concerned or conservative American a racist. Since the government cannot aggressively promote an ugly concept based on negative terminology, members of the media came up with a new marketing strategy that promotes racism through a positive concept called "Diversity."

Thanks to members of our corrupt media, our

corrupt governmental leaders can now stand proud and tall and tell all Americans to "celebrate our unity through our diversity," knowing full well that future conflict along racial lines will ensure the destruction of our America.

To help you understand just how insipidly destructive the concept of diversity really is, I have included the following article, written by Kishore Jayabalan, that recently appeared in the Rocky Mountain News:

> "Diversity means our national survival," said the speaker standing on a raised platform before an audience of 300 employees at the Bureau of Labor Statistics in Washington. "And diversity is the full utilization of all human resource potential," he said.
>
> I'd been told by my boss - the federal government - to spend three hours listening to Edwin J. Nichols pontificate on the importance of racial sensitivity in the workplace. Nichols is a member of the growing diversity industry, a loose conglomeration of business consultants who take their clues from *Workforce 2000*, a book anticipating the rise of minorities and women in the workplace.
>
> Nichols rightly said that minorities and women will continue to play larger roles in government and the corporate world. This simple fact, according to Nichols, will have important workplace consequences. Racial and ethnic differences, for instance, often lead to conflict. Workers must begin to understand and accept the many different cultures they will soon encounter in their colleagues he said.
>
> Nichols urged his listeners to "reflect inwardly on one's own cultural biases and transcend them for the greater good." Europeans, for example, view life

in "linear sequence," he said.   Asians, on the other hand, "conceive of the whole."

I was wondering what this could possibly mean - there's no such thing as an "Asian" culture, after all - when Nichols pointed to me, sitting in the front row:

"An Indian engineer might constantly bother his coworkers about what they're doing because he is so concerned with the whole project, not just his part," said Nichols. This situation would cause tension and stress among my co-workers, he said, since they don't understand my special Asian perspective. But with help from Nichols and people like him, my colleagues and I can get down to business without undue cultural interference.

Asians aren't the only people who are fundamentally different from Europeans (whom I now took to mean anybody white, even if they had never set foot in Europe).   Blacks and Hispanics, said Nichols, are less "object-oriented" than Europeans and much more interested in developing personal relationships." They also have a "spiral conception of time," he said. He backed up his claim by citing the old adage, "what comes around, goes around," which is apparently a very popular saying in black and Hispanic communities.

What this means in the business world, he said, is that we can't ask non-whites to maintain "white" standards. If a pair of black employees arrive late for a meeting, it's not because they don't have the company's best interests in mind. They may have been chatting in the hallway, developing those personal relationships.

Nichols pointed toward economic stratification

as the root of all evils. During the 18th century, he explained, the American workforce changed drastically. Most immigrants before the Civil War came from Europe and worked hard jobs as manual laborers. Afterwards, a new wave of immigrants arrived and held jobs as office clerks and bookkeepers. But since "all white people look alike," Nichols said, society had to categorize them as blue-collar and white-collar workers.

This supervisor-and-worker relationship replicated the old European lord-and-serf relationship, said Nichols. The difference in America was mobility - "the illusion that the more education you have, the more likely you are to move up the social ladder."

As higher levels of education made increasing numbers of people unwilling to perform manual labor, the country found itself with an oversupply of managers. Recent trends towards global competition have resulted in high levels of unemployment and higher levels of stress among the middle management classes, who are predominately made up of white men.

The rise of non-whites in the workforce disorients these middle managers, said Nichols. Whites have been trained from birth to believe that all unmarried black mothers are welfare queens and that Hispanics multiply like rabbits. White men buy into these stereotypes and fight to protect their own positions.

Nichols said his goal is to show how these stereotypes are invalid, so "we can all work together."

He went on to discuss the economic plight of young black males. They're systematically shut out of the workforce, he said. "They can't even get jobs at

McDonald's, because there aren't any McDonald's in Anacostia," he said.

A few phone calls later that day revealed that there are actually six McDonald's in Southeast Washington, but by then I had realized that Nichols wasn't going to let facts get in his way.

"The black man can't get a job outside of Anacostia because the white man didn't build a Metro (subway) stop in Anacostia until recently," he said. "The black man can't drive into the suburbs because the police out there stop every black man who drives a car."

He argued further that racism prevents minorities from earning the same income as similarly educated white men. Remarkably, no one in a room full of professional economists and statisticians questioned either Nichols' data or interpretation.

But then again, no questions were allowed at all. We were paid for three hours to hear Nichols expound upon "gatekeepers" (minority workers who are allowed into positions of privilege in order to maintain the status quo), tactics of oppression ("Math is used as a barrier to keep women and minorities out of high-paying jobs"), and the Bible ("The Book of Genesis is sexist because it's Eve who commits original sin").

Later that week, the personnel office wasn't pleased to have me poking around and asking questions about why it hired Nichols. ("Some people ought to just listen to what's being taught," barked one bureaucrat.) But I did manage to learn that he received $15,000 to speak at five three-hour sessions. The directive came from the Bureau of Labor Statistics

Commissioner Katherine Abraham, whose performance agreement with Secretary of Labor Robert Reich includes a diversity training provision.

It's been two months since my workshop. I still haven't noticed any difference in how my colleagues treat me, or how I view them. But maybe that's because I'm thinking in spirals again."1

This article would be humorous if it wasn't also frightening. To realize that this type of nonsense is being taught to all governmental employees is unbelievable. To know that Robert Reich is using our tax dollars to pay the high priced fees of people like Nichols to promote such outrageous programs of hatred is mind boggling. To understand that governmental employees can sit through hours of this "brain washing" and then go quietly on about their lives makes one wonder just how much other, even more sinister, programs of hate are being promoted elsewhere by our government. After reading this article, the words divide and conquer take on a whole new meaning.

Take a moment to consider the similarities of *Workforce 2000* and *Goals 2000*. When examined in the cold light of reality it becomes evident that our government is fostering Socialism simultaneously *on several fronts.* Our taxes are being used to fund an educational system that is de-educating our children while our government (through such idiots as Robert Reich) pays people like Nichols to brainwash our workforce. This is a frightening concept. If we sit back and allow this type of nonsense to continue, we will get exactly what we deserve - *A United states of Western Russia governed by madmen and women like Bill and Hillary who foster situational ethics where the truth constantly changes to fit the circumstance of the moment.* If we allow this to happen, our children will be dumb, divided, disarmed and helpless slaves serving the Bill and Hillary's of this world. Do visions of bondage, sexual exploitation and blood sports similar to those enjoyed by the Romans when they threw the Christians to the lions come to mind? They should. If we allow our government to continue to promote the likes of *Workforce 2000* and *Goals 2000* and *GATT*, we will find ourselves living in a country where our leaders enjoy the power to do whatever they wish to whomever they choose. In such a society, a morally bankrupt president with a strong sexual appetite for many different types of women or men could select any man's wife or any wife's husband or even their children to satisfy twisted sexual desires and we would be helpless to stop it.

The next time you hear members of either the government or the media discussing the merits of "diversity" training or celebrating our "unity through diversity," remember what you read here. Like sheep, we are being led to the slaughter. If we are to have a future, we must begin to speak up and to write about these things. We must let everyone know what is going on so we can come together to stop the insanity. If we do not, we are even worse than those who want to destroy our free country to further the cause of Socialism.

While our government promotes racism under the name of diversity, detractors in the private sector promote open hatred among all men through the utilization of negative terminology. These detractors work closely with the government to keep ordinary citizens enraged at each other so governmental deceptions can continue without interruption.

A perfect example of the absolute perversion of the term "racism" (made by detractors in the media) occurred when Ruben Perez, Vice Principal of Horace Mann Middle

School in Denver, Colorado, attempted to suspend ninety-seven disruptive Hispanic students. Even though, Reuben Perez, is Hispanic, the Hispanic community called Perez's actions Racist.

When incoming House Speaker Newt Gingrich first began discussing the need to cut back entitlement programs, Gingrich was called a Racist.

When the University of Colorado's head football coach Bill McCartney announced his retirement, in late 1994, McCartney recommended either Bob Simmons, CU's defensive line coach, or Elliot Uzelac, CU's offensive coordinator, be named his successor. When both Simmons and Uzelac were passed over for CU's first-year quarterbacks/receivers coach Rick Neuheisel, the fireworks began. The reason? Simmons, 46, had been with the CU Buffs' for seven years. Simmons is black. Neuheisel, 33, is white. Allegations of racism were hurled at CU's administration.

Even the very reverend Jessie Jackson, the head of the Rainbow Coalition, (and quite possibly the greatest detractor of all) got into the act by calling a national news conference to blast the selection process by the CU Regents. For several weeks, the college community was caught in the grip of national attention as the media fanned the flames of "Racism."

Ironically Jackson admitted he'd never met Simmons or knew anything about the criterion of the selection process. Jackson simply focused on the fact Simmons had been a coach at CU for seven years to Neuheisel's one. In Jackson's world, tenure must somehow be some sort of guarantee of upward mobility, especially if a "minority" is involved.

What Jackson conveniently overlooked during his tirade is the fact Elliot Uzelac has been a coach at CU much longer than Simmons. Of course Uzelac is white so I guess that doesn't count in Jackson's world of "equality."

I suggest Jessie Jackson and members of his Rainbow Coalition take turns looking in the mirror if they want to see individual racists. Jackson's argument that the University of Colorado was "Blatantly Racist" in hiring Rick Neuheisel as head football coach over Bob Simmons cuts both ways. If Simmons had been hired simply because he is black, then Elliot Uzelac and Bob Neuheisel would not have been hired simply because they are white. That is the basic logic of Jackson's argument.

Jackson prefers rhetoric to logic. Part of Jackson's rhetoric is the belief that in any given job opening where one of the candidates is a minority, the employer must hire the minority under the auspices of "affirmative action." In Jackson's world, to do otherwise is to be a racist. Before inciting people to hatred on a national level, Jackson should take a little time to read the Bakke vs. California decision in which the U.S. Supreme Court repudiates this type of reasoning.

Jackson's worse sin, however, is to claim that good people, who he has never met, conspired against another individual whom he has also never met, on the basis of race. Jackson's actions smack of prejudice. Prejudice is a preconceived notion or judgment of others based on their race or other "identifiable characteristics." Prejudice is perhaps the most insipid form of racism. It is Jackson who is the *racist* in this instance. It is Jackson who fuels the fires of racism by unwarranted allegations of hatred.

If we are to heal the deep "racial" wounds festering in this great country, all Americans must come together to consider themselves "Americans." Americans must stop referring to themselves as Afro-Americans, Hispanic-

Americans, Jewish-Americans, Puerto Rican-Americans, Irish-Americans, Indian-Americans, etc. Each of us of is part of the great melting pot called America. As Americans we must work together for the common good of all people of this great country; not for the special interests of any one race or creed (as the detractors and the government are causing us to do).

When Americans believed in the supremacy of God instead of the supremacy of man, America was not under siege by Americans at war with each other; we did not watch our cities burn nor witness brother turn against brother. If we can again believe in the supremacy of our Creator, we will once again become brothers where race and creed are irrelevant. If we continue to believe in the supremacy of man, men will continue to turn against men as all men seek supremacy over all other men based on the flawed theory of a hyphen.

If we can believe again in the supremacy of our Creator, the detractors will disappear because people will have no need of hate filled men preaching the politics of hatred. If all people will stop using the hyphen and just think of themselves as Americans then all people of this great country will begin working together to build a future filled with unlimited promise instead of overwhelming fear.

Right now we are witnessing the virtual destruction of black children by the liberal vision of *Diversity*. In several colleges, black children who scored above the national average on SAT scores are flunking out, because they are being placed in situations where they cannot possibly make it. Look at Berkeley. In a recent study it was shown that seventy-three per cent of the black kids admitted to Berkeley do not graduate. Why is this happening? On doing research I discovered the SAT scores of the black kids at Berkeley are above the national average. However, the SAT scores of white kids are further above the national average, and the SAT scores of Asian kids are even further above the national average than that.

Black kids are failing at Berkeley simply because we insist on putting them in a school where they are over matched. We do this in the name of affirmative action to discourage allegations of discrimination based on race. The result of these affirmative action programs is the failure of black kids who could be graduating, perhaps even with honors, at other colleges.

By insisting on body counts, our politicians and our courts are insisting on double standards of admission. The chief victims of double admission standards are the black and brown kids who are brought in to fail at Harvard or Yale, when they could have succeeded at Rutgers or some other college.

The current system has terrible consequences further down the line. The black student with a 954 SAT score flunking out of Berkeley could be a stellar student at Cal State. It's like dominos. Because of affirmative action programs, if Berkeley is going to take the black and brown kids who meet the standards of say San Jose State, that means that San Jose State is not going to have enough black and brown kids unless it accepts kids who meet the standards of some community college.

In the end we have all of these kids, who are perfectly capable of getting a college education and doing well in life, struggling and failing simply because they are mismatched with the institutions our government places them in.

This naturally produces predictable consequences. The psychological make up of these black and brown kids is damaged, and they have responses. One of the things that happens is that they carry on about how they've been discriminated against. They become angry and bitter young men and women who turn against society; many become criminals.

When Harvard or Yale offers a to accept a high school student, parents and children are thrilled. They can't wait to accept the offer. Often times the offer should be declined. The best thing for parents children to do is to look up the average combined SAT score at the school being considered, and compare that average SAT to the individual SAT. If the average SAT of the school is two hundred points higher than the individual SAT, don't go! You are asking for trouble. One of the messages we have to get out to parents in general and to black and brown kids in particular is that graduating from a second or third tier school is much better than flunking out of a first tier school.

The Affirmative Action plans implemented by the U.S. government in recent years have existed internationally for many decades. Affirmative action has been in Nigeria, India, Shrilanka, Malaysia, and so on. The results are pretty much the same everywhere. While they are a great help for those who were more fortunate to begin with, in many instances the poor are much worse off after affirmative action.

A study done in the United States some twenty years ago showed that while blacks with a college education and with long numbers of years of work experience advanced during the era of affirmative action, blacks who lack these two things fell further behind than ever.

The problem with affirmative action plans is that even when the empirical evidence shows such plans do not work, the evidence means nothing to those who believe in these programs. Supporters of affirmative action plans will tell you that affirmative action plans have created *opportunities* that would not have otherwise existed. I agree. Affirmative action programs have created limitless opportunities for failure. Naturally countless numbers of needless failures have followed.

If affirmative action has made us worse off why do we need affirmative action? To create conflict. Our government, fosters affirmative action programs, in the same manner through which it promotes diversity, to create discord in America. A country divided is a country that can be controlled by the very government that creates the division.

Internationally, affirmative action has led to violence. While violence caused by affirmative action has not yet erupted in America, we are heading in that direction. India has affirmative action much longer than the U.S. and in India it is very common for riots to break out where the lives of hundreds of people are lost. There is no more guaranteed way to turn groups against each other than through affirmative action plans. In fact affirmative action is just one of a whole set of programs that amount to nothing more than paying people to make people hate each other.

This is happening in America today. As a result of affirmative action programs, middle aged white males, are now the most discriminated against group in the United States today. These men, especially those in the South where affirmative action programs are given priority, expressed their anger in the November, 1994, elections by voting against liberalism and in favor of conservatism. This is why the South voted overwhelmingly in favor of representatives who promise to work to end affirmative action plans. We had better hope our representatives can end this insanity or the polarization that is taking place in this country will erupt in the same sort of violence we see in India.

The bottom line is this: If America is to survive,

Americans must put America first. We must come together to tell our government that we will not allow our tax dollars to be used to pay for high priced programs that promote the division of people. We must stop the detractors from diverting our attention from our government's actions. It is up to us. We can choose to sit back and do nothing or we can come together and act. If we do nothing then we are to blame for the destruction of our Country.

9

Entitlements
The Politics of Envy

"Welfare is the most clever and cruelest form of slavery ever designed by those in power. Welfare destroys the desire to work for a better way of life and the will to become educated to understand what the game of power politics is all about. The poor souls addicted to the benefits of welfare not only lose the desire to better their way of life but the ability to do so. Welfare recipients become slaves, dependent on the wills and whims of those in power."

"In 1965, the percentage of children born out of wedlock to single mothers was one-half of one percent. Today, over thirty per cent of our children are born out of wedlock to single mothers. Welfare benefits accelerated the breakdown of our code of morality. The statistics prove it. Today, single women choose to have children out of wedlock as a means to get a free ride.

- Mike Haga

Basic economics is not being taught in the American public school system. Most people have no real exposure to economics until they go to college where they take Economics 101, which doesn't really teach anyone anything of substance. The basic nuts and bolts of how economics work are not taught today. Of late, I have begun to wonder if this too is not part of some devious plan. Our leaders don't put much stock in teaching us the basic fundamentals of the free market system. It seems we have an almost schizophrenic view of the free enterprise system. In college, most professors seem to have a bias against the free enterprise system, and yet it is precisely the free enterprise system that has made this country great in spite of our government's repeated attempts to socialize our economy.

One of the things that is tragically missing from all high school educational requirements is the concept of how money is earned. By that I'm saying that when you or I decide to start earning a living we do one of two things: we either work for someone else or we work for ourselves. (Of course, when we work for ourselves, we end up working for someone else because we have to pay FICA and all other types of taxes).

In the work force there are two basic types of personalities. People who choose to work for others basically have a servant type of mentality. (I'm not talking about being a slave. I am talking about the type of person who does not want to take on the responsibility of owning a business.) The other type of person is someone who has the entrepreneurial spirit who wants to do something and is willing to take the risk to do it.

In a free society, people get income by pleasing their fellow man, making their fellow man happy. Take Bill Gates for example. Gates made many people very happy with Windows and all the other Microsoft products. Michael Jackson makes people happy. If I mow your lawn I make you happy. By making you happy or by pleasing you I get ten dollars for mowing your lawn. What that ten dollars represents is a certificate of performance. With that ten dollars I can go to the grocery store and demand ten dollars worth of what my fellow man produced. The grocer may say that before I can demand ten dollars worth of goods I have to prove that I have served my fellow man. The ten dollars is my proof.

Contrast the morality of the market system with the morality of government. Through our entitlement system the government tells me that I can sit on my butt and watch TV; that I don't have to please my fellow man because the government will take money from other working people and give me a right to make claims on the things other men produce. That's the immorality of government. Government is involved in coercion and theft whereby the market requires that we serve our fellow man.

Anybody who is a Christian has to support the market mechanisms because the requirement to get a claim on what your fellow man produces is that you must first serve him. This is a very important point that today's school kids do not understand. The better you serve your fellow man, the richer you are. Why does Michael Jackson make so much money and I don't? It's because people will plunk down thirty-five dollars to hear Michael Jackson sing. People will not plunk down money to hear me sing. Therefore, I have to try to serve my fellow man in different areas, in things that I am good at, like writing. This is what every American should be doing. Instead, the government fosters amorality, envy, and hatred through a system that steals from one man to give to another who always wants more for doing nothing. Contrary to popular belief, government entitlement programs are the epitome of evil because these entitlement programs are designed to steal from those who produce to give to those who do nothing.

In thirty years, the United States has moved from the War on Poverty to a war against unlimited handouts to those who choose to do nothing with their lives. I'm talking about people who *choose* not to work because they can be

paid more by the government for doing nothing.   The
Personal Responsibility Act, one of the ten bills designed to
enact the Republican Contract With America, has as its central
goal ceding to states "greater control over work programs,
benefit programs, and Aid to Families with Dependent
Children." The bill would prohibit mothers under the age of
eighteen from receiving A.F.D.C. or housing payments for
children born out of wedlock; states would have the option of
extending that prohibition to mothers from eighteen to twenty
years of age.

In the Personal Responsibility Act, states must
begin moving welfare recipients into work programs if they
have received welfare benefits for at least two years; families
may be dropped from the A.F.D.C rolls after two years if the
mother has spent one year in a work program, and states must
drop families from the program after they have received
benefits for five years. Moreover, Republicans are proposing
an overall limit on welfare spending, replacing food stamps
and child nutrition programs with a lump-sum payment to each
state, and, by so doing, ending what has become accepted as
a fundamental right to assistance to all who qualify that has
been central to the welfare policy since the passage of the
Social Security Act of 1935.

Naturally, the bleeding heart *liberals* are screaming
about the inhumanity of the Republican plan and the
heartlessness of Republicans. Are Republicans inhumane? I
don't think so. I don't think anyone else who believes in the
basic tenets that made this country great would disagree either.
The United States was founded on the premise of freedom;
freedom to succeed or to fail. It was a matter of personal
choice. If you chose to work hard, you could succeed - often
against overwhelming odds. Except for people on entitlement
programs who don't have to take chances, that same premise

holds true today.   Able bodied welfare recipients lack the
work ethic. They are a drag on the rest of society.   They
expect us to pay them to sit home and watch television while
the struggling taxpaying people of this country, hand over
more and more of our hard earned money to them. Naturally,
the standard of all working citizens has fallen as those on
entitlement programs continue to grow in number while they
demand more of our money. Naturally, corrupt politicians,
who rely on the welfare masses for re-election, are all too
willing to increase entitlement spending to ensure re-election.

This sad state of affairs has torn this nation apart
in the last few years. Working men and women are tired of
being taxed to support those too lazy to do anything with their
lives. We are rapidly reaching a point where open hostility
between the working and freeloading segments of society will
manifest itself in open warfare on our streets. This is a scary
thought. If we can't get the freeloaders off their butts and
back to work, then the future of America could be nebulous
indeed.

The Republican rout in Congress was the
culmination of angry voters giving Uncle Sam one last change
to stop the insanity. Working Americans are expecting the
104th Congress to uphold their Contract with America, while
the bleeding heart liberals that brought us to today's sorry state
claim it is a Contract on America; which makes one wonder
what the liberal agenda really is and whether the majority
rules anymore.

The liberal agenda is socialism. It is socialism!
Liberals want every working man and woman to be equal;
equally poor and manipulatable. Until November, 1994, it
appeared the liberals were well on their way to total success.
Today, liberalism appears to be under attack from all sides and
most working Americans are hopeful the Republicans will

bring back freedom and restore the work ethic.

Will the Republicans do this? I'm not optimistic. A lot of surface posturing is taking place but on deeper levels both the Republicans and Democrats appear to have joined forces to sell America down the river. In case you have forgotten the deeper issues, turn back and re-read the section on GATT and NAFTA. Turn to the chapter entitled *The Rush is Over!* and read the quotes at the beginning of the chapter. Through November, 1994, America lost 10,000 jobs thanks to NAFTA.

While Republicans talk about cutting back spending on entitlement programs, they turned right around and went along with the passage of the GATT Treaty which adds thirty-one billion dollars per year to the deficit to pay for a World Trade Organization that will decide the future of America's trading practices in the name of competition. GATT was one of the biggest lies ever fostered on the American people. Unfortunately the constant stream of political lies and deceptions is destroying America.

Will the Republican Congress make good on its promise to enact all provisions of the Personal Responsibility Act? I wouldn't bet the farm on it; not if you want to keep the farm. As I mentioned earlier, you can expect heated debates on the pros and cons of cutting back welfare programs. There will be so many debates and so little done most people will lose interest and the whole issue will in all probability be drowned with time. In fact, you can expect to see members of the liberal minded, socialist oriented, media devoting countless hours of prime time television coverage to focus on this issue. Unfortunately, members of our socialistically oriented media elite will use the Dan Rather's, Bryant Gumble's, Peter Jenning's, Connie Chung's, Oprah Winfrey's, and Sallie Jessie Raphael's of this country to show

how the heartless cruelty of conservative members of our society will create untold economic and spiritual suffering for the less fortunate.

Night after night, precisely during dinnertime, average Americans will witness a constant stream of poor people paraded across the television screen. Most of the poor will appear to be homeless and helpless. Most will not be wearing winter coats even though the cameras will bring in scenes of cold and snow in the wintertime. Americans, sitting in the warmth of their living rooms will lay down their forks and knives and look at each other in horror at the thought of so many hungry and hurting people. Precisely at this point, the media will intensify the scenes of suffering, by having several of the homeless, the helpless, identify themselves and talk about their sufferings; knowing full well Americans cannot tolerate having names and voices associated with such suffering.

In fact, I expect some of the finest most heart wrenching, soap-opera like editorial programs, aired in the name of news, to stream across the television screens of all Americans in the coming months and years. What average Americans must keep in mind is *that it is all staged for the benefit of the liberal agenda of socialism.* Most of the people portraying the homeless will have well scrubbed faces and sad eyes and probably belong to the Screen Actors Guild! Most of those playing with the hearts and purse strings of the average American will collect paychecks after filming the segments and will later utilize the best photos in their resumes.

While this may sound outrageous, keep one thing in mind; members of the media must find just the right types of actors to portray the homeless and the helpless. If members of the media were to focus on the real "homeless and helpless" segments of society, Americans would see sullen faced teenaged girls holding their illegitimate children while standing in the living room of their apartment in publicly financed housing projects the inhabitants are too lazy to clean up. In the background would stand a large screen television (which most average Americans can't afford) airing a segment of some popular soap opera or some emotional talk show where Oprah or Donahue or Sally Jessie Raphael is coyly talking with guests about whether it is best to wait until marriage before having sex.

If members of our socialistically oriented media elite were to air these scenes, the real scenes of those who are portrayed as helpless, most Americans would be outraged and would demand an immediate end to all welfare programs. Since our media elite are working together to erode the rights of freedom of all Americans, except for themselves and members of the government who will come together to effectively rule America while sharing the spoils in the process, you can expect members of the media to put together one of the greatest productions of all time. Don't fall for it! Some homeless people *choose* to be homeless and simply want to be left alone. If you do fall for the media hype you will become an active participant in the planned destruction of America.

On some television stations, the staged productions have already begin. Carol Simpson, one of the queens of liberal press, recently did a morning show on welfare reform with Nancy Landen Cassenbaum, the new Chairman of the Senate Labor and Human Resources Committee; John Ingler, Governor of Michigan; and a Catholic Priest.

The debate illustrated the historic welfare reform that could be coming if Americans don't fall prey to the media's attempts to stop it. The set-up piece started with a shot of a mother, the mother's daughter, and the daughter's daughter (a grandmother, mother, and daughter).   The grandmother was thirty-five years old and had been on welfare and A.F.D.C. her entire life.   The mother (unmarried) was fifteen years old, on A.F.D.C. and welfare.   The daughter was six months old.

Simpson was misty-eyed at the right spots in the piece, and the grandmother was talking about the fact she doesn't have a high school diploma.   When the thirty-five year old grandmother was asked, "What would happen to you if your welfare benefits were cut off," the grandmother cried and said, *"I guess I would have to get a job.   But you just got to give us a chance!"*

I found myself laughing.   It was late and I was tired.   I'd put in a long day at the office.   We'd finished dinner and I was paying bills, wondering which ones I could let slide until the following pay day, (a trait shared by ninety per cent of all working Americans - especially during tax time) while Carol Simpson talked *with a thirty-five year old grandmother who is worried about having to go to work.*   How touching!   How touching!   I'm worrying about how to keep a roof over my family's head while a thirty-five year old *grandmother* cries at the thought of having to go to work.   Even worse, the grandmother's daughter isn't even out of high school and she's already a mother herself.   And the government requires me to support the three of them.   That's all I need, three more mouths to feed.   But really, haven't these people had more than enough chances?   It's time to end the hand-outs.   If benefits were cut off, these people *would* get out and go to work.   If they were working, maybe we wouldn't see quite so many thirty-five year old grandmothers or fifteen year old mothers.   Restoring the work ethic could go a long way toward rebuilding the morals of this country.

Many people are probably in full agreement with

everything I've just said but wonder where we can possibly find jobs for those addicted to welfare. The jobs are there! The jobs exist. When you finish reading the chapter on Proposition 187, you will understand what all Americans can do to end not only welfare but also the illegal alien problem in America. If we require welfare to work we would have no place for illegal aliens to work; illegal aliens would go home.

While the Carol Simpson's of this country will call me a racist, I prefer to think of myself as a realist committed to improving the lives of every American currently working and giving those who are not working a chance to work and to make it, if they desire. If they choose not to work then we let them starve.

Just remember, the bleeding heart, socialistically oriented media coverage of those in need of your hard earned money will intensify in the coming months and years. The Carol Simpson's of this country will be given free rein to pummel all Americans with heaping portions of guilt.

The whining of America will be transferred from the health care debate to the welfare debate. Some public policy group recently came out and said if welfare benefits were just cut off some two and one-half million children will be prowling the streets for food. Naturally, this is a statistic that cannot be proved.

This stuff has got to stop. It's not so much the money, but it is the behavior patterns you change in people. We Americans want a great America! The only way we can return America to greatness is to have great people. The real impetus behind cutting off welfare benefits is love and compassion. Weaning people off this dependency cycle called welfare is compassionate. Many of today's welfare people think the only way they can get off welfare is if the government gives them a chance. A chance at what? People have choices.   Most working people didn't have their jobs handed to them; they worked for them.   Most Americans get an education and work hard to make something of their lives.

Work of any type seems beyond the realm of reason to most welfare recipients.   Most have made it very clear that, if they have to go to work, they will not work at what they feel are demeaning jobs.   Wouldn't it be nice if the rest of us had such a choice, or the time to reflect on what we will and will not do in the workplace.

Speaking of work, why is that after a major fire or some natural disaster like a hurricane or an earthquake, welfare people never get out and pitch in to help the displaced members of the working class whose taxes support those on the dole?   *I can never remember seeing even one picture of a welfare recipient lending a helping hand to a middle class working person in need.*

Ironically, the welfare recipients never fail to show up at the supermarket to cash their checks - the minute they get them; shopping for the best food and paying for it with food stamps in the process.   Why doesn't someone in the liberal press stop and ask why those on welfare never help anyone else in need?   Working people support the welfare class.   Shouldn't the welfare recipients lend a hand to middle class working men and women when they need it?

The Carol Simpson's of this world would probably be the first to say that welfare people don't owe anything to anyone.   After all, according to Simpson's reasoning, if people on welfare were to help others, they might miss an exciting segment of Oprah or Jenny Jones where other welfare recipients discuss how it feels to be treated as second class citizens by working class people.

The subject of orphanages is of particular interest to me.   While members of the liberal media try to paint pictures of orphanages as being nothing more than sweat shops of despair, I agree with Newt Gingrich's concept of sending many of the children from entitlement addicted homes to orphanages to give the children a chance at a better way of life.

I am the product of a broken home. I am one of three children whose lives were shattered when my parents divorced. I was nine years old. I was ten years old when my mother decided to marry another man; a man much older than herself. When my mother remarried, the lives of each of us three children were further damaged. Our lives were damaged because mother married a man who did not want children. Mother later told me she remarried for financial security. She told me she remarried *because* she had three children to think about.

Naturally, there was much discord in our new home. There was no love. We became a family at war with each other. I was the rebellious child. To vent my anger at my mother, I did everything I was told *not* to do. My rebellion resulted in my being sent to Staunton Military Academy in Staunton, Virginia, 2,000 miles from home (a private orphanage of sorts).

My first few months at the academy were not pleasant. I resisted authority. I was disruptive. Since the time of my parents divorce I had not done well in school. I continued not do well in school. But with the passage of time, I began to emulate other peers. I began to enjoy school. I began to behave.

By the end of my third year at Staunton, I could not stand the thought of going home; going back to a dysfunctional house. As fate would have it, temporarily declining fortunes dictated that I return home for my final year of high school. It was not pleasant. I remained but a short time before leaving home to live with two teachers for the remainder of the school year. These two teachers, Margaret Locarnini and Clara Reida, gave me the desire to go on to college and helped me complete the necessary paperwork that would enable me to obtain financial assistance. Over the last thirty years, these two wonderful women have given over seven other children of broken homes a reason to live, a home, and the drive to become successful individuals. All of their "children" have become successful men and women with children of their own.

Thirty years have passed since I left Staunton. Many things have happened to me; some bad, most good. I often reflect on what my life might be like if I had not been sent to a "private" orphanage. In my heart I do not believe I would be alive today, or if I were alive I probably would be a ward of the state or a drug addict. I consider myself one of the lucky ones to have had the chance to be removed from a dysfunctional home. Today, I often talk with my younger brother and my older sister and I am saddened by their lives.

My sister and my brother were not as fortunate as myself. Both my sister and my brother grew up in a dysfunctional home. Neither my sister nor my brother have happy lives. My sister joined the Air Force, the minute she graduated from high school. Within five years my sister was given a medical discharge from the Air Force because of a medical diagnosis of Bipolar Disorder. To this day my sister, who was such a gifted child, a child who could paint pictures that moved me beyond words, is dependent on Lithium and anti depressant drugs. My sister fluctuates between the world of reality and the world of madness. My sister has undergone twenty years of intensive therapy to exorcise the ghosts of a past fraught with so much sadness it breaks my heart. My sister is a prisoner of a past over which she had no control but one from which she suffers tremendous guilt. I am now attempting to help my sister break free of the chains of her past.

My brother is also a victim of a childhood filled with turmoil and tragedy. My brother failed in school. My brother married an older woman who turned out to be manipulative and unloving. My brother's marriage to this woman did not last. For years after his failed marriage, my brother turned to alcohol to escape the ghosts of his past. In recent years my brother was fortunate enough to find a good and caring woman to share his life. His mate came into his life complete with a son from a previous marriage. My brother has been with his mate for many years yet my brother cannot muster the courage to marry this good and loving woman because he is afraid she might try to take advantage of him. I hope someday my brother will recognize what a treasure he has found in his mate. Unfortunately my brother did not want children and although he tries to be a good father to his mate's child, he admits he cannot find the strength to love her child as his own. Ironically, my mother calls my brother's mate's son her *grandson*.

Today in America some 5,000,000 children are living in broken homes or single parent households. Most of these children do not know what it is like to live in a stable home environment. Most of these children are not doing well in school. Most of these children are disruptive. Most of these children crave discipline and order and love. Many of these children will grow into adults with lives much like those of my brother and my sister, unless we manage to take these children out of these dysfunctional households and give them a chance.

While the bleeding heart liberals play with the emotions of mature tax paying Americans, telling them that orphanages are creations of despair run by heartless characters intent on destroying the dignity of all children living in orphanages, I am living proof that orphanages are much better alternatives to life in dysfunctional homes that create future dysfunctional adults. Let's give children a chance. Let's put children from broken homes in orphanages to give these children a chance.

Let's turn our attention to the question of how we treat the aged in our culture as we talk about Social Security. It is a very touchy issue. Even the incoming members of the Republican Congress are going to be very reluctant to talk about it, and yet, most people under the age of forty know the system will not be there when they retire, *despite assurances to the contrary from politicians*. This has me quite disgusted. I see eight or nine per cent of my paycheck going every month to something I will never get. Social Security is an inter-generational transfer of income; that is it transfers income from young people to older people. The tragedy of Social Security, according to conservative statistics, is that a person entering the labor force in 1980 would have to live until he or she is ninety-four years of age to break even with what he/she put into the Social Security system, while a person receiving Social Security today breaks even in four years.

That is, a married couple receiving Social Security checks today break even with what they put in four years. The reason this is happening is because for a large part of their working life they only paid in sixty dollars a year in Social Security taxes. Today, many individuals, pay two or three thousand dollars per year into a system that will not be there when they retire. I'm not advocating the government break its contract with people who are Social Security recipients, but we should address the problem now before it gets worse. One of the ways to address it is to allow individuals to opt out of the current plan and set up their own retirement plan through the use of annuities etc. The new Congress must discuss and act on this problem.

The clue to whether a government program is good or bad is to see whether the government has to force people to be in it. Normally, in a program that's any good, you don't have to force people to be in it. But in something that is a losing proposition, like Social Security, you more than likely have to force people to be in it.

I am fearful members of the new Congress will table all forms of entitlement reform if demonstrators take to the streets to protest. Members of Congress are political animals. The very thought they could be creating anarchy will stifle much of the initial enthusiasm of the new members. However, if we are to return America to greatness, we must not let Congress break its promise to end entitlement programs and we must make Congress enact legislation that will give all people the right to opt out of the current Social Security program. If we do not allow working people the ability to save for their future retirement, when these people reach retirement age they will riot.

Face it. We have reached the point where we have no choice; we have got to get the government out of the entitlement business before the government destroys the country. While I have focused my attack on the welfare system, in this chapter, remember I previously discussed the need of eliminating all entitlement programs including, agricultural entitlements, entitlements for the Export-Import Bank, etc. We must eliminate all federal entitlement programs and most state entitlement programs if we are to restore America to greatness.

10

Proposition 187
Is Fair!

"We could end illegal immigration overnight by making people on welfare work at jobs filled by illegal aliens. Why not make welfare people work, we're already paying for their labor."

"Proposition 187 is about economics not race. American taxpayers cannot afford to feed, clothe, and educate the rest of the world."

"The Mexican people have one of the highest birth rates in the world. The Mexican people and their president are using the United States as a dumping ground for the excesses of their poor which are coming into the United States."

"If people come into the United States illegally, they should be immediately deported."

"Corporations employing illegal aliens should face confiscatory fines."

- Mike Haga

   During the 1994 Congressional elections, few issues demanded more national attention than California's Proposition 187. The evolution of this Proposition was the cumulation of a momentum that had been building for over thirty years. The people of California, including about fifteen per cent of Americans of Latin origin, were tired of the fact that not only low wage dish washing and agricultural jobs were being lost to illegal aliens, but that illegal aliens were taking over many good paying jobs as well, jobs such as bricklaying jobs, high tech jobs, well paying jobs like those of plumbers, electricians, aircraft manufacturing jobs, etc.

The old song still sung by people who promote illegal immigration is that illegal aliens take only the low paying jobs. This is absolutely not true anymore, especially in California. During the early 1980s, the California economy was booming. Employers began to hire illegal immigrants to make up for shortages in a very competitive job market. Employers looked upon illegal aliens as loyal employees who would not leave in search of a better job once they were trained. During this time, jobs were plentiful and even though most Californians knew that corporations hired illegal aliens, they didn't care; neither did the Governor nor the politicians. Times were good and it just didn't seem to matter that the taxpaying citizens of Californian were footing the bill for educating the children of illegal aliens and that they were paying for the health care of all illegal aliens.

In the mid 1980s, the California economy was struck by a severe economic recession. Cutting costs was the only way most corporations could hope to survive. Since labor costs are one of the biggest components of running a business, most employers began looking for ways to cut the cost of labor. It didn't take employers long to realize the significant cost savings that came by replacing legal American workers with illegal aliens. Not only would illegal aliens work for less, illegal aliens did not demand health and retirement benefits either.

For example, construction companies were laying off bricklayers with fifteen years experience who were making twenty dollars an hour plus benefits, and silently replacing them with skilled illegal aliens who would work harder, producing quality work, at a cost of ten dollars per hour with no benefits.

What seemed a trivial matter during booming economic times became a volatile issue during the recession as more and more Californians were losing their jobs to illegal aliens. As Californians lost jobs, they lost homes, and cars and so on and so forth. The one thing Californians did not lose was the ever present open hand of the tax man who demanded increasing tax revenues to educate and to provide medical attention for illegal aliens. These events set the stage for Governor Pete Wilson to bring Proposition 187 to the ballot for a vote by the people.

Written by and voted for by the majority of California residents, Proposition 187 prohibits the children of illegal aliens from receiving a free public education (at the expense of taxpayers) in the California school system. Proposition 187 also denies free medical services, funded by taxpayers, to illegal aliens.

Many Latin American people living in California and throughout the United States feel Proposition 187 is racist. Latinos feel they are being targeted and discriminated against by other American citizens. The moment the Proposition was overwhelmingly passed by the voters of California, the American Civil Liberties Union, ACLU, commenced an appeal process in the Federal Court system that prohibited California from enforcing Proposition 187 pursuant to a 1982 United States Supreme Court ruling which requires all States to provide, at State expense, education for the children of all people, legally or illegally living in the United States.

Nationwide, Latin Americans, Jews, Orientals, homosexuals, feminists, environmentalists, and so on and so forth, are also coming together to protest Proposition 187, claiming the proposition is racist. Hogwash! Proposition 187 is about economics not race. The people of California, struggling with job layoffs and a declining economic base, cannot afford to lose good paying jobs to illegal aliens willing to work for less while being required, by the Federal government, to fund at taxpayer expense, State programs that provide free education and health care for illegal aliens who do not pay taxes.

Before it's over, the United States Supreme Court will be called upon to rule on the legality of Proposition 187. The mixture of the United States Supreme Court has changed since 1982. Today, a few more conservative Justices are sitting on the bench than were in 1982. Will today's more conservative Supreme Court overrule its 1982 decision and uphold the legality of Proposition 187? Only time will tell. If the Supreme Court does not uphold the legality of Proposition 187, the ramifications will be immediate and not pleasant. States, tired of and unable to pay for unfunded federal mandates, may cause the downfall of our oppressive federal government and help return America to the Republic it was founded as. While all minority groups may revolt during the process, the healing of America could begin.

If members of the Supreme Court uphold their 1982 decision and declare Proposition 187 illegal, average taxpaying men and women may well revolt against oppressive taxation and regulation by the Federal government. Average citizens could set in motion the events which cause the collapse of the federal government and a return to the Republic America once was. In either scenario, the federal government will become less onerous, unless martial law is declared and regulations are tightened so fast that America becomes a socialist state. It should be an interesting, frightening, future.

Let's turn our attention to the real problem, the problem of illegal aliens coming into the U.S. I'm not an ivory tower theorist who writes about California immigration problems from half-way across the United States. At different times, I have spent weeks with the border patrol just outside San Diego, California. On these occasions, I have been completely overwhelmed, watching the incoming tide of illegal aliens pouring into America from Mexico, across our very porous and diffuse border.

Hundreds and even thousands of illegal aliens have been coming into America each and every night since the 1970s when we made the unfortunate decision to elect Jimmy Carter President. In fact it was Carter who gave aliens the name "undocumented workers." The fact is illegal aliens are not undocumented workers; they are people who have broken our federal immigration laws. Illegal aliens are criminals. They should be prosecuted. They should be sent back to Mexico. They are not prosecuted. In most instances, they are not sent back across the border.

Sometimes illegal aliens come across our borders with forged documents. If illegal aliens don't have forged documents when they come across our borders, they manage to get them in every major city of the U.S., shortly after arriving here. Possessing forged documents is a criminal act. We have laws to regulate criminal behavior. Why don't we use these laws?

It is very difficult to understand how our President can order the loyal men and women of the United States Army, Navy, Air Force, and National Guard, to set up detention camps in Florida to hold *known* illegal aliens, *like those from the recent Cuban boat-lift crisis*, while requiring American taxpayers to feed and house these illegal aliens, while our governmental leaders decide how many of these illegal aliens should *automatically* be given full rights and benefits of U.S. citizenship. President Clinton set up the same sort of detention camps at the American Military Base in Panama. Even the Panamian President made it very clear the refugees are not welcome in Panama and that the U.S. had better find homes for the refugees elsewhere.

During the detention process, the loyal men and women of the United States Army, Navy, Air Force, and National Guard are often attacked and injured by "restless" detainees who simply want to be given citizenship. Why is it that we don't simply ship at least the troublemakers back to the countries where they came from? Why is it our military personnel have to be subjected to violence and intimidation? What is wrong with our government? Why do our leaders allow Americans to be treated as second class citizens by illegal aliens? What is wrong with this picture? Why don't more Americans wake up and demand the madness be stopped?

I believe American citizens have been lulled into a false sense of security by the media. By the time American citizens realize what has happened, it will be too late. The arrogant ignorance of the foolish masses would be funny if the consequences weren't so tragic. *Our government is giving away our country, our rights, our future.* We, the legal citizens of America, *still* have the power to stop the madness; unfortunately, it seems we don't have the guts to stand up and do what is necessary and right.

As a practical matter, it is very hard for the Immigration Naturalization Service, INS, to do anything about the illegal immigration problem. I knew General Leonard Chapman who was the Chief of the INS before Leano J. Castillo was appointed by Carter. Through the INS, Castillo almost destroyed the border patrol, with, I might add, Carter's blessings.

The INS, which includes the border patrol, is one of the most under-funded understaffed agencies in the Federal government. Not only is the INS understaffed and under-funded, a basic organizational structure is nonexistent, and the technology used by agents of the border patrol is totally obsolete in detecting hordes of illegal aliens coming across the border.

Newt Gingrich talks about spending an additional three billion dollars per year to beef up the U.S./Mexico border patrol. Whether this will happen, or whether it will turn out to be nothing more than more governmental rhetoric, remains to be seen. Most *legal* American citizens are not optimistic. While we certainly need to beef up the border patrol, we also need to revamp the patrol. The INS should be put under the Department of Defense. After all, we are talking about defending America from an enemy that, in collusion with our own government, seems intent on enjoying the benefits of dollars paid by American taxpaying citizens while demanding ever increasing numbers of rights in the process.

Mexicans are demanding that Spanish be taught in the classrooms of American schools. We must remember, always remember, this is our country. *The United States of America does not belong to Mexico nor to Mexicans.* As legal American citizens, we have the right to dictate what is taught in our public school systems. Illegal Aliens have no rights, yet our leaders seem intent on subordinating the will of legal Americans to the will of illegal aliens.

How has it come to this? The major corporations in America, in conjunction with our governmental leaders, and the liberalist/socialist oriented media elite (who as we've seen earlier are receiving generous amounts of taxpayer dollars from the GATT Treaty to help mold public opinion to accept socialistic programs like GATT, while opposing initiates like Proposition 187) do not want the borders sealed off because to do so would stop the flow of cheap exploitable labor into the United States. California agriculture would come to a standstill without illegal aliens. So would the restaurant business, the service business, the textile industry, clothing manufacturing, and so on.

While there is a lot of lip service given to what we are going to do to stop illegal immigration, the reality, however, is that we would find it very difficult to compete in the international marketplace in a variety of fields if it were not for the illegal immigrants in the U.S.

In agriculture, many years ago, we had a guest worker program which was known as a *Brascero*, which means   "strong arm" in Mexican.   During harvest, the Braceros came in, we had nice places for them to stay, they had labor relations, and they were well thought of.   The Braceros harvested the crops, were paid, and then returned home to Mexico. Unfortunately, we discontinued the program. We should bring this program back into being again, especially in States like California, Colorado, Texas, and so on.

In the competitive worldwide labor market, Americans have access to a source of cheap labor who will work for much lower wages than Americans, *who have non-work welfare alternatives and unemployment alternatives*, because illegal aliens are willing to work for less money. Companies employing these workers, really do incur much lower costs that are passed on to consumers in the way of lower prices. Not only do corporations benefit, but consumers of products manufactured by corporation employing illegal aliens benefit by paying lower prices for those products. These people are the winners of the illegal immigration game.

The winners are offset by the cost of the social programs necessary for illegal aliens: health, welfare, and educational services. On balance, given the social costs, are we better off with or without the labor of illegal aliens? We are better off without it. America has the most generous immigration program in the world. If Proposition 187 had come into existence because of a fear of immigrants coming into the U.S. from all over the world, the people of California would not have supported it.

Proposition 187 roared to life because major American corporations are pouring millions of dollars into the Mexican-American Legal Defense and Educational Fund run by people who have a radical approach to the rights of Mexicans to enter this Nation. The major corporations of America are also funding radical student organizations, like MACHA Scholarships which are based solely upon race.

Earlier in this book it was pointed out that if the American people would only wake up and smell the coffee, they would realize we don't need illegal aliens as a cheap source of labor. Right now, the American people are giving forty million welfare recipients a free ride. Why don't we require that every able bodied man and woman currently receiving welfare benefits, help harvest crops, work in restaurants, etc.? Not only would this cut down on the amount of assistance these people need, it would cut down on the number of bureaucrats required to run benefit programs, and it would allow the government to grant an immediate across the board tax cut to every working middle class American. In the long run, having these people productively employed would lower the rate of crime, lower the cost of free health care (its a proven fact that physical exercise not only makes people feel better, it lowers the cost of medical care) provide people with a work ethic which provides a sense of self esteem. Hard work would also provide the impetus for many to go on to get an education (in the evening like the rest of us who work) and give perhaps something back to society.

American corporations would not only have access to a low cost and very plentiful source of labor, these same corporations could realize a tax cut in the process. Everyone would benefit. Even workers' receiving workers compensation for on the job injuries could be assigned to other tasks they could complete while their injuries heal. Not only would this cut down on the current and astronomically high costs of worker compensation programs, we would have far fewer workers (who simply want to stay home) claiming on the job injuries.

Liberals honestly believe that requiring able bodied people who are receiving public assistance to work for what they get is un-American because it smacks of involuntary servitude. I would venture to bet that if a poll were taken today results would show the average American worker feels he/she is being forced into involuntary servitude by the outrageous taxes required to support a non productive class of freeloaders.

If America's politicians don't have the guts to stand up and pass legislation that requires able bodied people receiving benefits to work at jobs currently filled by illegal aliens, then the least the politicians could do is to enact legislation that would allow employers to utilize illegal aliens *only during times of labor shortages* under a guest worker program similar to the one currently utilized in Germany.

Germany utilizes "Gast Arbiters" (guest workers). For years, the Germans have utilized gast arbiters, people at fairly low paying jobs who are imported from other countries. These people serve as a cushion during good economic times when there is a labor shortage. Then when Germany goes through a recessionary cycle, when the business cycle turns down, the first people to lose their jobs at the margin are the gast arbiters. Now they are out of work and they are sent home to whatever country they came from. As a consequence, the brunt of unemployment doesn't fall on Germans, it falls on the marginally employed gast arbiters. This serves a political as well as an economic purpose. Now that there is a recession in California, if California were operating under the German model, they could send home the marginal workers. But, of course, since workers in California are there illegally, they can't be sent home and the employers don't want to send them home either. It is a completely different situation in California than in other industrialized countries where they also bring in a lot of non-citizen workers.

Americans would do well to adopt the German model. Will this happen? It is doubtful. There are far too many self-serving politicians and liberal media types involved. Because of the self-serving nature of politicians and the media, Americans will be bombarded with all of the peripheral issues surrounding Proposition 187. The media will focus on the alleged racial overtones of the proposition, or talk about how it is the children who are being targeted. Politicians will play politics with the issue. Democrats will point to Republicans and accuse them of being cold and heartless. Republicans will, in turn, accuse Democrats of being irresponsible, and so forth and so on. People will tire of the mindless, surface trivia, and tune out, turning the issue over to self interest groups intent on completing their own objectives even if it means destroying America in the process.

Can American citizens stop the insanity? You bet!

First we have to change the mind set of most Americans. We have to establish alternative sources of news; real news. We have to get the word out. We have to have people willing to stand up and talk about these things; real people who are willing to address real issues. We need people who not only understand but who are willing to honestly tell all Americans what is really going on in America and what all Americans need to do to take back the America that rightfully belongs to them. These people cannot schmooze up to politicians and the powerful who have self interests to protect.

The Limbaugh's of this world are ok for superficial entertainment, but for hard hitting, really informative discussions of real issues, we need people that haven't been bought out, bought off; people like Chuck Harder, Paul Gonzales, and Jerry Hughes of The People's Radio Network based in White Springs, Florida. These people talk about hard hitting issues and tell all Americans what needs to be done to take America back from the special interest groups, the corrupt politicians, the elite who would enslave us all.

All Americans who want to get the Federal government off their backs, education and prayer back in the classroom, and freedom back in this country, need to provide financial assistance to organizations like For The People, the parent company of The People's Radio Network which has grown from a dream to encompass over 600 radio stations nationwide. We need to support Christians like Pat Buchanan who not only tells the truth, but also has no hidden agendas, and who really cares about what happens to America and all Americans in this time of detraction and deception.

We must find politicians willing to stand up and stop the give-aways. Have we found these people yet? No! Do you think Newt Gingrich is going to risk re-election or possibly even the presidency by cutting back on Social

Security benefits? Do you think Gingrich is going to alienate big business (and the money it means to his campaign) by proposing ending illegal immigration? NO!

On a recent segment of Meet The Press, Newt Gingrich said he was in favor of Proposition 187 for California, but that he could not support such a proposition in any other state because no other state is currently faced with an illegal alien crisis. Does Gingrich really believe this? *Don't bet the farm on it. Gingrich is a politician; an actor. We will never be privy to the real agenda Gingrich is shrewdly promoting.* Even CBS has carried a segment where firms like Tyson Chicken in Arkansas are openly recruiting illegal aliens in Mexico and shipping them to Arkansas.

The people of Arkansas, Colorado, Kansas, Missouri can no longer ignore illegal immigration. The fact that people like Tyson bring in illegal aliens because they can work the illegals like slaves and pay them next to nothing, takes jobs away from American citizens who work in the chicken cutting factories. The negative impact on all American communities is frightening.

In the interim, why don't we just open our borders and let everyone in. That's essentially what the new President of Mexico would like to see happen. When we said we have rules and regulations, he said, "They have human rights to come across your sovereign border, and I will defend those rights." Ironically, the Mexican, government will not tolerate illegal Aliens coming into Mexico from Guatemala, El Salvador, etc., which are continually flowing through Mexico on their way to the U.S. The Mexican government immediately arrests illegal aliens who are then placed in detention camps until they can be loaded into small boats and cast out into the sea, or loaded onto trucks and sent back across the border. People trying to come back into Mexico know they can be shot on sight.

Since Mexico will not tolerate illegal aliens coming into Mexico, isn't the Mexican government interfering in the foreign policy of the United States? It would seem so.

Aside from being taxed to support illegal aliens, most Americans are also angry at the effect of bilingualism in our schools. Bilingualism, in California and other states, is a very prominent educational force. By putting Mexicans in bilingual educational programs, we are not forcing them to learn English, the officially recognized language off the U.S. This keeps all aliens out of the mainstream of social, economic, and political life in America, which makes for cannon fodder for radical nationalist organizations.

Is this de-education process for children of illegal aliens planned? Do school administrators realize that bilingual education creates more friction between Americans and illegal aliens?   One would have to believe they must.   School administrators, though mostly ignorant of the requisites required for getting a good education can't be that stupid, can they? One would hope not! Though it seems that someone is purposely designing educational curriculum to foster division. With what we've learned so far in this book, it would not be surprising to find some convoluted reasoning surface somewhere along the way that helps us make sense of the current immigration nightmare and subsequent de-educational process our politicians and court systems not only tolerate but seem to foster.

If our government would simply mandate that entitlement recipients work for a living, we would all be better off. We would not need another bureaucracy to oversee a national work ID card that smacks of big brother and Revelations. Even if the government implements a national ID card, someone somewhere would find a way to forge it.

In forcing people on entitlement programs to work for a living, just like the rest of us, we will re-build the work ethic in America, lower the crime rate, improve the overall health of the nation. We will unify a fractionalized American people and discover, in the process, that we do not need illegal immigrants, but that we do need all Americans working together to Take Back America.

If Newt Gingrich and the new Congress have the will to stand up and immediately implement legislation requiring to a generation of lazy, arrogant, sullen, freeloaders to either work for their benefits or go hungry, illegal aliens will be out of work and on their way back to Mexico and the healing of America will begin overnight.

11

Gun Control
The Ultimate Lie

"The United States Constitution guarantees the right of each and every citizen to bear arms."

"Not one provision in the Constitution regulates the types of arms the American people can own."

"The Brady Bill is a farce. It is a cleverly constructed media ploy designed to help in the disarming of American citizens in a process to make American citizens helpless."

"The Federal government and the Federal Court system of the Unite States have enacted gun control laws in violation of rights specifically granted to each and every American citizen by the Constitution of the United States."

"People in government are constantly pressing for more and more gun control laws in spite of the fact we have in excess of 22,000 of them and they have no effect on crime."

"The American people should demand that laws in violation of the Tenth Amendment of the United States Constitution be repealed. It is time to get the Federal government off our backs, out of our bedrooms, out of our classrooms, out of our lives."

"It is time for Americans to take back America. "

- Mike Haga

Gun control people have grabbed ahold of the wrong end of the horse. They want to arrest guns, imagining that will reduce crime. Criminals, of course, don't buy guns they steal them. Why someone who is willing to expose himself to serving twenty years to life for robbing a bank is supposed to be inhibited by getting five years for stealing a gun is beyond me.

When I read the Founding Fathers, the Federalist Papers, and the Anti- Federalist Papers, what I see is a profound belief in the collective wisdom, judgment, prudence, and sagacity of the American people, along with a great trust in the individual citizen to do the right thing. What I see in people who are pressing for ever more restrictive laws on the use of firearms is just the opposite; a distrust of the American people, a belief that we cannot allow the American people to have this kind of semi-automatic firearm or that kind of hand gun which doesn't make any sense to me.

Beyond the issue of gun control, one can draw a much broader conclusion. It is not just the Second Amendment that is under attack. In trying to abrogate to itself all power, the federal government is increasingly encroaching on the rights of the states, individual citizens, and the communities in which citizens live.

Remember the Wizard of OZ? It's as if the Emerald city in the Wizard of OZ is now located in Washington D.C. where the Wizard now sits behind the green curtain, sending off colored balls of smoke, shining lights off mirrors, and pulling levers to create different effects to terrify people in a desperate attempt to entice them down the yellow brick road where he will grant them their every wish if they only give him all their money and allow him to make every decision for them.

That wasn't how the country was invented. I'm appalled by the arrogance of the members of our federal government. More and more these people are intruding, not just on our rights to bear arms, but on our rights to control how our property is used, how our children are educated, how we worship, and in giving Salamanders and Spotted Owls equal status with human beings.

To further show the aptness of the Wizard of OZ to our federal government, one must remember that the Wizard, the man behind the curtain, the man we were not supposed to pay any attention to, was Frank Morgan's wonderful rendition of a con man. Most thinking American citizens now view our President and most politicians as being nothing more than con men and yet Americans continue to remain complacent.

Why do most of these con men want to disarm America? These con men want to render American citizens helpless to defend themselves. If the con men can disarm law abiding American citizens, the con men can rule America and take what they please in the process. Where will it end? In civil war? It could. It could if we allow these con men to continue to erode our rights.

To help demonstrate the insanity of today's gun control laws, simply consider the following:

In December, 1994, in Denver, Colorado, forty-eight year old Ron Coleman, a neighbor of Senator Pat Pascoe, was arrested for investigation of first-degree assault, after he shot and paralyzed one of two suspected burglars breaking into the senator's home.

Ironically, Pascoe, a gun-control advocate, said she called 911 about 11:15 A.M. when she saw two men trying to break into her home through a back door. After calling 911, Pascoe ran out the front door and over to her next door neighbor, Coleman. Coleman, a retired policeman, ran out his back door, chased the alleged burglars down the alley and fired several shots from a hand gun in the process. One of the two alleged burglars, 18 year-old Jeffrey Nowman, took a bullet in the spine and was rushed to a local hospital. Later, the hospital's spokeswoman said of Nowman, "His condition is not life-threatening, but it is life altering."

Wasn't Pat Pascoe lucky that she had a neighbor who was on hand to come to her aid. She was also lucky that Coleman had a gun and knew what to do with it. Not so lucky was Nowman who may be permanently paralyzed. One wonders if, after this episode, Pascoe will still favor gun control. Imagine how helpless Pascoe must have felt while dialing 911, knowing the police could not possibly arrive in time to help her. If she had a gun, and she had known how to use it, would she have felt so helpless? I doubt it.

This episode brings up a number of questions about what the law ought to be, what public policy ought to be in relation to the ownership and use of guns in America. Do we live in an increasingly vigilante society where the citizens are taking the law into their own hands? Is there a better alternative?

In this case, if Coleman hadn't been there, the two burglars might have gotten into Pascoe's house, ransacked it, and stolen whatever they could get and fled. The police would have arrived on the scene, too late, gone through a cursory investigation, apprehended nobody, and then these two guys would probably have gone on to burglarize other houses. Instead of that, thanks again to Coleman, one of them was shot. The one who was shot will probably turn in his friend by the time all this is over and we have two fewer burglars, potential murderers, on the street.

The alternative is to tighten up gun control laws, laws that would punish citizens for taking the law into their own hands. Most Americans now believe we should liberalize those laws.

In every city and small town in America the police are working as hard as they can and they can't keep-up with the lawlessness taking place in today's society. People must be given the right to help curb the lawlessness. If they are not given these rights, then lawlessness will continue to increase until anarchy prevails. Part of Americans Taking Back America requires citizens to defend themselves, with force if necessary, in all instances of defense of self and/or property.

While it would be nice, if we did not live in a society where so much lawlessness prevails, the fact is we do live in a lawless society, and that means citizens will increasingly have to *effectively* defend themselves. It always troubles me when a citizen, effectively defending himself or herself, winds up in trouble with the law.

Ability, opportunity, jeopardy, and conclusion are the current tenets of self-defense. Today, most Americans would expand this definition. In the Coleman case, Coleman shot a fleeing suspect. Most people would amend the law to allow people to shoot a fleeing suspect, even recognizing innocent people are going to be shot, too. Those are the times in which we live. It's a jungle out there.

While it is true that people deserve protection from being in the wrong place at the wrong time, it's a trade off right now. People inclined to commit crimes would be less likely to commit crimes if they thought there were more people like Coleman out there. That's the trade off. That's the benefit. While there is a downside, there is a plus side, too.

The trade-off is this. In cases of a flood, an earthquake, a hurricane, we call in the National Guard and declare Marshal Law because of our concern of looting. When we do that, we sacrifice some of our liberties. We have to go along with a curfew, we suspend Due Process. People can be arrested under conditions that in normal times they wouldn't be arrested. We don't want to do that, but we are forced to do it and we do it prudently because of a trade-off; because the situation has deteriorated to such a point we feel that to protect ourselves we must give up some things.

In today's society with so much violence and so much crime, we have to give up some of those safety concepts and take some additional risks as part of the trade off. As Robert Heinly once said, "An armed society is a polite society."

In advocating a loosening of gun control regulations, it is understood that society will still have to adhere to narrow definitions of when it's okay to shoot at people. The necessary legislation can always be enacted. In today's violent times, we have got to allow people more room to defend themselves and their property.

In order for a person to claim self-defense under Colorado's "make my day" law, that person must be in a dwelling, believe that the intruder committed a crime or is about to commit one, and fear that he or she may be harmed. This definition of self-defense is too narrow. Roger Coleman should not be prosecuted. Colorado's law needs to be changed so that what Coleman did is not prosecutable. I'm not saying we should give everyone a carte-Blanche ticket to shoot at will. I'm not saying our cities should become modern day versions of Dodge City, Kansas, where gunfights were common place in the 1800s.

The laws on the books right now were crafted in

order to protect potential perpetrators, and they protect them too much. I understand that innocent citizens will be, to some greater extent, in greater jeopardy if we loosen gun laws. I am willing to suffer that risk, in the short-term, to take back our streets and protect our homes, businesses, and families.

If a poll were taken in the Coleman case, most people would probably vote to give Coleman a medal for stopping the commission of a crime and for possibly permanently removing a criminal from the streets. Most people would probably feel that Coleman was doing a policeman's job. Most people would probably vote to pay Coleman for what he did from the same city coffers used to pay the police.

Is Coleman being given a medal? No! Coleman is going to be prosecuted by a misguided legal system that views Coleman's actions as being reckless. Most citizens are outraged. Many citizens have set up a legal defense fund for Coleman. To the average person, Coleman is a hero.

I am in favor of concealed weapon laws like the one in Florida. If more people were given the right to defend themselves, then the rate of crime would fall. I chose to use Florida as an example of gun control relaxation because of what has happened since Florida allowed citizens to carry concealed weapons. Remember when Florida was held in the grip of a crime wave that threatened to destroy its tourist business? Remember the countless stories of car hijackings and murders of just a couple of years ago? Do you hear of this happening today in Florida? No! Why? Because the Florida legislature, in response to a crime wave, loosened the laws on gun control. When people were allowed the right to carry concealed weapons, the car jackings and murders stopped! Why? Because criminals are afraid of being shot. The tables have been turned. Score one for the law abiding.

Why doesn't the federal government recognize the benefits of less gun control? I believe most members of Congress do recognize the benefits. Unfortunately, being the political animals they are, our politicians tend to legislate in accordance with the hidden desires of their peers, the other con men, and with the dictates of the media.

Previously, we examined the hidden agendas of our major media conglomerates. Most of the powerful people in the media today are very liberal leaning pseudo-Socialists. What is the aim of Socialism? To make, with the exception of the ruling class, everyone equal; equally poor, equally ignorant, equally defenseless. What better vehicle than the nightly news and newspapers to slowly mold the mind set of average citizens.

Gun control is a perfect example of media manipulation of the masses for a desired result. On a daily basis, American citizens are constantly reminded of the hidden dangers of guns and the need to control guns. Each and every night, the nightly news flashes gruesome pictures of people shot to death during gang altercations, robberies, burglaries, domestic disputes; shows pictures of children accidentally shooting other children when playing with mommy's or daddy's gun, while the newscasters talk of the need to get all guns out of the hands of middle class America to stop the violence, the deaths.

Average Americans, hearing about and seeing the most gruesome scenes, day after day, subconsciously begin to believe the only way to stop the violence, the deaths, is to get rid of guns; to round up all the guns from all the households in America so people can't hurt each other anymore.

After planting the seeds of doubt, the media then begins to focus on the most despicable of the gun toting people. After seeing creepy looking people carrying guns, threatening other people, average Americans begin to think that only creepy people carry guns. Naturally, no one wants strange people toting guns around; God knows, anyone could be shot.

Ever so slowly, Americans begin to privately discuss banning the ownership of guns; private discussions then become public discussions. The media fuels debates through thought provoking articles which conclude the only way to stop the madness is to stop gun ownership. The populace finally agrees. The next step is to vote on the issue. By then, the media, if the campaign is successful, leads voters to vote according to the original plan; in this case, for gun control. The populace buys it hook, line, and sinker.

It is only much later, after some crisis, that people wonder what made them vote for something that made them unable to defend themselves and their property from the criminal element, especially since most criminals have guns and no one is safe anywhere anymore.

If the American people could only stop and rationally think about the subtle thought control techniques utilized by the media, most Americans would be outraged at how the media dupes them every time.

On the issue of gun control, why can't average people simply look at the statistics. The majority of guns in this country are owned by middle class people. How often, in proportion to the number of middle class gun owners, do middle class people use guns illegally? Not often. Less than one per cent. These are the people the government wants to take guns away from.

On the flip side, one asks, how many criminals own illegal guns? Estimates vary so widely, it is difficult to assume any relatively accurate figure. What we do know is that the criminal element, in relation to the general population, is small (though growing). Ironically, this small segment of society uses illegal guns to commit ninety-nine percent of all crimes involving guns. Most criminal acts involving guns are committed by criminals. If the government institutes gun control, would these people turn in their guns? Not hardly.

If the American people are dumb enough to allow the government the power to institute increasingly stricter standards of gun control, only the law abiding middle class segment of society will comply. The result will be a middle class held hostage by *both* the government and by the criminal elements of society (which, by the way, are often one in the same).

As an historian, I am appalled at the ignorance of the American people on the issue of gun ownership. From the day this country was founded, American citizens have owned guns. America's founding fathers, realizing that an armed populace is a safe populace, specifically granted to all American people the unconditional right to own guns. This right is spelled out in the United States Constitution; the cornerstone of the foundation of the United States of America.

From 1776 to 1960, Americans enjoyed the freedom to own guns of all types. During this period of time, were American citizens subjected to drive-by shootings and other random acts of sheer insanity? Were people so afraid of every stranger that came through their neighborhood that they put bars on their windows and doors? No! In the summertime people often sat on their front porches and talked to all types of people.

What has changed? What has happened to America since 1960? Why has hatred and violence overtaken decency and honesty? Why does our government want to take away more of our freedoms to attempt to control hatred and violence, only to find an increase in both? Why do American citizens continue to look to Washington for answers when Washington is the problem?

The answer is simple, though the process is complex. We, as a nation, have turned away from the tenets that made this country great. We have turned away from the belief in the supremacy of our Creator, to embrace the belief in the supremacy of man. Unfortunately, we keep looking for a man deserving of our belief in his greatness. Since no such man exists, we have begun to turn inward, believing in the supremacy of ourselves over all others. Naturally, everyone, every man and woman, wants to reach the top of the heap of humanity. This is why we see Whites, Blacks, Latinos, Feminists, Homosexuals, etc., uniting with others of their same race or creed demanding more rights for themselves in the process. Each race and creed is attempting to gain the upper hand over all other races and creeds. Unfortunately, these short-sighted often pathetic people do not understand they are fighting a loosing battle that may, in the process, destroy the very country that allowed them the freedom to pursue the interests of self over the interests of the collective whole.

Through legislation designed to enhance the differences between us, our politicians in Washington continue to add fuel to the destructive forces they helped create. When politicians and the courts banned prayer in the classrooms and prohibited the very young, the very impressionable, from reciting the Pledge of Allegiance, they set in motion the very destructive forces that are coming together to destroy America.

The Pledge of Allegiance and prayer are symbolic of the commonality of all Americans, based on the supremacy of our Creator who demands that we respect and love each other in spite of our differences. When these basic tenets were ripped from the fabric of our lives, the fabric began, unnoticed, to fray. Through the passage of time, that fray has become a tear that threatens to completely unravel America.

Instead of addressing the real issues, setting about to repair the very damage they created, our arrogant Judges, educators, and con men politicians began patching the failing fabric of America. Unwilling, unable, or perhaps with full knowledge of what they were doing, they began creating clever diversions to distract society's attention from their dastardly deeds, to cover up the cause of America's illnesses. These distractions have taken the form of increased legislation, higher taxes, more regulation, less freedom, and gun control.

Many people believe gun control is nothing more than a cleverly designed ruse to disarm America; to make All Americans helpless to defend themselves in the event of total governmental control, or to keep Americans from taking back America when all Americans wake up and acknowledge the cruel hoax that has been played on them.

One thing is certain. Gun control became an issue when Americans of all races turned away from the belief in our Creator to embrace the belief of man. Along the way our society has suffered and our people have become cold, jaded, cynical, un-trusting, dishonest, and afraid of each other and even of themselves. Through this cultural breakdown, Americans have seen the streets of every city and town turned into jungles of crime with death coming from vollies of bullets.

Instead of addressing the root cause of America's moral decay, politicians have enacted increasing numbers of laws to control the ownership of guns, which politicians have convinced American citizens is the problem. Gun ownership is not the problem. The problem is the loss of morality that came with the belief in the supremacy of The Wizard of OZ. We have reached the point where each race and creed believes in their own supremacy and in trying to prove that supremacy, races and creeds are not only shooting other races and creeds but other members of the same race and creed.

When the Brady Bill was passed, Americans heaved a collective sigh of relief believing a background check on people purchasing guns would end the gun problem. Predictably, it did not. When that did not work, politicians set about banning certain types of guns, telling the American people the gun problem had been stopped. It has not.

Politicians then said, let's ban the ownership of all guns. While this has not happened yet, it is frightening to see just how many ignorant Americans are willing to go along with such an insane scheme.

If all gun ownership is banned, only the politicians and the criminals will own guns. With guns only in the hands of criminals and politicians, no law abiding citizen will be safe. The real issue is not about gun control, the real issue is about morality. Until the American people turn back to their Creator, turn back to the cultural foundations that made America great, America will continue to drift along the current path to destruction.

Americans must look to their Creator for the strength and the guidance to help them take back *their* America, a nation founded on Christian values and a belief in the work ethic.. To do less means Americans are willing to relinquish control of their America to Clinton's "New America," a nation of situational ethics, unity through diversity (which results in chaos) with no respect for those who work honestly; a nation where crime is rampant, where violence continues to increase until anarchy prevails.

To emphasize the magnitude of the deceptive game politicians are playing in the name of gun control, we simply have to look at what happened when politicians and federal law enforcement personnel turned their destructive forces loose first on the Weaver family and then on a group of individuals, The Branch Dividians, both of whom professed beliefs not viewed as being politically correct.

Randy Weaver lived with his wife and four children, in an isolated cabin on twenty acres of Ruby Ridge, in the Idaho Mountains, forty miles south of the Canadian border. Mr. Weaver was a white separatist. He did not favor violence against blacks or any other race, but merely believed the races should live separately. Because of his odd beliefs, Mr. Weaver was targeted for a government undercover sting.

In 1989, an undercover agent for the Bureau of Alcohol Tobacco and Firearms, approached Mr. Weaver and sought to get him to sell sawed-off shot guns. Mr. Weaver refused. However, the agent was persistent and even showed Mr. Weaver exactly where to saw-off a shotgun barrel. Mr. Weaver eventually relented to the undercover agent's demands and sold him two shotguns with barrels cut off in exactly the place indicated by the agent.

The agent then identified himself to Weaver as an undercover agent for the U.S. Bureau of Tobacco and Firearms, and issued Weaver a citation to appear in court for violations of federal firearms laws because the barrels of the guns were one-quarter of an inch under the legal minimum required by law.

A court official then sent Mr. Weaver the wrong date to appear in court. After Mr. Weaver did not show up on the actual court date, a Justice Department attorney, who knew Weaver had been sent the wrong date to appear, then secured a warrant for Weaver's arrest.

Federal agents then launched an elaborate eighteen-month surveillance of Mr. Weaver's land and cabin. David Nivin, a lawyer involved the subsequent court case, noted later, "The marshals called in military aerial reconnaissance and had photos studied by the Defense mapping agency. They had psychological profiles performed on the Weavers and installed $130,000.00 worth of solar powered long-range spy cameras. They intercepted the Weavers' mail. They even knew the menstrual cycle of Weaver's teenage daughter, and planned an arrest scenario around it."

On August 21, 1992, six U.S. Marshals trespassed onto Mr. Weaver's property, outfitted in full camouflage and ski masks, carrying sub-machine guns. Three agents circled close to the cabin and threw rocks at the cabin in order to get the attention of Mr. Weaver's dog. As Mr. Weaver's fourteen year son, Sammy, and Kevin Harris, a twenty-five year old family friend, who was living in the cabin, ran toward the cabin to see what the dogs were barking at, U.S. Marshals shot and killed one of the dogs.

Sammy Weaver fired his gun in the direction from which the shots had come. Randy Weaver came out from his cabin and hollered for his son to get into the cabin. Sammy yelled, "I'm coming, Dad," and was running to the cabin when a federal marshal shot him in the back and killed him. Kevin Harris responded to Sammy's shooting by fatally shooting a U.S. Marshall. Later, federal agents testified in court that the U.S. Marshall had been killed by the first shot of the exchange. However, evidence later showed that the Marshall had fired seven shots from his gun before he was shot during the exchange. In other words, the federal agents purgered themselves.

The death of the U.S. Marshall sent the U.S. Government into a frenzy. The commander of the FBI's Hostage Rescue team was called in from Washington, D.C., and ordered federal agents to "shoot to kill" any armed adult male outside the Weaver cabin, regardless of whether that person was doing anything to threaten or menace federal agents.

Thanks to the surveillance, federal officials knew the Weavers always carried guns when outside their cabin, as do many people in the Idaho mountains. With the massive firepower that the federal agents had in the area surrounding the cabin, the automatic weapons, the deadly accurate sniper rifles, the night vision scopes, this was practically an order to assassinate the alleged wrongdoers. Four hundred government agents quickly swarmed in the mountains around the cabin.

The next day, August 22, Randy Weaver walked from his cabin to the little shack where his son's body lay, to say one last goodbye to his boy. As Mr. Weaver was lifting the latch on the shack door, he was shot from behind by FBI sniper Ron Hirauchi. As Weaver struggled back to the cabin, his wife Vicky stood in the doorway, holding a ten-month old baby in her arms, calling for her husband to hurry. An FBI sniper shot Vicky Weaver in the temple, killing her instantly. The FBI is very proud of its talented sharpshooters. Mr. Hirauchi, testified in court that he could hit within a quarter of an inch of a target at a distance of two hundred yards.

Though federal officials now claim that the killing of Mr. Weaver's wife was an accident, the FBI capitalized on her death to try to psychologically torture the survivors during the siege.

As a *Washington Times* writer Jerry Seiper, whose excellent reporting has helped keep this issue alive reported: "Court records show that while the woman's body lay in the cabin for eight days, the FBI used microphones to taunt the family. "Good morning, Mrs. Weaver. We had pancakes for breakfast. What did you have?" Asked the agents in at least one despicable exchange."

Neither Mr. Weaver nor Mr. Harris fired any shots at government agents after the siege began. Mr. Weaver surrendered, after eleven days. An Idaho Jury found Mr. Weaver innocent of almost all charges and ruled that Kevin Harris' shooting of the U.S. marshall was legitimate self-defense. Federal Judge, Edward Lodge told Mr. Weaver, "You've suffered probably far beyond what the court could do. I think you are a good person."

Judge Lodge then condemned the FBI, "The actions of the government, acting through the FBI, evidence a callous disregard for the rights of the defendants and the interests of justice and demonstrate a complete lack of respect for the order and directions of this court."

Judge Lodge issued a lengthy list detailing the Justice Department's misconduct, fabrication of evidence, and refusals to obey court orders.

Recently, officials of the United States Department of Justice launched their own investigation of the Weaver case. A three hundred page report was completed in early 1994 condemning the FBI's handling of the Weaver case and recommending possible criminal prosecution of federal officials. Yet, senior officials at the Justice Department, have disregarded the report's findings and are refusing to release the report to the public or even to Idaho Senator Larry Craig who has fought doggedly to try to get the truth out on this case.

Instead, portions of the report appear to have been leaked to journalists trusted to write pro-government stories on the killings. One of these pro-government stories, written by Mr. Patrick, appeared on the front page of *The Washington Post* on December 4, 1994. (Remember it was the *Post* that promoted NAFTA and GATT and is now being paid two million dollars per year of taxpayer money under the terms of the GATT Treaty. That's money that the government took from you and me in the form of taxes.)

In the *Post* article, Mr. Patrick concluded that

while there was evidence to show that government agents intended to shoot Mrs. Weaver, "The former Vietnam War hero who represented the government, when negotiating Randy Weaver's surrender declared that the government's profile of the Weaver family recommended killing Mr. Weaver's wife. I believe Vicky was shot purposely by the sniper as a priority target because the profile said, if you get a chance, take Vicky Weaver out."

After his lengthy article, Mr. Patrick concluded that because of the government's profile of the Weaver family the FBI's actions against the Weaver family did not involve, "Excessive force." The FBI effectively decided in this case that a family that had defended itself against the defacto ambush by U.S. Marshals, practically, automatically deserved the death sentence to be administered by FBI snipers.

Vicky Weaver was targeted by an out of control FBI hostage rescue team. The FBI hostage rescue team and The Bureau of Alcohol Tobacco and Firearms ought to be dissolved. We can't have this sort of thing going on in the United States of America.

Worse yet, the Clinton Administration has indicated there will be no prosecutions of federal agents involved in the killing of fourteen year old Sammy Weaver or his mother Vicky Weaver, during the 1992 government siege in Idaho. Devo Patrick, Assistant Attorney General for the United States Office of Civil Rights, effectively overruled a Justice Department investigation that urged prosecution of the agents involved for, among other things, violating the U.S. Constitution. Instead, the Clinton Administration is signaling that government agents can practically never violate the rights of gun owners, even when they kill a man's wife and his son.

Mr. Patrick's whitewash of the Idaho killings echoes what Attorney General Janet Reno did after the WACO debacle. The Justice Department report released in late 1993 blamed the Branch Dividians for their own deaths and ludicrously portrayed the gassing and the defacto bulldozing of a compound with live people inside as a "non-aggressive FBI tactic." Again, it was the FBI hostage rescue team that created the WACO disaster. P.J. O'rourke said, "The government felt there was a bunch of Religious nuts with guns down there." And as O'rourke points out, "This country was founded by religious nuts with guns." The Justice Department's final evaluation of the final assault at WACO repeatedly praised FBI agents for showing "remarkable restraint," even when FBI tanks pumped the potentially toxic gas banned from use in international chemical warfare into closed areas occupied by women and children.

If this is not excessive force then don't U.S. agents have the right to kill anyone suspected of a crime who happens to possess a gun? Can we expect federal sharp shooters to be gunning down women holding babies anytime that some supervisor feels his agents may face some distant threat, however remote?

The Weaver and WACO cases present a great challenge to the competency and courage of the new Republican Congressional leadership. Either or both the House or Senate Judiciary Committees must investigate these travesties of justice. If the Republicans let the Justice Department and The FBI get away with what may have been murder, then they will be accomplices to the deceit and repression of American people.

It's astonishing that these type of things are permitted to go on in this country. It is even more astonishing to think that someone like Ron Coleman, with whom we began this chapter, will spend years and countless thousands of dollars fighting to vindicate his name for trying to help a neighbor, for trying to help protect his neighborhood, by shooting an alleged burglar, when federal agents can shoot and kill innocent people and be praised for it by the likes of Janet Reno and company.

American's had better wake up and smell the coffee. Members of our corrupt federal government will continue to try to take away the right of average Americans to own guns by showing just how dangerous guns are. Don't buy into it! The only ones using guns irresponsibly and in the commission of criminal acts are criminals and agents of the government. If we allow our government to disarm law abiding citizens, then there will be nothing to stop the criminal acts of our government. We will be helpless. We will be sitting ducks. There will be countless thousands of Vicky Weavers. Don't laugh. You or yours could be next. Remember the lessons of history. Hitler managed to convince a nation to follow him.........

Keep in mind it is not only members of federal and state governments who seem to have lost all reason on the issue of gun control. Many of our nations largest corporations have instituted very strict policies prohibiting employees from defending themselves in the workforce.

It is the philosophy of our armed forces that troops never surrender; never give up, when violence is directed against them. Why can't the same philosophy prevail in the private sector when employees are defending their employer, their own personal property and lives? Recently at a Quick Mart on Benson Highway in Tucson, Arizona, a convenience store clerk, twenty-eight year old Eric Baxtom, a family man with several kids, was being chased around the store by a robber wielding a machete type knife. After Baxtom fell down and the robber blocked Baxtom's route of escape, Baxtom pulled a pistol and shot the robber. The robber is alive but is now paralyzed.

Baxtom chose to work to provide for his family; to be a law abiding taxpaying citizen instead of being a criminal. Because Baxtom chose to shoot a man who was attempting to rob the convenience store, Baxtom was fired by Quick Mart and left to his own devices to justify his actions.

In doing investigative research on the policy of Quick Mart and other convenience stores like Quick Mart, I quickly realized that most stores have policies that prohibit employees from carrying guns to defend themselves. I think that is wrong. In today's lawless society, to disarm the law abiding citizens makes every law abiding citizen easy prey for the criminal element.

In the Quick Mart example, if Baxtom had not pulled the pistol and shot the knife wielding robber he would have been chopped up with a machete. Would that have violated Quick Mart's policies? Probably not. You know what the people of Tucson should do? Until the people of Quick Mart reinstate Baxtom and publicly commend him for doing what he did, the citizens of Tucson should take their business to Seven Eleven and all other convenience stores. Nobody ought to go anywhere near any Quick Mart stores. If business owners do not value the lives of their employees, they sure don't value the lives of other customers!

The Quick Mart case is not an isolated example. This type of thing is happening all across America. On November 8, 1994, the American people began taking their country back from one undesirable element. Now we need to take our streets and businesses back from the criminal element.

How do we do this? We do this by flooding the halls of Congress with letters and faxes in which we tell Congress to throw out all gun control laws. If our

Representatives choose to ignore us, we vote them out in 1996.

One of the Senators we may need to vote out of office in 1996 is the newly elected Senator Bob Kerry of Nebraska. Recently, Senator Kerry appeared in an advertisement on gun control. I have found a bit of dishonesty in the ad that perhaps most people haven't picked up on. In the ad, Kerry talks about assault weapons. Kerry, being a decorated veteran of the Vietnam War, a man who was awarded the Medal of Honor, ought to know how the United States Government through the Department of Defense defines an assault weapon. According to the Department of Defense, an assault weapon is one that through the action of a selector switch is capable of fully automatic fire. If you push the switch down and press the trigger the gun will automatically empty the magazine. The weapons which were recently banned in the so called Crime Bill are strictly semi-automatic; they are by definition not assault weapons.

First of all, Kerry calls an assault weapon something which it is not. But then, when he refers to the weapons ban and says people don't want these weapons banned, in the background is a weapon firing full automatic; an AK 47. The AK 47 was not banned in the Crime Bill. There is so much deceit going on in the ad.

But even more significant, during the November elections, Kerry promised his constituents in Nebraska that he would not infringe on citizens rights under the Second Amendment. Kerry promised each of his constituents that he would never vote for any laws banning firearms and their use. Not only is Kerry's commercial deceptive, the point is he did not keep his word with his voters. That counts with me. I was raised to believe if you promised something you were supposed to stand by that promise.

This is still a free country. This is still our country. *This is still America. If we want to keep our country, we must be vigilant and we must exercise our most important right - the right to vote.* If we catch any elected official telling us something that is not true, or if our elected officials stray from their campaign promises, we must vote them out of office at the first opportunity.

As this is being written I have learned that members of *the new Republican dominated 104th Congress* are considering the possibility of passing a very repressive gun control law that would effectively prohibit private individuals from owning guns, in violation of ARTICLE II of The Bill of Rights of the United States Constitution.

ARTICLE II of the Bill of Rights states: *"A well regulated militia, being necessary to the security of a free State, the right of the people to keep and bear Arms, shall not be infringed."* According to sources, the new Congress is considering a law that would allow only members of the military and of the National Guard the right to bear arms by twisting the meaning of ARTICLE II to mean that only members of the militia have the right to bear arms. I hope you don't feel so smug now about having a new Congress who we have been told is going to restore Constitutionality to America. We must not let this transgression take place. To understand how we can throw out the unconstitutional laws of the federal government, turn to the **Appendix** and read the information contained therein very carefully. The life blood of the United States is contained in the documents included in the appendix. If you want to be free people living in a free land, you must memorize these documents and make certain that every friend and family member memorizes them as well.

NOTE: Because of public pressure, our esteemed director of the FBI recently announced that he was going to discipline some of the agents engaged in the Weaver massacre. On January 3, 1995, (over two years after the Weaver massacre) the FBI announced that several agents of the FBI and the BATF were being suspended for fifteen days *without pay* as punishment for the killings of Vicky Weaver, her fourteen year old child Sammy, and her unborn child. *However, the director of the FBI also made it very clear that at least one of the agents is being recommended for a promotion after the suspension period has Passed.*

God help us!

12

The AMA and The FDA
Animal Rights Activists
Environmental Idiots

"On the wall in my study hangs a little plaque which says, "The more people I meet, the more I like my dog!" From my perspective, there is a lot of truth in that statement....... A lot of truth."

"At times I believe there is a massive conspiracy of silence on the part of the American Medical Association and its member physicians in the testing of drugs and medical products <u>on unsuspecting human beings</u>. Silicone gel breast implants are a perfect example of this conspiracy of silence. Why was there silence? Money! Lots and lots of money!"

"Why does our federal government pass insane laws that protect the rights of common birds and animals like the Spotted Owl and the Kangaroo Rat? The government passes such laws to allow the government to seize private property in violation of the United States Constitution."

"Who cares about Spotted Owls? A number of environmentalists who make a lot of money getting five dollars from little old ladies to save Spotted Owls in spite of the fact every Spotted Owl saved costs hundreds of hard working American citizens in Oregon their jobs."

"Why does our federal government forbid loggers in Washington and Oregon from making a living by declaring

sacred the forests in which Spotted Owls live when Spotted Owls often live and nest in commercial highway signs?"

"Why does our federal government spend so much time and energy protecting the rights of wild animals only to turn a blind eye to unspeakable animal cruelties performed by members of the government through such illustrious governmental organizations as the National Institutes of Health and the Food and Drug Administration?"

"Why are animal rights activists, other than members of People For The Ethical Treatment of Animals, so willing to overlook animal atrocities performed by government labs and yet be so willing to condemn a farmer who ran over a Kangaroo Rat when plowing his field? Money! Lots and lots of money!"

"At times, one has to wonder if most animal rights activists aren't working <u>for</u> our federal government!"

- Mike Haga

When I was younger, I had the privilege of working in the operating room of one of the largest hospitals in Denver, Colorado. I've seen the mutilated body parts of people involved in automobile wrecks, industrial, and farm accidents. I've watched plastic surgeons reattach severed limbs, and brain surgeons remove cancerous tumors. I have witnessed open heart surgeries and liver and lung transplants. I am aware of how fragile the human body is.

I grew up on a ranch. During my childhood I learned a lot about the miracles of nature. I have helped cows in trouble deliver their calves. I have seen bears grab trout out of a swiftly moving stream. I have heard the eerie cry of an Elk during mating season. I have seen a mountain lion kill a new born deer. I have hunted and I have killed animals, not for the sport of it, but for food. I have learned much about the differences between animals and humans.

The physiology of human beings and the physiology of dogs, cats, rabbits, mice, and other animals is considerably different. Animals can safely ingest things that would kill human beings. Human beings can safely ingest things that would kill animals. For example, an Owl can ingest cyanide with no discomfort while human beings use cyanide for the lethal injections of condemned prisoners. Rabbits can eat certain types of mushrooms and just get fat and happy from the mushrooms. If a human being ate even a tiny portion of the same mushroom, death would quickly follow.   When Sir Alexander Fleming discovered penicillin, for example, if he'd had any Guinea Pigs handy to test it on, there would have been a problem. Penicillin is lethal to Guinea Pigs while it is beneficial to mankind. Chloroform was not used on humans for many years because it will kill dogs.

The reason I bring up the physiological differences between humans and animals is simple; why do humans utilize animals to test the safety of medical devices and drugs that will be used by humans? Since humans use animals to test the safety of medical devices and drugs that will be used by humans, perhaps this is why so many humans die when new drugs that have been declared safe in animal tests are initially approved for use by humans.

If animal testing is not a reliable way to test the safety of medical devices and drugs that will be used by humans, why does the American Medical Association, The

Food and Drug Administration, the National Institutes of Health, and countless numbers of university animal laboratories (funded by the federal government) foster the use of animals in tests that are often inhumane and even cruel? Not only do helpless animals often suffer indescribable pain and horrible deformities in these tests, humans often find out decades later they have been the victims of what could only be deemed cruel hoaxes fostered by flawed research precisely tied to the differences in the physiological make-up of humans and animals.

Silicone gel breast and other types of silicone gel implants provide ample evidence not only of flawed research findings but provide ample evidence that distinguished members of the medical community kept quiet for decades after they discovered silicone gel implants could cause life threatening diseases. Even worse, members of the FDA, the AMA, and the medical community continued to promote silicone gel implants in humans who were continually reassured the implants were safe. Why was this done? Perhaps members of medical community were conducting long-term human testing or perhaps the medical profession simply looked the other way because so many people made so much money.

While we will never know the truth, we do know the lives of countless numbers of individuals have been diminished or destroyed because of Silicone gel implants. We also know many members of the medical profession continue to deny silicone gel implants are capable of causing diseases in humans while the manufacturers of the implants simply said "Oops!" and decided how much monetary compensation would be necessary to wash their hands of the matter so the medical profession and manufacturers could move on to devote attention to newer and better and more lucrative medical products.

    I know first hand the devastating effects of silicone gel implants. As a young man I was afflicted with testicular cancer. I was mortified. After the surgery, chemotherapy and radiation treatments, for a while I was just thankful to be alive. Later, not wanting to appear deformed, I asked my urologist what could be done. With full assurance of complete safety I became the recipient of silicone gel testicular implants. I was ecstatic. I no longer thought of myself as a freak. I had my life back, or so I thought. It was not long thereafter that the medical nightmare really began. I began to suffer one unexplainable medical illness after another. I developed an insidious disease called Sarcoidosis which the medical community defines as, "A multisystem disorder of unknown origin characterized histologically by the presence of noncaseating epithelioid cell granulomas in affected tissues."1 According to members of the distinguished medical community, "Accumulated evidence supports the importance of immunologic factors the pathogenesis of Sarcoidosis."2

    In short, the medical community believes Sarcoidosis is caused by something that causes the immune system to run amok. For years, the fragile state of my health perplexed and angered me. I am active. I have never used drugs. I do not abuse alcohol. I do not smoke. In fact, I work out quite regularly and try to take care of myself. Yet my medical condition deteriorated. I developed excruciating headaches. I became irrational. I signed blank checks and gave them to stockbrokers who in turn made bad investments that cost me millions of dollars. I traveled around the world even though I am mortified of flying on airplanes. I do not remember most of the trips although I have photographs. My family thought I had developed schizophrenia. My marriage failed.

Years later, baffled by my continued and excruciating headaches, my physician ordered an MRI of my brain which showed swelling in the ventricles and some atrophy (brain destruction caused by the swelling). Since there was not a tumor or anything else causing my brain to swell, my physician ordered a spinal tap. The results of the spinal tap showed noncaseating epithelioid granulomas consistent with Sarcoidosis. Since Sarcoidosis, which is a relatively rare disease to begin with, and very rarely permeates the blood/brain barrier, my prognosis suddenly did not appear all that promising. Further testing showed the same noncaseating epithelioid granulomas in my lungs, my eyes, my joints.

My physician was baffled. Nothing in my family history indicated anything that would cause such a profound disease. I was started on Prednisone, an anti-inflammatory drug, to help control brain swelling and joint pains. The Prednisone worked, although the side effects of the drug are not pleasant; bone loss, weight gain, cataracts.

More years passed by. Along came the silicone gel breast implant controversy and the subsequent settlement by Dow Corning and other manufacturers with women who have the implants and who have been impacted by unexplainable diseases. On reading about the controversy, I asked my physician if my silicone gel testicular implants might not be the cause of my medical nightmare. My physician considered the possibility and had me visit other specialists all of whom told me, "Perhaps, although it is such a gray area."

They then tell me the only way to know is to have the implants removed to see, if in time, I don't improve. At this stage of my life, and having a good mate beside me, the cosmetic issues seem somehow trivial to getting my life back, to feeling good again, to living life without pain and the need of Prednisone. Only time will tell if removal of the prosthesis will restore my health. But one thing is for certain, my faith in our illustrious medical community has, to say the least, been shattered.

Members of the AMA, the FDA, and members of the medical community in general, are quick to point out that the vast majority of drugs that have been tested on animals have been proved not to have negative consequences on humans, although there will always be exceptions to the rule.

Members of the AMA are also quick to point out the various procedures, drugs, and techniques that are under consideration often can be utilized to alleviate problems with animal health. I don't think it is the exception at all and that it is frightfully dishonest to paint it that way. Extrapolation is the number one problem if you don't care about animals but you do care about the validity of experimentation or research. For example, the rat, which researchers are so happy to tell us are used more than any other animal so that we will go away and stop feeling sentimental, has no gallbladder. Rats are obligate nose breathers. Humans are not. Rats are nocturnal. Humans are not. Rats manufacture their own vitamin C; they metabolize things twenty times faster than humans. If fact, a lot of studies on rats and other animals have led us down a path which has ended in hurting humans. A good example of this is the new Hepatitis drug which has now killed five people. This drug went through the animal tests with flying colors. So while animals have certain things in common with humans like feeling pain, suffering, becoming fearful, not liking life in a cage, the AMA conveniently forgets this and tries to concentrate on the similarities. But humans are not giant rats. Humans are not just different looking dogs. If we want to put money and time into productive ways of researching cures for our illnesses then it is time we looked at funding more human clinical studies.

The AMA is quick to point out that of the two hundred fifty some new drugs tested in animals in the U.S. each year, only five reach the stage of being able to be tested in human beings.

According to the World Health Organization, seventy per cent or more of today's what we call diseases of affluence, cancers, heart diseases, and strokes - are preventable. The AMA, instead of lobbying for more money to shove substances down rats and rabbits throats, should ask for this money to go into prevention. We would save a lot more lives. In a study of six different drugs, there were seventy-eight negative effects seen in human beings while only twenty-six of the same negative effects were seen in rats and mice. This is typical. If you read any of the pharmacological journals, you will find people debating back and forth how they can overcome the archaic regulations, circa 1920s, from the FDA that say the way to decide whether you can put a drug for human use on the market is just to force feed it in massive doses to other animals. What happens is it comes back to haunt us, especially the elderly, and especially the very young.

We have Arthritis drugs, that have, in some cases, actually killed the elderly because of archaic research. The AMA is quick to point out that while prevention is a very important strategy, we need to remember the information we currently have relative to prevention came out of animal research. The AMA also points out that *the federal government is attempting to legislate prevention* which will become a part of any national health care plan, if one is adopted. (In essence, national health care reform would come with mandates telling Americans what they can and cannot eat and so on. Ironically, Bill Clinton who favors greasy Big Mac's would be exempt - because he is a member of the government - from the mandates. It is frightening to think how close we came to more governmental control over our lives hidden under the reassuring rhetoric of something free for everyone).

One of the things that appalls me is to see our President and members of our Congress, relatively young people, with their guts hanging over their belts because they are steeped in fatty foods. These people are obviously candidates for coronary disease. We also see young girls smoking cigarettes because they want to look like adults while most adults no longer smoke because they have better sense. If we just took care of our own bodies an awful lot of research and legislation would not be necessary.

I am also appalled that several new Senators in conjunction with the FDA are attempting to ban health foods as being unhealthy. Talk about an invasion of our rights of freedom. Why doesn't Dan Rather or Connie Chung speak of this? Better yet, why not 60 Minutes? There is far less risk in ingesting health foods than in most of the so called wonder drugs produced by our governmental/medical establishment. For instance, I have known many people once afflicted with Arthritis who took every known Arthritis drug with no success only to find complete relief by ingesting massive doses of vitamin C. Members of the AMA, some of the same of whom tell me they are uncertain of the side effects of Silicone gel implants, are quick to tell me this is nothing more than a logical fallacy.

After my own experiences with the medical community, my discussions with members of the AMA and the FDA, I am opposed to animal testing simply because of the differences in physiology between human beings and animals. Also, the cruelty involved in animal testing disturbs me greatly. Using the Blalock Press and the Sigler Chair is outrageous. The Blalock Press is a device that has sort of an automobile spring compressible by tightening four nuts. By tightening the nuts, researchers can compress rigid plates together with the pressure of five thousand pounds per square inch, which is used to crush the muscles in an animals legs without crushing the bone so researchers can theoretically study crushed muscles.

Members of the AMA state that the Blalock Press is a wonderful device to help members of the medical profession understand what they will be dealing with in a typical emergency room situation. What an outrageous comparison. Most injuries seen in emergency rooms result from things people do to themselves or have done to them by other people. To advocate doing the same thing to helpless animals is insane. Perhaps members of the illustrious medical community advocating the utilization of the Blalock Press on helpless animals should themselves be subjected to the device. The best training for emergency rooms is in the emergency rooms.

By taking some helpless dog or cat and deliberately torturing it to see how it responds to different types of pain is unconscionable. Why take a cat and put its head in a mechanical device that holds its mouth rigid and then take out its eyes? Why inject a helpless dog with toxic chemicals to see if it develops cancer? Members of the illustrious American Medical Association tell us that there is simply no substitute for animal testing at this time.

In fact I don't know how the AMA can hold its head up because it has such a lousy track record. What I think of when I think of the AMA is a doctor in a white coat on television telling us which brand of cigarettes we can smoke. The record on health issues is abysmal. The AMA gladly accepts millions of dollars of "donations" from the alcohol industry and the tobacco industry. Most recently the AMA accepted money from Monsanto to issue some sort of statement that there's no human health risk associated with Bovine Growth Hormone which is injected into cows and passed in milk to humans. The AMA has no idea if there is a health risk associated with the growth hormone.

The AMA always defends the cruelties of animal testing labs, telling Americans that the alleged cruelties do not happen when in truth there have been expose after expose of conditions in animal testing laboratories which would make anybody with a grain of compassion weep. The United States Department of Agriculture and The National Institutes of Health just came out and upheld the findings of People For The Ethical Treatment of Animals at Wright State University where investigators found people bludgeoning pigs to death with a hammer just so they could take them home and eat them after the experiments.

They found eighteen violations of the federal Animal Welfare Act and believe me this is no huge standard. This is something that just says animals who are chronically ill, who are suffering enormously, such as one little dog at the Wright State lab left overnight to die of her own recourse in pain, should be given anesthesia. Yet the AMA has been up there on Capitol Hill fighting the smallest little consideration for any animal, saying, "no," they don't need to take a step in any direction, even if the animal is in a cage for ten years. According to the AMA animals don't need psychological enrichment even if they are primates like ourselves.

The AMA says it is concerned for kids, the sustenance of both the human and the animal races. Unfortunately, the AMA has shortchanged them all. The

AMA needs to go off in a corner and let someone who is reformist minded do some work so that human beings will get the benefits of quantum pharmacology of the new cancer tests that don't require just sticking substances into animals but instead use human cells in vitro.

The AMA says that it and all of the "reputable" biomedical research advocacy groups are in full agreement with members of PETA in using adjunctive technology, technology that is used along with animals. The AMA says there is a gross dichotomy between what members of PETA believe and reality. The AMA says it is in full support of animal advocacy but that members of PETA are talking about literally re-creating animals as humans.

What the AMA does not talk about is the fact that all the research showing how diseases like heart disease, and specific types of cancer, can be prevented has been done by epidemiological and clinical research on humans. Animal research has contributed nothing to that effort although countless numbers of animals have been sacrificed for experiments. Animal research was used by the tobacco industry for a long time to prove "smoking does not cause cancer" because the AMA tried giving massive doses of cigarette smoke to Beagles in laboratories and they did not get cancer. Based on the tests of the AMA, the tobacco industry argued smoking did not cause cancer.

When discussing the necessity of animal research with members of the AMA, the members speak in the broadest most emotionalistic terms; "Saving babies; Scurrilous filthy rats; If we don't have animal research we'll all die." When you get down to specifics, the AMA does not want to talk about the truth. The AMA will try to switch over and start indulging in emotionalistic propaganda. The AMA tries to avoid discussing the factual realities of animal research which is a dirty business. It is a big business. There is a lot of money in it. There is a lot of manufacturers of equipment for laboratories, breeders of animals, who are paying the salaries of members of the AMA because it is big money for them.

The AMA will reply that it has heard these same arguments for years and that the arguments simply are not true. With respect to the Tobacco Institute, members of the AMA say they do not support the Tobacco Institute's data which the AMA says is fraught with an enormous amount of problems. As to the cardiovascular areas of research, the AMA says there are probably three hundred thousand open heart surgeries performed each year in the United States. Every one of those operations requires the use of the heart-lung machine. According to the AMA, the heart-lung machine came from experiments which utilized dogs and pigs. According to the AMA, there are many people in this country which have elevated cholesterol levels. The drugs used to treat high levels of cholesterol were developed using animals. According to the AMA, the Nobel Prize for the development of the low density lipo protein receptor, the LDL receptor, came from dog and chicken experiments.

The AMA will quickly point out that heart disease kills more than seven hundred thousand people in the U.S. each year and that while members of the AMA believe that a prudent life style, low saturated fat, exercise, and all those other good things that preventive medicine colleagues have been telling us for years are in fact quite appropriate but that is not going to take care of a large segment of heart disease. There are genetic diseases which we simply do not have cures for and which cannot be prevented by the healthy lifestyles that are being promoted by animal rights zealots. According to the AMA, animal rights zealots really use two things to explain away all of what we know in medicine; they say it is better public health and that it is better nutrition; that while better public health and better nutrition have indeed improved morbidity and mortality, they have not been the only thing.

The problem I have with the AMA is that a good physician will certainly tell his or her patient that the Framingham Heart Study said if you have a cholesterol level of one hundred fifty or less you are not going to have a heart attack. The time to know what to do about your diet is not after you have had one heart attack or two, it is before you get there. This is where the AMA falls down on its job, among other places.

Since the 1920s, the Food and Drug Administration, FDA. has required that all drugs go through rat and dog and monkey animal studies. What this does is several things. It gives us misleading information that is not necessarily applicable to the human condition. It also delays having good medicine come on the market. It also puts bad medicine on the market. The following is list of drugs that were not tested on animals but were approved by the FDA to treat everything from high blood pressure to epilepsy to depression. These drugs were discovered by clinical studies on humans: Propanol, Valium, Lidocaine, Phenobarbital, Estrogen, Progestin.

In tests of the Dalcon Shield on Baboons, one in eight of the Baboons died yet A.H. Robbins marketed the Dalcon Shield anyway. Where was the AMA? Where is the AMA when money is taken out of the health care budget and given to experimenters at the National Science Foundation or the National Institute of Health, or even the military to do things like take the tops off the heads of birds to see if it affects their mating calls. To look at the sexual habits of tree frogs?

Animal rights activists are currently raising over three hundred millions dollars a year in their fight to stop the inhumane cruelty of animal testing yet the AMA continues to use animals for the most inhumane tests.

Each and every American possessing even an ounce of decency needs to speak up and stop the insanity of animal testing. Animal testing is nothing more than an elaborate charade to raise enormous amounts of money that would be better utilized in the medical treatment of all Americans thus reducing the outrageous medical costs of all Americans.

I believe, with the exception of members of PETA, other animal rights activists are nothing more than overpaid detractors who help the government use animal rights in a cleverly disguised attempt to infringe on the private property rights of all Americans. Prohibiting loggers from cutting trees in forests where Spotted Owls live is insane.

As I said previously, Spotted Owls often nest in barns and on top of commercial sign posts. Comparing the plight of Spotted Owls to the plight of countless numbers of helpless dogs and cats caged in labs funded by governmental tax dollars is also insane. It seems that once again our illustrious politicians conveniently talk out of both sides of their mouths. How politicians can pass laws prohibiting logging in forests where Spotted Owls live to save the lives of Spotted Owls, when these same politicians approve hundreds of millions of tax payer dollars be sent to laboratories where animal cruelty is a common phenomenon is beyond belief. I believe our politicians exploit the emotions of the uninformed to infringe on the rights of all citizens while these same politicians set around and laugh about the great hoax they have created in the name of medicine. The Emerald City and the Wizard of OZ are amazing.

Wake up, America. Wake Up! If you want to stop animal cruelty then demand the government stop funding animal research projects with your money. Demand that Congress repeal laws that infringe on the property rights of American citizens. This will not only end the sufferings of helpless animals and humans but will allow members of mankind to utilize the resources of the earth which God gave mankind mastery over.

Just as I advocate the efforts of PETA, I berate the efforts of environmental groups. While mankind has in fact taken over and built upon much of the earth that once was once rugged and pristine, environmental activists are nothing more than Socialists who advocate subordination of individual rights to the rights of the government while championing the causes of Mother Nature who really needs no help from mankind. In America there are over two hundred environmental organizations with dues paying members who promote such items as educating all American citizens about the wise use of natural resources. Most of these organizations can aptly be compared to the likes of the United Way which issues emotional pleas for money and depends on the donations of many to support the lush lifestyles of the few administrators who dole out minuscule amounts to various causes. Most can be compared to reverse giant Ponzi schemes; they do nothing for anyone other than to provide good livings' for the organizers and employees of the organizations.

A perfect example of one of these meaningless organizations is the National Wildlife Federation which, by the way, is aptly headquartered in the Emerald City. The National Wildlife Federation was founded in 1936. The National Wildlife Federation (NWF) "is a conservation education organization of private citizens promoting the wise use of natural resources." In essence the NWF supports the subordination of individual rights to the collective rights of the government in the name of conservation. I'll bet most of the NWF's dues paying members haven't a clue they are supporting an organization that promotes the taking of private property for public use - Socialism.

The NWF and others like it would be inconsequential but for the fact the NWF has a membership of some 5,800,000 dues paying idiots who pay $16.00 per year to an organization that may often work against many of its dues paying members. The NWF manages to raise, from dues alone, approximately $92,800,000.00 which is used to pay the lavish salaries of the top echelon and then to promote the subordination of individual property rights to the rights of the government. In fact, I've known ranchers who were members of the NWF before discovering the NWF worked in conjunction with members of the federal government to seize ranch land and set it aside as "wilderness areas" for the benefit of all humanity. Some of the ranchers who contributed to the NWF found their own land seized by the federal government thanks to the concerted efforts of the NWF. Talk about a rude awakening. Don't laugh. If we don't stop these whackos, the government will one day own all of the land in America and each of us will reside in tenements provided by the largesse of the government.

Wake up, America. Wake up before it is too late and America has become the next Russia.

13 Women in the workplace And Other Such Horrors!

"The number one silent killer of men in America is not heart attacks, it is feminism!"

- author unknown

"San Francisco, the shining city of moral decay, recently passed an ordinance permitting women to wear pants in the workplace. No wonder there is so little heterosexual romance in San Francisco."

- Mike Haga

According to the *liberal* media machine, to be a woman in America at the close of the 20th century - what good fortune. That's what we keep hearing, anyway. According to the *liberal* media, the women's fight for equality has been won. In the corporate world, women have so many opportunities they no longer need equal opportunity policies. Women can enroll in any University, apply for credit at any bank, sit on the board of any company, even serve in the military, fighting in the trenches just like men. Women can become policemen, firemen, postmen. Women can become anything *other than women*.

According to the *liberal* media, women are free of the chains of womanhood, motherhood, and *conformity*. Women are so equal now, lawmakers say, that we no longer need an Equal Rights Amendment. According to the *liberal* media, at last, women have received their full citizenship papers.

And yet . . .

As Susan Faludi says in her national bestseller, *BACKLASH; The Undeclared War Against American Women*, "Behind this celebration of the American Woman's victory, behind the news, cheerfully and endlessly repeated, that the struggle for women's rights is won, another message flashes. You may be free and equal now, it says to women, but you have never been more miserable."1

According to Faludi, "This bulletin of despair is posted everywhere - at the newsstand, on the TV set, at the movies, in advertisements and doctors' offices and academic journals. Professional women are suffering "burnout" and succumbing to an "infertility epidemic." The *New York Times* reports: Childless women are depressed and confused" and their ranks are swelling. Newsweek says: Unwed women are "hysterical" and crumbling under a "profound crisis of confidence."2

Faludi is right! Today, working women and professional women alike are depressed and angry. I know many single "professional" women who would give up everything they have achieved in the professional world just to find a good man with whom to settle down and raise a family.

Even founding feminist Betty Friedan has been warning that professional women are suffering from identity crises, loneliness, and alienation; which brings us to the central question of this chapter: How can American women be in so much trouble at the very time they are said to be so blessed? If the status of women has never been higher, why is their emotional state so low? If women got what they asked for, what could possibly be the matter now?

According to Faludi, "The prevailing wisdom of

the past decade has supported one and only one answer to this riddle: it must be all that equality that's causing all that pain. Women are unhappy precisely *because* they are free. Women are enslaved by their own liberation. They have grabbed at the gold ring of independence, only to miss the one ring that really matters. They have gained control of their fertility, only to destroy it. They have pursued their own professional dreams - and lost out on the greatest female adventure."3

From this point, Faludi launches into a five hundred-plus page dialogue on why feminism in America will ultimately prevail and why all feminists will ultimately find true happiness in both their professional and private lives, with or without men, children, homes, or even love. From this point, I feel sorry for Faludi who obviously lacks love in her life and who understands nothing of the history of the United States. If Faludi understood history, she would understand that we are witnessing the end of the feminist movement in the America - for at least the next thirty years that is.

Feminism in America is nothing new. Feminism is a product of economics. Feminism comes with good economic times and feminists disappear during bad economic times. During tough economic times women seek tough but tender hearted men to protect them from the terrible reality of hardship. During good economic times, women turn away from their tough and tender hearted men, in fact from all men, because women can enjoy the fruits of freedom without the fear of hardship. The main thrust of feministic thought can be summed up by the title of a recent and very popular pop song, "Girls Just Wanna Have Fun!" When economic times are good, girls just wanna have fun without the chains of marriage and children. When economic times are bad, women just wanna have fun with Mr. Right who will protect them and coddle them and ensure the fact they will not suffer undue hardship, even if Mr. Right demands a home and children and supper on the table at the end of a long day.

In the 1920s, the Roaring Twenties, seventy percent of working age women voluntarily chose to join the labor force. In the 1920s, seventy percent of all working age American women chose to work in either clerical positions in sterile offices or in demanding professions. These women voluntarily chose to turn away from Mr. Right and to break free of the *chains* of motherhood and homemaking to grab hold of the golden ring of equality and independence.

During the 1920s, working women laughed at the thought of marriage and children. Working women were free and free they were. They partied and danced and smoked cigarettes and slept with whichever man suited their passing fancy and reveled in their independence. Throughout the 1920s, authors devoted volumes of gushing prose to the supremacy of independent females. "Men," as May West said, "Who needs them?"

During the 1920s the small percentage of women who chose to marry, to have children, and make homes for their husbands were viewed as little more than traitors to the cause of women's rights. And women had rights in the 1920s. Women had the right to vote. Women had "protective labor policies," and so on.

In many respects the period from 1910 through 1929 resembles the period from 1974 through 1994. During both periods, women eagerly sought freedom and independence. During both times women flocked to join the workforce. (In 1994, seventy-five percent of working age women were in the workforce. The remaining twenty-five percent who chose to marry, have children and make homes for their husbands were viewed as little more than traitors to the cause of women's rights.)

In fact by the late 1920s most social commentators held the belief that women's rights had been secured. Political science scholar Ethel Klein writes of the 1920s, "The dissipation of interest in the women's movement was taken as a sign not of failure but of completion."

Of great interest is the fact that most women began to lose interest in feminism by the end of the 1920s because the economy wasn't all that hot and it was tougher to make a living. Except for a few radical feminists who captured the attention of the nation because of their outrageous demands, most women of the late 1920s, found life alone harder and no longer yearned to live without men but yearned to live with one special man. Most women had also grown tired of freedom and longed for the security of a traditional family setting. In fact, by the late 1920s, women were flocking to physicians in search of some miracle cure for the loneliness that had overtaken their lives. F. Scott Fitzgerald captured the mood of all women of the late 1920s in his classic book *The Great Gatsby* where Daisy (the principle female character who lived her life surrounded by vast material wealth and spiritual emptiness) longed to find a man who would make her feel like the woman she was.

Perhaps the most interesting parallel to be drawn when comparing the 1910-1929 time period to the 1974-1994 time period is the marked decline of the family unit and all the associated problems that come with it. From 1910 to 1929, and from 1974 to 1994, the children of emancipated women became problematic in schools, became addicted to drugs, ran in gangs and showed little respect for authority. During this period of time crime was rampant in our cities and senseless murders reached epidemic proportions.

In 1929, the world was thrown into an economic depression of unparalled magnitude. During the 1930s interest in feminism died in all women. Women in the 1930s were happy to find a mate with whom to ride out the tough economic times. Naturally, interest in the home and family became paramount. Women who did not settle down were treated with open hostility. Family unity became paramount. Problematic children straightened up under the guidance of both parents. People turned away from a belief in the superiority in the sexes to a belief in the superiority of God. Civility returned to America and America was a much better place.

Today, we are witnessing the decline of feminism for precisely the same reasons as occurred during the late 1920s. The economy is not that hot and it is getting tougher to make a living. Except for a few radical extremists like Eleanor Smeal, Susan Faludi, and the so called chic career women who belong to the National Organization of Women, who continue to garner media attention because of their outrageous demands, *most* single women of today are finding life alone harder no longer yearn for freedom from men but long to find good and tough and tender hearted men and to build a life with one very special man. We can see evidence of this phenomenon everywhere.

Today, the workplace has become a battleground *most women long to escape from.* Women no longer desire independence and freedom. Women want to find mates, to settle down, to build homes, and to raise children.

In my opinion, this is why there is so much chaos in the workforce today. On any given workday morning we find roads clogged with lines of cars carrying single women to their offices. At every stoplight women work frantically to put on their makeup while intently studying every other car that carries a single man. If the man is young and makes eye contact with one of the women, the woman lights up and seems to silently ask, "Are you available?" "Will you take me away from this madness?"

Often, long after the light has turned green, one of these women continues to sit lost in thought in her motionless car, dreaming of the possibilities of wedded bliss until, the sound of car horns blaring behind her breaks her revery and she lurches forward often through a red light where she collides with another car driven by another woman lost in daydreams. Don't laugh, statistically speaking, most car accidents occur between the hours of 8:00 A.M. to 9:00 A.M., and 4:30 P.M. to 5:30 P.M., precisely when most women are commuting to and from the office while frantically searching for Mr. Right.

On the freeways of California, single women have even learned how to put on their makeup while switching lanes at sixty miles an hour - at the same time they are checking out single men. A reliable source says some single women have gone so far as to advertise their availability via bumper stickers which say, "Single! Fertile! Available!" "Marriage Material."

But it does not end here. Once in the office, most women spend most of their time catching up on the office gossip. Of particular interest (especially after a weekend) is finding out who got engaged, who is pregnant, who gets to get married and get out of working for a living. It is true. Most working women no longer know anything about office policies, procedures, or deadlines. But every working woman knows every little thing about the personal lives of every other member in the office. And God help the single young bachelor of the office. He gets more attention than anyone has a right to get. It's especially hard on us older, married, men who find we cannot hope of getting satisfactory work from love starved single women dreaming about marriage.

On any given workday at any given time, customers often find they are unable to contact anyone in any office with whom they do business because the phones are perpetually busy. Secretaries, catching up on the latest gossip from distant girlfriends who just got engaged or just got back from honeymoons are to blame. You can plan on the newly married girlfriend of your secretary tying up your office *phones* for at least three hours a day. At first you become angry, then you become desperate. With all the federal regulations in place that effectively prevent you from firing the secretary, you ultimately succumb to the temptation of attempting to find an eligible bachelor for your secretary just so he will marry her and whisk her away, forever out of your office, so you can get some work done.

Ironically, and as I detail in another one of my best selling books entitled *ON THE BRINK, How To Survive The Coming Great Depression,* I firmly believe our country (and the world) is on the brink of an economic depression that will make the Great Depression of the 1930s seem mild in comparison. When this next Great Depression hits, feminism will die-out completely just as it did during the Great Depression of the 1930s, because feminism is an economic phenomenon. With the death of feminism will come the return of family unity, extreme conservatism, and the return of the family unit. The battle for supremacy by the sexes will be replaced by the return of the belief in the supremacy of God over both sexes. After much chaos, civility and *romance* will return to America. It will be a wonderful time to be alive.

By the year 2025 (if the world survives that long) feminism will once again make its presence felt in the lives of all Americans. If the world survives till 2025, people will discover that the economic cycles will continue. This means that by the year 2025 good economic times will return to

America. With the return of good times will come the desire of women to be free of men, to be independent, to have fun! Chaos will return. The war between the sexes will again begin and a new breed of feminists will be fueling the war of women's independence. Thankfully I will be retired, and as an old man, I will find much amusement watching the chaos from a safe distance. During the coming depression and through 2025 at least most people will be able to call most businesses and not get a busy signal.

Beverly LaHaye, founder of the New Right's Concerned Women for America when asked about feminism recently responded, "Feminism is more than an illness. It is a philosophy of death." Susan Faludi and other feminists would do well to heed the words of LaHaye. While Faludi continues to promote feminism, the coming economic decline will render all remaining feminists to the scrap heap of outmoded thought. And I, for one, am not going to be sorry to see the self centered Faludi's of this world fade.

As a nation full of self centered, cynical, jaded, and empty husks of humanity, being able to witness the return of reasonable God fearing women like LaHaye is like a breath of fresh air; a light in the darkness; a sign that God is coming back to reclaim the hearts and souls of those of us who will listen and who will respond. I am one of those eager souls in waiting for God's goodness to cleanse our troubled country.

To all feminists I say, "Put on a dress, go to church, and find yourself a good man, build a good home, and raise some good children. If you do this, you will find the true meaning of happiness; you will discover the true meaning of life, and you will discover that God and only God is supreme. If you do this, America will begin the long process of healing its broken children, broken homes, broken lives. And romance and laughter and love and respect will prevail.

As I said before, as feminism fades in 1995, the liberal media will still focus on the actions of a few extremists thus giving most people the distorted perception that feminism is gaining ground. In 1994, a few examples of the sheer lunacy of the remaining extremists in the battle between the sexes could be seen.

In December, 1994, a thirty-five year old airline mechanic named Steven Serling successfully battled Texas Women's University to admit men to all its programs. Female students were enraged. A dozen females marched outside the Student Center, toting signs that read, "Better Dead Than Co-ed," and "Raped By The Regents." Students also staged a sit-in at the Admissions Office. Many of the women said they were not anti-men, they were simply trying to preserve the University's ninety-one years of traditions, one of which is not to admit men.

Earlier in the year, a female student successfully sued to be allowed to attend all programs at the Citadel, an all male military academy, claiming it was discriminatory for the academy to accept public funds and admit only males. Women around the country were ecstatic with the Citadel ruling, including some of the women attending Texas Women's University. Later, when the same female student sued to stop the Citadel from requiring her to shave her head, a tradition the men had adhered to for decades, women around the country cheered her on, claiming women should not be subject to male rituals.

Both of these cases illustrate the absurdity of the actions of the American people, and the rulings coming from our legal system. Our citizens have embraced the flawed teachings of our liberal education system that demand total equality, and our courts have, in the name of eradicating all forms of "discrimination," created chaos for everyone. I just wish our courts, and our misguided judges, would let everybody alone. Let the men go, if they want to, to all male schools. Let the women go, if they want to, to all female schools. Let everybody else go to co-ed schools, if they want to. We operated under this "voluntary separation" system for decades, and the system worked. Perhaps it worked too well for our liberal judges who can't stand to leave alone the tenets that made this country great.

Judges can issue a million insane rulings in the name of eradicating sexual discrimination and one fact will always remain; men are different from women. Men have always been different from women and men will always be different from women. God made men and women different for a reason. Fortunately, man cannot change those differences, even though he seems bent on trying to do so. In the process of trying to change God's laws, men and women are creating chaos and strife that is undermining the tenets that made this country great. As men and women choose to make war with each other in the name of equality, the family unit is being torn apart in the process.

Women are beginning to hate men and vice versa. Instead of loving each other, we seem locked in a war for superiority over each other. Women want to prove they are better and brighter and stronger than men. Men are stronger than women, yet women won't accept the biological differences in power. In the process, both sexes have become cold and hard toward each other. God did not create men and women to go to war against each other. God created men and women to love, honor, and respect each other and to raise children to ensure the future of mankind.

Today, as the war between the sexes rages, women leave home, leave behind their family responsibilities and set off to compete with men, destroying marriages and children in the process. The feminists are to blame for this tragedy. The feminists do not want equality between the sexes, the feminists want women to dominate men. Far too many rational women have, through our dysfunctional educational system, unwittingly gotten caught up in this battle for superiority. It is a tragedy in the making. And the longer the battle rages, the weaker our nation becomes.

To the feminists, I say, "go home!" Go back to your roots. Go back to the Bible. Go back to the things that made this country great. What's wrong with women making homes out of houses? God gave women the innate ability to transform the home into a place of warmth and sustenance. Men don't have this ability, even those who try. Why would women consciously choose to enter the sterile arena of the work world where everything is transitory and shifting, when they could utilize their God given talents to create an air of permanence and tranquility in a home that forms the very basis of society? Have our leaders and educators so twisted, so distorted the truth? It certainly seems so.

Let's work together to get rid of what, *in my opinion*, is nothing more than a corrupt liberal media machine intent on destroying America. We can start restoring reason in America by canceling subscriptions to such leftist newspapers as *The New York Times*, *The Washington Post*, and *The Los Angeles Times*, which foster trans-genderism, lesbianism, homosexuality, condoms in the classroom, and permissiveness in the home. These newspapers are intent on destroying the family unit and they just might succeed unless we prevail in our quest for the return of decency and morality in America. Tell the leftist media machine they are not welcome through the one medium they still understand: *MONEY!* Boycott their advertisers and their products, and these purveyors of filth and trash and vermin will disappear.

14

Keep your private life private!
Lesbians & Homosexuals

"Be proud of who you are not what you are"

- Barry Holthus

The medical profession recently changed its position regarding homosexuality. There was a time when members of the not so illustrious American Medical Association said homosexuality was a mental illness. The AMA has backed off from this position. The AMA now says that while there is no hard scientific evidence to *prove* that homosexuality is other than a life style choice, recent research *indicates* there *may* be a genetic predisposition.

I believe that research will eventually prove that homosexuality is genetic. Homosexuals have been a part of mankind from the beginning. Homosexuality occurs naturally in nature in every species of animal and I'm not so sure animals consciously choose their type of life style. According to the AMA and some Biblical fundamentalists, animals are not even capable of the logical thought processes that would give them the capability of deciding upon a particular life style choice even if they wanted to.

I don't understand why the medical community still has such a difficult time with the whole issue of homosexuality. (But then this is the same medical community that once assured women of the safety of silicone gel implants and now wants to ban all vitamins as hazardous substances, while promoting the most cruel forms of animal testing.

That's not much of a track record, is it?)

Most homosexuals will flatly tell you that they knew there was something *different* about themselves; that they felt some strange attraction to members of the same sex long before they even knew what sex was all about. Once most homosexuals realize what they are they enter into a period of denial and/or repression.

Most homosexuals instinctively know they cannot change their sexual desires anymore than they can change their sex; except through surgical intervention. But to change anything there has to be the desire to do so. Many homosexuals tell me that they have wanted to change but that they cannot. Some have undergone professional therapy in an attempt to change, but they cannot. Most homosexuals say they would like to change because they do not want to live life as members of one of the most persecuted segments of society.

At this point, many homosexuals marry members of the opposite sex in an attempt to overcome their feelings of attraction to members of their own sex. Sadly most of these marriages are the result of the homosexual's drive to be accepted by parents who would disown their homosexual child if they knew their child was homosexual. Unfortunately few, if any, of these heterosexual marriages have proved long lasting. These marriages simply destroy the hopes, dreams, and lives of many *innocent* women and men unwittingly caught up in a real life game of family charades.

Failing family acceptance, many homosexuals migrate to urban areas where large groups of homosexuals are known to reside. For a while many homosexuals are simply overwhelmed by the realization there are so many others just like them. Some quickly lose all inhibitions and irregardless of AIDS and other sexually transmitted diseases become promiscuous in an attempt to embrace every sexual impulse they once ran from. Most, however, quickly realize there is nothing magical about standing up and proclaiming to a rather bored world. "I'm gay!" Most quickly tire of dimly lit bars and superficial lives. Most find it best to return to the often quiet towns they came from. Most realize the whole issue is much to do about nothing.

In reality, who really cares what two consenting people, who have reached the age of legal consent, do in the privacy of their homes? Other than a few dysfunctional mothers and fathers, who can't love their children because they can't accept the fact their child did not turn out to be the person they planned, a few radical members of the so called Religious Right who utilize the Bible as an instrument of hatred to justify their own hidden agendas (many are probably homosexuals themselves), and all members of the liberal media who like to discuss every *irrelevant* thing that goes on in our society, no one cares. *The fact is no one really cares about anyone else's sex life!* The only thing all members of society should care about is that people live by a moral code of right and wrong. All of us know that promiscuity is immoral.

In fact, most homosexuals would probably find themselves living in a much more tolerant society if they would simply grow up and *shut up*. The average person in America just wants homosexuals to shut up and live quietly. In reality, most homosexuals do manage to find someone to share life with. Most homosexuals live in quiet homes on quiet blocks in just about every community in America. These conservative homosexuals rarely encounter any form of prejudice.

Members in the military have told me that a "known" homosexual in a military unit is extraordinarily disruptive of unit cohesion, bonding, and fighting effectiveness. However, if an individual is not known to be a homosexual, there isn't any problem. Homosexuals have been serving in the military for years. Before the radical elements of the homosexual community began "coming out," homosexuality was not an issue because people kept their private lives *private*.

There are a great number of homosexuals who resent being painted with the same brush as those who belong to Queer Nation, ACT UP and other extremist groups. Some have said to me, "Look! I would never think of going into a Catholic church and desecrating the alter anymore than I would go into a Synagogue and paint Swastikas." For radical homosexuals to do that in the name of homosexuality unfairly taints all homosexuals.

Heterosexuals should remember that the antics of ACT UP and Queer Nation are not representative of the majority of homosexuals. I choose to believe members of ACT UP and Queer Nation represent just a minuscule segment of the homosexual community and are not in any way the majority.

I also believe all the hoopla about the AIDS epidemic is merely another mindless campaign by members of the liberal agenda to foster feelings of hatred and division between homosexuals and heterosexuals. The following is perfect example of the misdirected mind set of the liberal media: "AIDS volunteers preventing death, making a difference," was the headline in a recent edition of *USA Today*. Of course, we regularly have AIDS recognition day in which a lot heterosexual people worldwide take part in keeping the issue on the front burner.

We regularly hear from such groups such as ACT UP, demanding immediate action to find a cure for AIDS. In fact, most AIDS activists say they don't want words, they want *action*. What kind of action do these people want? We've got more money and research going into AIDS than into any other disease, and far more people are dying of cancer than of AIDS. AIDS is preventable! To control the spread of AIDS, activists and members of our dysfunctional government want more condoms to be passed out in schools, in bars, in community centers, but we know condoms aren't the answer. The answer is to not be promiscuous.

Thomas Perrin was the U.S. Surgeon General from 1936 to 1948. He won the battle against syphilis by demonstrating that the over-arching need to protect the public health required identifying the carriers. Perrin's son believes that his father would not comprehend how today's AIDS victims, with the support of the ACLU have cowed our elected officials into banning the proven protocols of infectious disease control. Perrin's son believes that Perrin might even be more astounded by the contrast between the strident demand that science find a cure for AIDS while manning the barriers to controlling its spread from mother to child. The real question we should be asking is simple: what's the bottom line?

According to Dr. Stan Monteif and a lot of other physicians, if we want to control the spread of AIDS we must apply the standard hygienic principles that have always worked. We must identify carriers, and quarantine them if necessary (which in many cases it is not). We also need to make it illegal for a person to have sex with other people if a person knows he or she is a carrier of the AIDS virus. In my opinion, the bottom line on the whole thing is morality. *Morality!* It's the thing the most radical segments of the gay community don't want to hear, *"Zip up your pants!"*

When AIDS activists say they want more action

they will turn right around and dictate what type of action they want. AIDS activists continually scream for the governments of the world to "do something now." But when governments talk of quarantining, the activists recoil in horror and say, "Oh no! We don't want that kind of action." In reality that's precisely the type of action that worked with tuberculosis and syphilis and with all the other communicable diseases.

Since there are certain portions of our population which seem to be unable to control their sexual urges, we will, in all probability, have even more mysterious sexual viruses crop up in the future. The more global the world becomes, the easier it is for viruses to circle the globe. While one civilization may have built up a resistance to a local virus, international travel provides a host capable of carrying the virus to another culture having no immunity to the virus. Mysterious illnesses and even deaths result. When the white man first came to America he brought with him the viruses that cause Smallpox and Measles. Since American Indians had never been exposed to these viruses, many Indians died.

It would be bad enough if the cycle ended here but it does not. Viruses often mutate when introduced to new areas with other similar viruses. These mutated viruses have the capability of destroying entire civilizations. Remember the Black Plague? We could witness something much worse than AIDS in these chaotic times. if women *and* men don't learn to pull down their dresses and pull up their pants.

We can always scream for others to do something. But the real issue for many viruses, especially those transmitted through sexual contact, is to look in the mirror. If you sleep with animals, you can expect to die like an animal. Morality is the key. Members of ACT UP should ponder that, then look in the mirror and decide what path they choose *because AIDS is about choice.*

When Bill Clinton campaigned for the office he was a strong advocate of "Gay Rights." Naturally, members of the gay community voted overwhelmingly for Clinton. Clinton, like many gay activists,, does not have a strong sense of morality. Clinton often says one thing and then acts just the opposite. Clinton, like the members of ACT UP, should learn to stand up or shut up!

While members of ACT UP scream for the government to do something to stop a disease *they* can control, as they continue to lead promiscuous lives so hypocritical to their cause, President Clinton continues to speak out of both sides of his mouth. While the President continues to tell gay people he supports their cause, the Clinton Administration recently made an interesting decision regarding a 1993 gay rights ballot initiative in Cincinnati, Ohio, that was very similar to Amendment 2 in Colorado in 1992.

In the coming months the Cincinnati Court of Appeals is going to be hearing arguments in favor of overturning a lower court decision which held the initiative unconstitutional just as Amendment 2 in Colorado had been ruled unconstitutional.

Members of the not so illustrious Clinton Administration had been considering a Friend of The Court Brief, presenting arguments for the benefit of the court supporting the lower judge's ruling to declare the initiative unconstitutional. Of course Gay Rights activists were hoping the Clinton Administration would do precisely that. In fact two members of the Justice Department, Deval Patrick, head of the Civil Rights Division, and Eleanor Atchison, head of the Office of Policy Development, favored filing this brief agreeing with the judge's ruling that the initiative was unconstitutional, a position that would please gay rights activists.

The Clinton Administration decided not to file a brief in the case because of the November 1994 election results. Many feel this is the first test of the Administration's commitment, since the elections, on the issue of gay rights.

The administration also decided not to appeal the Keith Minehold case in San Francisco. Minehold was an enlisted man in the Navy; a sonar operator who publicly declared his homosexuality in a 1992 television interview. Minehold was discharged under old military regulations that were replaced in 1993 by the don't ask don't tell policy.

Under the don't ask, don't tell policy, Minehold would still have been released from the Navy. I suspect the Administration's decision not to appeal the Minehold case was well in the works prior to the November, 1994, elections.

Clinton, it seems, was willing to crawl in bed with members of the homosexual community just long enough to get elected. Once in office, faced with the political winds of conservative change, Clinton has decided it best to go quietly home.

If all gay rights activists would go home and love moral lives everyone would be much better off. Unfortunately our society chooses not to live by a moral code so we will witness even more insanity in the coming years.

San Francisco, the shining city of moral decay, just provided more fodder to the whole gay rights issue by enacting a far reaching civil rights law protecting members of the transsexual community from discrimination. "Very seldom do we have the opportunity to make history, to reach out beyond the mundane, to make justice," said Supervisor Terrance Holland, chief Sponsor of the anti-bias legislation. "We are doing it here, we are creating a civil right." In December, 1994, the Board of Supervisors unanimously approved the ordinance, which will make it illegal to discriminate against those individuals who fall under the category of "Transgender." (They mean of course, transsexuals).

"Transgender" is an umbrella term for people ranging from cross dressers to transsexuals. "They can't hurt us anymore. They can't bar us from stores. They can't kick us out of our housing," a tearful Tamara Ching, who was born male but now lives as a woman said after the board's vote. "Finally, we have protection."

Transsexuals are people who have undergone hormone therapy or surgery, or both, to transform from male to female or vice versa. Transvestites, drag queens and cross dressers, like dressing in clothing usually identified with the opposite sex. The transex community also includes people who have sex organs of both sexes, or undefined sex organs (whatever that means). They are big on social justice in San Francisco. They are very big on individualism. *San Franciscans also have one of the most dysfunctional cities on the face of this earth.*

I guess the bottom line for all homosexuals is simply this: Keep your private life private! Be proud of who you are not what you are. Don't demand special rights to protect yourselves from discrimination when your outrageous actions are the cause of people's negative actions towards you. Don't hold "gay rights" celebrations and then act like a bunch of depraved animals copulating in public when the camera's eye is trained on you. Just shut up and be the best you can be in all that you do and others will come to respect you for who you are not what you are. If you do this, no one will care what you are, they will simply care about you.

15

The Rush is Over
Limbaugh!

"The Rush is over"

- Steve Gross

"A new jobs report on NAFTA issued by Rep. Byron Dorgan (D-ND), revealed that 127,000 jobs were created as a result of NAFTA, but that 137,000 jobs were lost. This means there is a net 10,0000 jobs lost through September 1994 as a result of NAFTA. The report draws the conclusion "that NAFTA has not increased U.S. employment, but rather increased global access to Mexico's low-wage labor supply, as reflected in the growing shipments of capital goods and production inputs to Mexico, from the U.S. . . . This report was completed in November, 1994, and should have had a significant impact on stopping the passage of GATT. Why? Because if it cost the U.S. 10,0000 jobs to open free trade with Mexico, just think of the jobs it will cost us when we open ourselves up to free trade with the world. Unfortunately, the report wasn't released until the day after Congress voted to pass GATT."

"Buried in the GATT Agreement is a provision that will now allow an employer to reduce a lump sum payout to a retiree by about twenty-per cent. The sharks are circling the retirement island." Why doesn't Rush talk about this?

- Larry Bates, Author of The New Economic Disorder Will You Survive

Once in a generation, someone comes along who manages to reach out, shake up and wake up the slumbering masses of the silent majority, giving them the impetus to return enmasse to the voting booths to vote out of office almost an entire generation of corrupt political leaders. In the last decade of the Twentieth Century, Rush Limbaugh became the lightening rod for a generation of ordinary working class American citizens who had it with the lies and deceit emanating not only from Washington, D.C., but from State governments across America. Because of Rush, millions of conservative Americans rushed to the polls to hand liberal Democrats their first major Congressional defeat in decades.

When Rush Limbaugh first invaded the airwaves he not only entertained people, he made each and every loyal listener very much aware that they were not alone in their feelings of distrust and disgust with the status quo. As word of Rush spread across the land, millions of people turned on their radios and tuned in to listen to Rush's litany of rationality in an un-rational period of time. From humble beginnings, Rush became a phenomenon, a powerful force capable of singlehandedly stopping the encroaching madness that seemed to paralyze this great Nation.

When ordinary people needed to talk about the sorry state of the U.S. educational system, they called Rush and in talking with him, they were also talking with millions of other Americans equally fed up with the declining standards of a public school system sinking in a cesspool of decay. When ordinary businessmen and women needed to vent their frustrations over increasing taxes and insane regulations, they, too, called Rush and felt solace in knowing they were not alone. When Rush blasted the politicians and the political system the politicians had built, men and women across America began talking with each other, coming together to tear down a corrupt system that, before Rush, seemed impenetrable.

In lambasting the socialists among us, Rush gave heart to those of us who believe in the fundamental goodness of freedom. Rush was like a light in the darkness, debunking the hidden agendas of the feminists, environmentalists, gay rights activists, politicians, and educators. When the liberals attacked Rush, every conservative felt attacked and conservatives finally struck back in voting booths across the country. Many of us believe the Republican Rout in the November, 1994, elections occurred in large part because of Rush, and we thank Rush for giving us the courage to speak up; to begin the long process of taking back America.

Unfortunately, it seems every leader ultimately succumbs to the seductive influences of wealth, power, and corruption. Many of us now wonder if Rush has crossed the line and become one of those he used to condemn. In the process of creating the beginnings of a conservative revolution, it seems that Rush has perhaps fallen prey to the ultimate and totally corrupting forces of money.

Today, a lot of ordinary people, Steve Gross and myself included, no longer have faith in much of anything Rush Limbaugh says. Our loss of faith began with tiny nagging voices of doubt, after listening to Rush extoll the virtues of NAFTA. Those seeds of doubt continued to grow and perhaps blossomed in outright distrust after listening to Rush come out and fully embrace the questionable GATT Treaty. Perhaps we are wrong in our feelings. Only time will tell. But the Rush of today seems far different than the Rush we once looked to for truth.

In discussing the passage of the GATT Treaty, Rush does give one reason to pause and wonder. As to GATT, Rush says that many people were convinced that

moments after the deal was signed that America would cease
to exist, as we know it. That many people are convinced that
everything you own will, one day, be subject to being taken
over by a foreign government. He goes on to say that one of
the arguments that had been raised by the anti-GATT people
as a means of persuading people to join them is the child labor
issue. There are people saying, "I just refuse to buy
something made by a child of ten working twenty hours a day
in a factory that is ninety-five or one hundred degrees. And
until we can change that I am not going to buy that product."
 Rush says GATT doesn't allow us to define how people are
going to conduct their affairs; that we can't do anything about
the child labor laws of another country with GATT. "So what
is it about GATT that makes you people think India can tell
us how to run our affairs. It's this kind of thing the Anti-
GATT people are saying that I can't support. It is not true."
Come on, Rush. Even in the world of trade as it existed
before GATT, Presidents Clinton, Bush, Carter, etc., have told
other countries the U.S. will not trade with them unless those
countries do something about human rights violations.
Remember the China flap, Rush? Under GATT, 129 countries
can collectively gang up on the 130th country and dictate what
that country must do to be a player in the arena of world
trade. Do you honestly believe one lone country will dare go
against all the others? I think not. While I think most people
would want their governments to stand up against a country
that permits children to work in sweat shops, what happens if
129 countries tell the U.S. its workers make too much money
or produce too many goods?

       According to Rush, *all of the concerns that people
have about GATT have been addressed by both Gingrich and
Dole in the implementing legislation.* Unfortunately, as we
discussed in Chapter Two, both Gingrich and Dole are
members of the Council on Foreign Relations which seems

committed to the implementation of world socialism. Rush goes on to state there are side agreements that specifically state that no U.S. law will be subject to change by some outside tribunal or agency. That's probably true (although I don't think any one individual knows exactly what sort of legalese is buried deep in the 22,500 page treaty). But what good are internal laws when an external tribunal enacts trade policies dictating the rules each country must adhere to if that country, say the U.S., wants to sell goods in the world marketplace. Won't those external policies really supersede internal policies? Logic would certainly indicate this is what the ultimate outcome will be.

Rush says the anti-GATT people portray a situation where American jobs are vanishing; where American industries are shutting down; where we are losing our competitive edge. Rush says that as of January, 1994, our manufacturing industry is better off than it was in 1960; our productivity is higher, and that we are responsible for sixty-six per cent of all the goods and services produced around the world. According to Rush, the notion that the United States is falling apart, is being destroyed externally and internally, just cannot be made. He talks about how the anti-GATT people talk about how rotten things are already and how they are saying things are just going to get worse under GATT.

According to Rush, we are all predisposed to believe the worst. We will believe the worst without facts. We will believe there are conspiracies that have been at work for the longest time to destroy the country, and yet when we hear good news we want proof. When proof is given, people say, "That isn't enough for me." When we ask why it isn't good enough it's because someone else said something else to support the worst case scenario. While it is true that it is human nature to suspect the worst when faced with change, it is also true that the American people have good reason to suspect the worst case scenario in all cases of change because so much that has happened in America (thanks to our politicians) has turned out to be the worst case scenario. Our rights have been eroded, our streets are not safe, our children are learning less and becoming more violent and disobedient, our debt and deficit keep climbing, our inner cities are decaying, and 40 million Americans on welfare just sit on their butts watching game shows expecting the rest of us to continue to give them more of what we make, while our blue collar workers (once the bulwark of the middle class) are being thrown out of work thanks to the implementation of new technologies they cannot begin to comprehend.

Charles Murray, author of *The Bell Curve*, is right on target when he says we are becoming a society in which the cognitive elite are leaving the rest of the masses far behind, doomed to lead lesser lives. What have our politicians done in response to this situation? They have bent over backwards to implement Outcome Based Education that penalizes bright children and rewards children who are dumb or lazy. Not only do our children suffer, the future of our Nation is placed at risk.

Why are we predisposed to think the worst, Rush? Most of us live lives of quiet desperation, simply struggling to keep our heads above water, our children safe in schoolyard's, our pensions from disappearing, our home mortgages from becoming past due, while battling bureaucratic red tape, telephones, faxes and deadlines, before even considering what new little wrinkle our politicians are planning for our lives. You must remember that success provides the monetary cushion to escape the repetitious rigmarole most of us face each and every day. Remember what it was like, Rush? Never forget your roots. Never bite the hand that feeds you.

Never become too friendly with friendly politicians; they may be using you! That would be the cruelest hoax of all; especially for your loyal followers.

Rush does not even want to consider the possibility of any type of conspiracy theory. Neither do most of the rest of us. But one certainly has to stop and at least *consider* the possibility. It certainly seems that every new piece of legislation is designed to further erode the quality of life of each and every ordinary working man, woman, and family. If there really is no truth to the conspiracy theories, there certainly is overwhelming evidence that, as our society has turned away from believing in a Supreme Being to believing in the supremacy of men, we continually set ourselves up to be disappointed and disillusioned. There is not one man among us that cannot be manipulated either wittingly or unwittingly, for the benefit of another man or woman or group of men and women pursuing personal power. There is certainly nothing wrong with people pursuing success or power, it is the driving force that makes people and countries great. The corruption of that power for purely selfish reasons, however, can also destroy a civilization.

Recently, Rush said that to believe we are in the last days, either Biblically or politically, as a way of life, he cannot relate to. He does not want to walk around thinking we are in the process of being destroyed, especially since he does not see evidence of it. When did you last walk down a city street, Rush? When was the last time you jumped in your car and drove through a middle class neighborhood only to see gang members brazenly hanging out on street corners in daylight; the same street corners that become battle grounds at night where casualties are far too often innocent bystanders caught in the cross fire of bullets? When was the last time you ran into a convenience store only to wonder if the weird looking guy behind you was going to pull out a gun and shoot the cashier for twenty bucks? When was the last time you looked out your office window at the Excellence In Broadcast Network and lamented over the sorry state of the New York City streets littered with garbage and graffiti? The last time I came to New York City to meet with a publisher, I couldn't believe my eyes! For the longest time I thought I was walking on sidewalks in some third world country. Even the publishing house had a fleet of private guards patrolling the elegant lobby, personally escorting people to their destinations within. You don't see it anymore, Rush, because you've become insulated, protected, complacent.

You've surrounded yourself with the Bennett's and Kemp's of this world and you let them tell you they know what is best for America. While you expose the moral and perhaps legal misdeeds of Clinton and his cronies, it would be wise to ponder the private agenda of your political pals. Remember the story of the Trojan Horse? The collapse of every great country has come from forces within, not without.

At times, Rush mystifies listeners by his inconsistencies. When refusing to even consider the possibility of a conspiracy in relation to the GATT Treaty, Rush turned right around and pointed to the possibility of a conspiracy in the Bosnian mess. He did this when he said that the war in Croatia was being allowed by members of the U.N. and NATO. According to Rush, the reason the War had not been stopped was because political members of the U.N. and NATO were sitting around in long tailed jackets, wearing ascots, dividing up the countryside according to their political agenda.   Rush then made the same sort of mystifying statement in relation to Ted Turner. When discussing TNN, Rush laughed and said, "Turner forbids members off his news organization to use the word 'foreign' when discussing foreign affairs." Then Rush went on to say, "they did this before GATT was implemented. They went global before GATT." On December 23, 1994, when discussing GATT, Rush again confounded many of us when he said David Rockefeller had recently told him that GATT was a mechanism to "export liberalism worldwide," and this is why the Japanese and other cultures are beginning to experience the problems we have in America.

Perhaps Rush is not even aware of his inconsistencies. Perhaps I read too much in the inconsistent statements made by Rush - perhaps. Then again, perhaps Rush has crossed the line and gone over to the other side. I doubt anyone will ever truly know.

For myself and many others like me, Rush has lost his luster. *The Rush is over.*

16 The False Economy!

"The mid to late 1990s will be remembered as a dark period in American History."

"A day of reckoning is coming. For the las thirty years, Americans have been living beyond their means, piling debt on debt. The bills are coming due. The birds are coming home to roost. Many entitlement programs will disappear overnight! Welfare addicts will riot! The government may declare a state of emergency to take even more of our freedoms in the name of safety!"

— Mike Haga

"Most of our major banks have over two hundred per cent of their equity tied up in derivatives."

"Cash, at the crash, will be king."

— Larry Bates

Americans are being offered record numbers of credit cards. One of my neighbor's sons, who is fifteen years old, recently had an offer of a five thousand dollar line of credit. Adam is just a high school student. I believe two things are happening:

1. In a desperate attempt to make more money, banks are increasing people's lines of credit to, **2**. Get people more deeply into bondage to the false credit based financial system.

In Proverbs it is said; "The borrower is servant to the lender." Today, most working Americans are little more than slaves for their lenders and their government.

Should people take advantage of this additional credit? Unless you have existing credit card debt on which you are paying a very high rate of interest and you get an offer of a card with a lower rate of interest which will allow you to retire the card with the higher rate of interest, throw the new card offer in the trash.

Even though most people know they should not continue using their credit cards, credit card borrowing just keeps going up. From September through November, 1994, MasterCard and Visa had their best months ever. People are borrowing like it is going out of style. In the long run this trend has an adverse effect on the economy. As people are paying back the high cost of credit card bills there is natural slow-down in economic growth.

Today the FED and its member banks are raising interest rates. The prime rate is going up along with the discount rate. The Chairman of the Federal Reserve, Alan Greenspan, indicates that he will continue raising short-term interest rates. Why is he doing this? Greenspan says that inflation is in the pipeline. Inflation is manifesting itself in the financial markets. Until mid 1992, a lot of people and municipalities made tremendous profits in the financial markets. Since mid-year, 1992, a lot of people have suffered heavy losses in the financial markets, including Orange County, California, once the richest county in America. Orange County recently lost $3.5 billion dollars in risky investments known as Derivatives.

Greenspan believes that if he doesn't move now inflation will get so far out of control that the Federal Reserve will have to raise interest rates back to levels not witnessed since the Carter years when interest rates topped twenty-two per cent.

Inflation is the result of inflating the money supply. Webster's Ninth New Collegiate Dictionary defines inflation as, "An increase in the amount of money in circulation resulting in a fall in its value and a rise in prices." Typically, increases in credit increase the money supply resulting in inflation. Ordinarily there is a time delay between the time the new money (credit) is put into the financial system until the time inflation shows up in the form of price increases. The average time varies with the velocity of the movement of money in the system, but generally inflation begins to show up within twelve months of when the money supply is increased.

Today, America has a total debt structure of $12.5 trillion dollars with a mere $3 trillions dollars of actual cash to pay off that debt. In essence, America has a $9 trillion dollar problem. Debtors are bring asked to pay back $9 trillion dollars of debt *with cash that does not exist*! This is impossible. The flip side of this problem is that this $9 trillion dollars represents money that you and me and countless numbers of foreign investors have loaned to banks, to savings and loans, to insurance companies, governments, corporations, brokerages, and so on and this money either: 1. Won't be paid back because of default or 2. The Federal Reserve will have to print the money to pay the debt. Either way, we lose. That's how tenuous this entire economy is. It could go at any time. It could go without warning. The only glue that is holding this entire economy together is nothing more than the reassuring platitudes coming out of the mouths of politicians and central bankers.

This is why our politicians and bankers continually reassure us that everything is fine. The sad part in all of this is that people want to believe it. Ironically it is that belief that keeps everything going. It is a con game. The Wizard of OZ is working hard in Emerald City to make certain the con game does not stop. But the con game will stop. The natural law of economics will stop the con game. When the con game stops, there will be anarchy in America.

Take a moment to take a dollar bill out of your wallet or your purse. Take a moment to study the dollar bill. The dollar bill is a Federal Reserve Note. What is a note. A note is an IOU. Try to find on that dollar bill what is actually owed to you. It is an IOU *nothing*. We are paying debt with more debt. We have a debt based economy. Inflation is the natural part of a debt based economy. In a debt based economy, the people who save and invest often get wiped out overnight. The day is coming in America when people are going to be wiped out overnight. There is no way around it because people are not willing to accept the pain it will take to straighten out this economy.

As I briefly mentioned earlier in this book, in *ON THE BRINK, How To Survive The Coming Great Depression*, I take a long hard look at long-term economic trends from an historical perspective. I believe we have reached the point in our current economic cycle where we will experience either hyperinflation or outright deflation. In either scenario, most Americans will be wiped out, financially.

Our government will be forced to declare bankruptcy. People will be left to their own devices to make it through very turbulent times. *Since most people have saved nothing, most people will lose everything.* That's a frightening thought. Think about that when you sit down to dinner and then retire to spend several hours watching mindless sitcoms on TV.

In fact, I believe our deep seated and structural economic problems will stop the Republicans from doing much of anything of substance to correct the current problems facing all Americans. That is a sobering fact. That is a frightening fact. That is a fact you need to prepare for.

On a personal level, if prices continue to rise, this means that most Americans will have to run faster and faster just to stay even. This means all Americans will have less and less income to service their existing debts. What most people will experience is a double declining event. In short, no matter how fast each person runs it will not be fast enough to make the income needed, save money, and to pay off existing debt in an arena of rising interest rates necessary to slow the economy down. This means all Americans will experience declining living standards. Many people believe this is being done by design; that it is part of the New World Order Plan. As we have repeatedly seen throughout this book, the New World Order is a plan for world *Socialism.*

In his new book, *THE NEW ECONOMIC DISORDER Will You Survive?* Nationally recognized financial expert Larry Bates says that, "The Socialists intend to level everybody out. The Socialists intend to make everybody equal; equally poor. That way, if people are equally poor and struggling to keep up, people are not a resistant force to the New World Order."

At The recent World Summit in Cairo, the leaders of most countries made it clear that the standard of living of all people in the U.S. has to be brought down to the level of Third World Countries. *Do You hear this, Rush?* America is well on the way to becoming a Third World Country. Unfortunately few see this yet, and no one is talking about it yet (*especially the infinitely ignorant Rush Limbaugh who is leading his uninformed followers right up to the edge of the financial cliff over which they will willingly jump when Rush tells them too*) because everything appears to be fine on the surface and no one has taken the time to look beneath the surface to examine our economic superstructure which is collapsing under the weight of debt.

In December, 1994, Orange County, California, filed for bankruptcy under Chapter Nine of the Bankruptcy code when the county lost $3.5 billion dollars in its investment fund. The investment fund was investing in United States Treasuries Securities and highly leveraged instruments called derivatives.

Derivatives are a very sophisticated and artificial investment instruments whose value is derived from the underlying value of the stocks, bonds, securities, or currencies that are underlying the derivative contract. Essentially, derivatives enable investors to leverage investments to extreme levels. The County Treasurer in Orange County took $7.5 billion dollars of the county's money and parlayed it into a $20 billion dollar portfolio. When interest rates started going up, bond prices started going down, resulting in the $3.5 billion dollar loss. Each of the taxpaying citizens in Orange County essentially picked up $2,500.00 in debts for investments for which they will never see the benefit of. Of late, many other municipalities across America are beginning to admit that they too have losses.

Our so called financial geniuses (bankers and brokers and bond houses, etc.) have created over $40 trillion dollars worth of derivatives. This is equal to eighty-five percent of the value of all the stocks, bonds, and currencies in the entire world.

A derivatives fund manager was recently quoted in

the American Banker Magazine as saying, "This is man's attempt to create wealth out of nothing. "To limit derivatives is to limit creation. In the beginning, we separated light from darkness and to limit derivatives is to limit creation." We didn't separate light from darkness, God did. Does this fund manager think all fund managers are God? In the beginning, God set up a system of honest weights and measures. Derivatives and our whole economy, our whole investment system, is based on a dishonest set of weights and measures. Our whole monetary system is also based on a dishonest set of weights and measures. We will reap what we have sewn.

In Amos, Chapter 8, verses 4-5 it is said, and they made the Shekel (the dollar larger) and the ephah (the bushel) smaller, where it bought less grain and cheated with dishonest scales. Today, we are inflating the dollar (making it worth less) at the same time it looks the same to people. Our financial system, like everything else about our government, is dishonest

Mayer Rothschild, of the Rothschild banking family in Germany said, "Give me control of a nation's monetary system and I care not who writes their laws." We have the Federal Reserve, who is neither Federal and who has doubtful Reserves, in charge of creating paper money. We gave the FED a monopoly on this in 1913. Ever since that time we have had the peaks and valleys the booms and busts, in the economy. It is not a phenomenon nature, it is a result of deliberate policy actions by the policy makers.

Bankers are like sharks. When they see blood in the water, they zoom in to protect their interests. Since we have such a small amount of liquidity in this economy, if the average person on the street really understood what was going on, we would have panic in the streets.

On November 8, 1994, right after the votes were

counted, the insiders were preparing how to sabotage the will of the American people. The will of the people is that we have less government, less taxes, and more individual responsibility. But I believe what we are going to see is that this New World Order Crowd, which intends to have a one world Socialist system, will do several things.

They will create conflict in America by attempting to end entitlement programs. Since conflict brings progress but controlled conflict brings controlled progress. We will have racial and civil disorder to force members of this new Congress to stop the attempted reform of our government. The second thing we will see is contrived crises in the economy that will force the Congress to inject even more of our tax dollars in all entitlement programs to further socialize this economy to keep the New World Order scheme on track. This means taking money from other segments of the economy which increases the social stress. This is the leveling out process.

For the New World Order crowd to be successful in their attempts to further Socialize America, American citizens must either be willing participants or foolish sheep who say nothing. I believe we can still take back America. I believe we can stop the destruction of America if we are willing to come together, to let our voices be heard, and do whatever is necessary to end the tyranny of our government. This may require all Americans to actively defend their individual rights of freedom. If this means armed and open conflict, so be it. This is why we must not allow the institution of gun control laws. A disarmed populace is a helpless populace. Our government, our leaders, want to make us helpless.

The only way we can take back America, to restore freedom to America, is to fight the forces of evil which seem bent on destroying us. When we hear the pleas of the homeless and the welfare addicts, we must remain strong. We must let these people know *they* have choices. We must let these people know they can either choose to work like the rest of us or they can starve. The choice is theirs.

We are living in critical times. Critical times require critical choices. The choice is ours to make not only for ourselves but for our children and their children.

17 We Can Stop the Insanity

"It's like the whole world has gone nuts."

- James R. Lewis

"Will the new Republican Congress really make a difference? Maybe. But I wouldn't bet the farm on it."

- FESSUP

In spite of what the liberals claim, a lot of ordinary Americans voted Republican in the November, 1994, elections to get the government off their backs. It's a great idea. Somewhere along the way government ceased being our servant and became our master, controlling almost every aspect of our lives. In the process, elected representatives continually demanded higher taxes for ever increasing numbers of absolutely insane governmental programs dealing with everything from saving Spotted Owls to passing out condoms in public schools.

Naturally every new governmental program required a fleet of bureaucrats just to make life more difficult for *working* Americans. I believe Hillary's grand plan for the monumentally monstrous governmental takeover of health care was the straw that finally broke the poor Camel's back.

Thanks to Hillary, (*we do owe her such a debt of gratitude for waking us up and giving us the desire vote against the corrosive liberal agenda responsible for so many of our problems)* most Americans *hope* they've finally gotten the monkey off their backs. I wouldn't bet on it, though. Every time a new crop of politicians goes marching off to reform *Babylon by the Potomac*, very few, if any, ever return home victorious. In fact, very few ever return period. They just seem to take up permanent residence and become part of the problem, creating and passing increasingly complex legislation that strips average citizens of rights and hope. Although I am a conservative, I believe the new crop of Congress men and women will muddy the water and detract Americans from the real issues thus allowing professional politicians and the governmental machine to continue the destruction of America unless all Americans take a stand to stop the insanity.

Most politicians seem puzzled by the sour, cynical mood of productive members of our society. They don't understand why Americans have grown tired of everything that emanates from Babylon by the Potomac. But why should they? Politicians remain above the laws and regulations they enact.

People, average working people, no longer *believe* they have control of anything anymore. A perfect example of this helpless feeling most of us have is the recent passage of a postal rate increase. It now costs 32 cents to mail a letter that may never reach its destination because a postal employee threw it in the trash along with thousands of other letters. Can people boycott the Post Office? No! The Post Office has a monopoly on the mail system. If that letter fails to reach its destination, and it contains a payment, is the Post Office liable for a ruined credit rating? When pigs fly.

Like most working, tax paying American citizens, I have had it! I am fed up with the lies and deceptions of our politicians, journalists, economists, and educational

administrators *who seem bent on destroying this great country!*
How did we ever come to the place where not only elected
officials, but members of the news media and even *some* talk
show hosts look upon us, the middle class working men and
women voters, as nothing more than pawns in an elaborate
chess game of deceit and deception?

I'll tell you how! We've gotten soft! We're lazy!
We're a spoiled rotten, selfish, lazy, and arrogant people! We
give every impression that we don't care about anything that
happens outside the confines of the comfort of our own living
rooms where we gather each night (after working in often
dead-end un-fulfilling jobs) to watch, with bored smugness,
idiotic sitcoms where the most thought provoking scenes are
deciding what to wear, who to sleep with in order to gather
a little more dirt to be used as ammunition for moving up in
the corporate or political world, who to eliminate (blow away)
to keep secrets safe while living in mansions and speeding
around in exotic cars; all of this being intermittently
interrupted by equally mindless commercials telling us how to
keep our teeth white, our breath fresh, our skin forever young,
and our hemorrhoids under control.

Just think how far backwards we've come in the
last fifty years. Most of us just sit in front of television sets
watching perfectly groomed perpetually smiling hosts of
various nightly newscasts flash countless scenes of death,
mutilation, and destruction, while we calmly eat spaghetti and
discuss the minute details of office politics.

How can we do this? It's simple. During the work
day, most of us are faced with completing endless tasks of
unrewarding work assignments for large corporations of which
we feel we have neither a vested interest nor hope of ever
achieving not only recognition but a promotion to a level
where we feel we can make a difference. Therefore, we just

put in our time and hope nothing bad happens while looking forward to a retirement where we fantasize we will finally find happiness, only to realize, when we reach retirement, that, too, is a big disappointment because we can't afford to do anything more than sit home watching the same *stupid* television programs that kept our mind occupied while dreaming of better days.

In the end most of us become silently bitter, quietly hostile, perpetually depressed, and often placed on Prozac. We can't understand what happened to us. We can't believe that life could hold no more excitement than a weekly trip to the shopping mall where we try to *charge* our way to happiness, hoping happiness can be found in a new dress, a suit, a pair of shoes, because maybe, if we look like the successful people that dance across our television screens, we can find not only happiness, but success, wealth, power. Power to break free of the mediocrity of our lives. But that, too, is an illusion, a deception. In attempting to *charge* our way to happiness, we become more deeply in debt (most of us are already well in over our heads anyway) thus ensuring our continued servitude chained to the very jobs we dream of breaking free from.

By now, most have summarized what a catch-22 we face. What most do not understand, however, is that it is a catch-22 of our own making. In seeking security and safety, we do not spread our wings and take a chance to soar with eagles. No, we choose to stand in fenced fields with the rest of the turkey's who look forever upward envious of those who are free to fly.

In choosing comfortable chairs, whiter teeth, and the newest cars over taking the chance of breaking free and trying to create something most of us can call our own, we allow those in power, the politicians, judges, journalists, economists, educators (the eagles) to tell us turkeys when it is safe to go outside in the sunshine, what to wear, how to act, what *not* to do or say in the name of (how I hate these words) *Political Correctness.*

We rely on those in power to fling to us whatever scraps they feel we deserve, and like the turkeys we are, we struggle to be the first to reach the feeding trough often trampling each other in the great shopping mall of America.

We have reached a point where the eagles (who not only are very crafty but can also be merciless hunters when they catch a turkey that has gotten out of the fenced field and is timidly taking a few steps to freedom) not only control us but perhaps own us. Isn't it time for all the turkeys to come together and break free? Without question, there are infinitely more turkeys than eagles. While some turkeys may be lost in the revolution, at least they will go down in history books as heros. At least they will have the sense of doing something exciting, something more than just sitting in front of the same television set each night eating spaghetti.

Just imagine how many of today's turkeys could be tomorrow's *uncorrupted* eagles helping America become *America, the land of the free, the home of the brave, once again?* It could happen. It has to happen if we are to have a future. It must happen if we are to become free. At times I think something good is beginning to happen, that there is a glimmer of hope on the horizon. Perhaps that is why the eagles want to disarm the turkeys, to take away the budding blossom of freedom before it has the chance to bloom. If this happens, the eagles will ultimately throw the turkeys to the vultures; the feminists, the judges, the environmentalists, the animal rights activists, the televangelists, the new age new world crowd who would enslave all who do not practice political correctness, and all will be lost.

As I said before, there is a sense of optimism in America. Since the Republican Rout in the, November 1994, Congressional elections, there is a belief that rational voices of conservative Americans will now prevail thus effectively stopping the socialisticly oriented insanity that has slowly enveloped not only Washington, D.C., but the rest of the country and even the world.

While there *may* be cause for optimism, I believe it much too premature to believe that anything has really changed. It will take time to see if the new crop of faces coming to Washington will do more than take-up where the old faces left off. Politics makes for strange bed fellows and power structures are not easily dismantled. Eagles are cunning. They plan their strategies. Turkeys are foolish, they have no memory and they keep falling for the same deceptions time after time.

Even before members of the new Congress took the reigns of power away from the Democrats, a lot of sinister posturing seemed to be taking place. Bob Dole and Newt Gingrich came out in favor of the GATT Treaty which a large majority of literate Americans feel very uneasy about. Is GATT going to transform world trade creating millions of new American jobs in the process? Parts of the Treaty sound good, but other parts sound equally bad. Shouldn't the American people have had the right to have the Treaty examined fully and fairly and then *told* the Congress what to do with it? In a true Republic that is what should be done. But, as most literate American citizens know, the United States of America is no longer a Republic.

Liberals not only believe they *know what is best for everyone, they enact legislation most citizens do not want in the belief they are acting in everyone's best interests.* Hillary's grand plan for health care is a perfect example of this father knows best attitude. Do Gingrich and Dole feel is now their duty to carry on where the liberal Democrats left off. If so, does this not make Dole and Gingrich liberals in conservative clothing? It certainly makes one wonder. It should also make most people *mad as hell!*

Where do these people get off? How could Dole and Gingrich enter into a contract with the American People where one of the first promises was to balance the budget and then vote for a treaty that immediately adds thirty-one billion dollars to the deficit? I am afraid most of us are going to regret what we did at the polls. Prior to the election all of us should have logged onto the Internet and come up with some names of unknown Americans and agreed to vote for them as write in candidates. If we had done this, completely cleaned house, perhaps we would have something to truly celebrate. By 1996, we may well choose this route!

Between now and 1996, I believe we are going to witness an incredible amount of posturing and name calling, which in all probability will be carried on with great fan fare, mostly to keep us occupied while the new Congress passes new legislation which will create even more governmental control of everything. It would be funny, if the consequences weren't so tragic for all of us!

By the time you finish reading this book, I hope you will be ready to pitch in and take America back from crooked politicians; put feminists back in the kitchen; tell homosexuals to shut up; put educators back in the classroom to teach traditional forms of education; place environmentalists in shock therapy before turning them out to live in trees with owls or beneath rocks with the snakes they are; give convicted murders the ultimate and final shock treatment; put welfare addicts to work on chain gangs until they *decide to get an education and go to work* like the rest of us (who don't always enjoy working either); ship illegal immigrants back where they came from *after we cut off their benefits* only to find them voluntarily asking us to send them home; turn the religious right back to the Bible to learn that God did not tell them to go forth and preach hatred of everyone that does not think exactly as they do; disband all federal bureaucracies and put all bureaucrats to work on the same chain gangs with the welfare crowd *until they, too, decide to get an education and work at real jobs just like the rest of us* (just think how much less money we will have to spend on health care with the elimination of all the stress bureaucrats inflict on the rest of us, not to mention the sheer enjoyment of watching them get off their fat butts for a change).

Imagine how grand and glorious this country could be without the likes of the EEOC, the NAACP, the NOW crowd, the IRS, the EPA, OSHA, and on and on and on and on.......

Could it happen? "Sure," you laugh and say, "When pigs fly and cows jump over the moon. When spotted owls learn to roost on signs and reformed environmental rights activists no longer dictate whether a logger has a job. When the people at PETA no longer invite turkeys to sit down and partake a Thanksgiving dinner of tofu *with* them! When Bill gets Hillary to shut up, put on an apron and learn to make Big Mac's and fries at home. You bet! Then it could happen! Anything and everything is possible in our dreams?" But dreams still come true! They do, you know. You just gotta believe and work for them.

Unfortunately, not many Americans are willing to work very hard for anything anymore. But we must come together and work together if America is to survive. Sources tell me that members of the left, who are promoting the socialist agenda in America, are working hard to organize splinter groups across the country to hold massive demonstrations in the event the Republicans attempt to cut entitlement programs. Members of these splinter groups plan will ultimately create civil disorder and riots in the months and years ahead. These protests will give the government an excuse to implement emergency powers to take even more of our civil liberties. We must not fail! We must not give in! We must not give up! If we do, all freedoms could be lost!

We must realize members of our federal government are attempting to destroy the freedoms of all Americans by pitting all Americans against each other. We can't allow this to happen. If we do, we are doomed.

We must begin working together, on a grass roots level to find people who will work for all Americans. We must then work together to get these people elected to offices where they can work to implement legislation beneficial to the common working man and woman. If we do this, then we can begin taking back America; to restore America to greatness.

In the coming years our weather will become more severe and many people will try to convince us we are living in the end times. Don't fall victim to these scare tactics. Only God knows if we are in the end times. Severe weather, however, is merely part of a natural change in the long term weather cycle which occurs every fifty years. I detail the weather cycle in another book I recently wrote titled, *ON THE BRINK, How To Survive The Coming Great Depression.*

The next World War is in the making as this book is being written. *History is repeating itself.* To help you understand what this means for our economy, I again urge you read *ON THE BRINK, How To Survive The Coming Great Depression.*

18 EPILOGUE

"We have staked the whole future of American civilization, not upon the power of government, far from it. We have staked the future of our political institutions upon the capacity of mankind for self-government; upon the capacity of each of us to govern ourselves, to control ourselves, to sustain ourselves according to the Ten Commandments."

- James Madison

"Men, in a word, must necessarily be controlled either by a power within them, or by a power without them; either by the word of God, or by the strong arm of men; either by the Bible, or the bayonet."

- Robert Winthrop, 1852

By now you are probably angry and depressed. Many of you may be wondering if we even have a chance to take back our America from the politicians who seem to have us in straightjackets. Do not despair! If we come together, starting at the grass roots level, to work together to take back our country, we can win! It is up to us, now, to have our voices heard, to make our presence felt.

The Republican Contract With America is not the radical hate filled agenda members of the liberal media make it out to be. The Republican Contract with America is simply a way to begin throwing out the failed policies of thirty years of liberalism. The Republican's Contract with America simply

says that within the first 100 days of the 104th Congress, the
new Republican majority promises to bring bills to the House
floor on:

1. Term limits for members of Congress.
2. A balanced budget and line-item veto
3. Family and middle class tax cuts
4. The Economic Growth Act, containing a cut in
   the capital gains tax
5. An effective crime bill
6. True welfare reform
7. Common sense tort reform
8. Tax fairness for senior citizens
9. Strengthening traditional values
10. Strengthening traditional families

In fact, if the Republicans make good on their
promise to begin reformist legislation in the ten areas listed
above, they will have done little more than pave the way for
truly historic reform in the future. This future historic reform
will hopefully include the abolishment of the entire federal
government. But I wouldn't bet the farm on it. I believe
members of the 104th Congress will, in reality, do little more
than slow down the pace of encroaching Socialism.

Fortunately, the majority of taxpaying Americans
have made it clear they want more personal responsibility, less
government, and less taxation. These are the very tenets this
country was founded on. This fact gives me *some* hope that
we can stop the Socialists. If we become complacent, we will
fail.

Today we have over forty million American
citizens who choose to do nothing with their lives other than
to live off the masses. Today we have more people riding in

the wagon than people pulling the wagon and those who are pulling the wagon are wearing out, giving up. We have to get those members of society who have been riding in the wagon out of the wagon to help pull the wagon.

Today, in Washington, D.C., a single woman with one child who receives all four available entitlement benefits actually receives an annual income of $21,000.00. If this same woman were holding down a minimum wage job, she would make just $8,800.00. From her perspective it makes perfectly good sense not to work. We have to stop this. We have to end entitlement programs that promote the belief that working for a living is just not worth it. We can do this. It is up to us.

Today in America there are farmers who receive well over $100,000.00 per year not to plant crops. We have got to stop this. We can stop this. It is up to us.

Today in America more people send charitable contributions to large and often anonymous organizations like United Way than they do to local charitable organizations often working in their neighborhoods. This is insane. Time after time we hear stories about the corruption of the administrators of these large charitable organizations and yet we keep right on sending money knowing full well that 60 per cent of every dollar goes to provide lavish lifestyles for the administrators of these organizations. Quit sending money to United Way that spends more of your money on itself than on those in need. Take the time to find out which local charity needs help, and then help that charity. This way you can see if your money is being spent to help the needy.

The list goes on and on.......

Unfortunately, most Americans are hopelessly in debt. Most Americans have been living beyond their means for well over thirty years. Most Americans can turn this around by throwing away charge cards and paying down their debts. This will not be easy, especially for people accustomed to instant material gratification. If people begin to realize that material wealth does not provide permanent happiness, people will begin paying down their debts.

We have to instill a sense of morality in all American citizens. We can do this if we stop believing in the supremacy of men and restore a belief in the supremacy of God. If we return to a belief in the Supremacy of God, we will adhere to the Ten Commandments; we will have no need for legislation in the areas of abortion, equal rights, education reform, governmental reform and so on, because each of us will be living according to the tenets of God, our creator. We can do this! It is up to us.

Think about how insane the abortion issue has become. It will become worse yet, until women and men begin living moral lives. We can legislate and demonstrate; we can protest and we can kill each other in the abortion battle and it will change nothing. There is only one way to end the abortion issue and that is by ending the need for abortions. The only way the need for abortions will be ended is when all men and women live by a moral code.

In December, 1994, after Paul Hill was sentenced for murdering an abortion clinic doctor and his escort in Pensacola, Florida, Hill was asked whether his actions might spawn more killing. "Indubitably," he replied Hill proved prescient, when in January, 1995, a gunman opened fire at two abortion clinics in Brookline, Massachusetts, killing two people and wounding five others. Attorney General Janet Reno (whose governmentally hired killers gave us the Weaver Massacre and the WACO debacle - for which no governmental murderers will be prosecuted) has promised to beef up security at all abortion clinics in the United States. With the track record of Reno and Company I shudder to think about the consequences for all of us.

To think that members of our federal government can kill people with impunity, foster immorality, and have the audacity to condemn the rights of law abiding peace loving individuals in the name of progress is frightening. To realize that our government with the willing participation of a corrupt media can create such chaos in our country would have been unimaginable to our Forefathers. To know that millions of American citizens even bother to turn on their televisions to watch the likes of such superficial people as Bryant Gumble and Katie Kourac discuss such irrelevant issues as *feminism* is beyond belief.

While our country is under siege by illegal aliens and our laws are manipulated by a corrupt legal system; while our children are afraid to play in schoolyards and criminals have taken over our streets; while 42 million Americans choose welfare as a way of life and live off the sweat and taxes of a shrinking middle class struggling just to stay ahead of bill collectors; while members of our esteemed Congress continue to legislate our rights away while spending us into bankruptcy; while members of the FBI and the BATF randomly and with impunity continue to kill Americans who attempt to flee the madness or come together to insulate themselves from the madness of our government's actions; while our children are being taught to turn away from the tenets of freedom and to embrace the corruption of socialism pursuant to the creation of national educational standards that are giving us dysfunctional and illiterate children who will become adults dependent on welfare as a way of life; while our government fosters racism in the name of affirmative action plans designed to cause people to fail, the esteemed members of our media elite (while taking $1 billion of our tax dollars under the table) choose to list all the reasons why prayer should not be allowed in the classroom.

While I am not so naive as to believe we can quickly instill a sense of morality in most Americans, I believe we are standing at a critical crossroads where forces beyond our control will necessitate most of us returning to the basic tenets of the Ten Commandments. When we return to these tenets, we will have no need of external governmental control because every man woman and child will be capable of self government. Ironically, the basic premise on which this country was founded was that each individual be self governed and that government (as we know it) simply protected our Sovereign borders.

If we are to be successful in taking back *our* America, we *must* dismantle the entire federal government. We must return all power to the individual States, we must return to the Constitution and we must return to God! We can do this! We have the power to take back our country if we come together to work together *to defeat the powers of greed and darkness that are trying to destroy us!* But we can only come together when we stop using that destructive little line, the hyphen, that we have been using to define ourselves as Afro-Americans, Irish-Americans, etc. We must face the fact that we are all Americans fighting for freedom and for justice for all. Remember, it was Martin Luther King who said that, *we are all Americans and that we are all equal.*

We must work together to radically reform our current and totally corrupt legal system. Today, our courts are more concerned about the rights of the accused, than about the safety of most Americans. Putting the rights of the accused above the rights of the law abiding has left most law abiding Americans living lives of fear in houses with barred windows and double bolted doors.

To reform the legal system, we must abolish all civil and criminal statutes currently designed to delay justice just to fatten the wallets of corrupt lawyers and judges. We must return to the realm of reason. We must make law-breakers aware that breaking the law will result in justice that is sure and swift. If public executions of convicted killers will help make this point, then we must institute televised executions.

Jurists must return to basic laws to allow ordinary jurors to make common sense decisions and return realistic verdicts. We could take a giant step in legal reform by simply throwing out ninety per cent of all federal statutes designed to usurp state's rights. We can do this. We must do this!

Hopefully, in the O.J. Simpson murder trial, we are witnessing the last sensational murder trial to capture the attention of our nation as the 20th Century comes to a close. If the liberal media would focus on critical events we would all be better off. This would also go a long way toward legal reform. Today, many people are committing sensational acts of violence in order to make the news. Why give destructive individuals more impetus to commit outrageous acts just to see themselves on the television? We must make punishment severe and swift. People need to stop creating memorials out of places where senseless murders are committed and work toward preventing senseless murders to begin with. If you feel the need to lite a candle for someone do it in a church or synagogue

We have the power to stop programs like *Goals 2000, Workforce 2000*, and *GATT*, if we want to. It is up to us!

For many months I have been told by reliable sources that our government is establishing a series of "detention camps" in almost every state of the nation.

Curious, I traveled to Oregon to personally see (from a distance) one of these camps. I have also seen one such camp being set up in Southern Colorado. If the two camps I have seen are any indication of other camps, I am concerned. The general population has not heard much about these camps. These camps are not identified by names. These camps are run by people in military clothing. My sources tell me these camps are to be used in the event of civil disturbance in America. If civil disorder arises, dissenters will be rounded up and detained in these camps. My concern is who defines the term dissenter? Janet Reno and members of the FBI would certainly define dissenters differently than would I. Hitler created such camps in Germany just prior to the Holocaust.

To talk with Americans of this, most Americans say, "This is America, for God's sake. Don' be so paranoid." Each of us knows deep inside that the America we love is under siege. These are difficult times. During difficult times some of the most outrageous acts of man occurred often almost *overnight.*.

By late 1995 or early 1996, the Federal Reserve will have replaced every existing dollar bill (of whatever denomination) with re-designed dollar bills to stop (or so we are told) counterfeiting. I have seen some of these new dollar bills which have been radically redesigned. On the face of each and every existing dollar bill, regardless of denomination, we see "THE UNITED STATES OF AMERICA". On the new currency, the portrait of every President has been enlarged and moved to the left effectively covering the word "UNITED." When looking at one of the new and multi-colored dollar bills, one sees "THE STATES OF AMERICA." Is this part of some plan to unite Canada, Mexico, and the United States? Only time will tell. We can stop this if we want. We have the power.

If we continue to allow our government to divide us, our government will conquer us and we will lose our America. We must work together to become one America so that we can take back the America that is rightfully ours.

To take back our America, we must, initially, return all power to the individual states. Once we accomplish this, we must dismantle the federal government and restore our Sovereign borders. We will utilize members of our military to maintain our Sovereign borders and to turn away illegal aliens attempting to illegally gain entry into our country. Once we do this, we will be able to keep more of our money in our home states and in our homes. With more money at home, we can return to the traditional family unit where one parent works outside the home and the other parent works in the home to raise the children. This will allow us to return romance to our lives and bring love back into our houses. With parental nurturing, children will begin to excel in schools where we know what is being taught. If we do this, we can take back our America. We can do it if we work together. *WE CAN TAKE BACK OUR AMERICA!*

The most important part of our collective fight in taking back *our* America is to network with other concerned Americans. At this time, I believe the following organizations provide reliable sources of information to help all American people understand what is really happening in this country.

To that end, join forces with members of the First American Monetary Consultants, FAMC, a Christian think-tank located in Fort Collins, Colorado, whose members so graciously provided pieces of the critical information contained in this text. I urge each of you to become subscribers of FAMC's monthly newsletter, *Monetary & Economic Review.* You can contact FAMC by calling 1-800-336-7000 or by faxing 303-223-4996. FAMC offers a myriad of economic and market forecasting services along with seminars covering critical social issues facing each and every American. Members of FAMC can be heard on various Christian radio stations across America. Contact FAMC, obtain a listing of local radio stations carrying programs produced by members of FAMC. Listening to these programs, you will learn about such controversial topics as Unraveling the New World Order.

Through FAMC you can order a copy of Larry Bates most recent book, *THE NEW ECONOMIC DISORDER, Will You Survive?* Larry Bates, an economist, is publisher and editor of *Monetary & Economic Review* and Unraveling The New World Order. He is a former member of the Tennessee House of Representatives and Chairman of its powerful Committee on Banking and Commerce. A former bank CEO, Bates is a nationally recognized expert on political systems, the Federal Reserve, and how they affect the economy and your investments.

Join forces with the American Patriots of the People's Network, Inc. in White Springs, Florida. You can obtain information about the People's Network by addressing your letters to 3 River Street, White Springs, Florida 32096. The People's Network publishes a monthly newspaper called *The News Reporter* and has a bookstore called For The People, devoted to the publications of conservative and Christian authors. You can obtain a listing of highly important books by calling 1-800-888-999.

The People's Radio Network is also a division of the People's Network. The People's Radio Network is devoted to exposing governmental corruption while discussing the critical issues that face this nation. Programs produced by the People's Radio Network can be heard on over six hundred radio stations coast to coast. Find out which local radio stations carry these programs. Write to the People's Network and request a listing of local stations carrying their programs; tune in and listen and learn.

Subscribe to *The McAlvany Intelligence Advisor* by Don McAlvany, a conservative and very thought provoking publication committed to informing all Americans about the dangers of encroaching Socialism and what to do about it. For information on this publication write to *The McAlvany Intelligence Advisor*, P.O. Box 84904, Phoenix, Arizona 85071.

May God help us and have mercy on us and on our children in the dark days ahead!

RESTORING THE AMERICAN DREAM

First I would like to thank you for having purchased and or read this book. If nothing else, I hope you will stop and take a moment to reflect on what it means not only to live in America but to be an American.

In the future I plan to do a series of books similar to this one. As such, I am interested in your life, your hopes, your dreams. If you care to participate and your response is selected for inclusion in a future work, you will receive a free copy of the book your response is contained in.

I am interested in your response to the following series of questions:

1. I was born in........(State, City) Year of birth is optional
2. My family was........class (lower, middle, upper)
3. My father was a......(factory worker, etc.)
4. My mother was a......(housewife, secretary, etc.)

5. I was one of.........kids (Discuss your family life)
6. What was your family was like?
7. When I was little I dreamed of being..........
8. Did you go to college? Where?
9. Have you realized your dreams? If so, why. If not, why not?
10. *What has happened to the U.S. during your life?*
    From the perspective of your city, town, background.
11. *What do you see happening in the future?*
    To yourself. To your children (if any)
12. *Are you confident about the future?* If so, why. If not, why not?
13. If you had the power to restore America to greatness, how would you do it?

You can mail your response to me at the following address:

Mike Haga
The Economic Outlook
P.O. Box 200262
Denver, Colorado 80220-0262

I would like your response to be in an essay format. I do not care what you write but I do request that you limit your response to ten pages or less.

Appendix

THE TEN COMMANDMENTS

1.
Thou shall have no other gods before me.

2.
Thou shalt not make onto the any graven image.

3.
Thou shall not take the name of the Lord
thy God in vain.

4.
Remember the Sabbath day, to keep it holy.

5.
Honor thy father and mother.

6.
Thou shalt not kill.

7.
Thou shall not commit adultery.

8.
Thou shalt not steal.

9.
Thou shalt not bear false witness.

10.
Thou shalt not covet.

Is America adhering to the law of God, or to the false law of man? Compare the "wisdom" of men in the Communist Manifesto (below) with the wisdom of God in the Ten Commandments. Then compare the "wisdom" of men in the Communist Manifesto with the wisdom of our founding fathers who adhered to the law of *God* in the **Law of The Land, The Declaration of Independence, The Constitution of the United States, and the Bill of Rights.**

When you finish comparing the Communist Manifesto to the Law of The Land, The Declaration of Independence, The Constitution of the United States, and The Bill of Rights, ask yourself the following questions: (1. Am I living in America or Russia? (2. Is it any wonder the United States is in such terrible shape morally, economically, spiritually? (3. Did this happen because we the people turned away from a belief in God to embrace the belief in the supremacy of individual men each of whom has failed us and who will continue to do so? (4. Is there hope?

Yes! There is hope! To restore America to greatness, we must nullify the power of the federal government which has usurped the Constitutional law of this country. To understand the limitations of the federal government, read the document entitled Federal Jurisdiction (below) provided by Ken Creamer. When you have finished you will understand what we must do to return to the tenets that made this country great. We must return to a belief in the supremacy of a Sovereign God, and we must adhere to the Ten Commandments. We can do this! The choice is ours! If we do not, America will perish!

* * * * * * *

TEN PLANKS OF THE COMMUNIST MANIFESTO
(which also seem to be the policies of our federal government)

1. Abolition of property in land and the application of all rents of land to public purposes.

2. A heavy progressive or graduated income tax.

3. Abolition of all right of inheritance.

4. Confiscation of the property of all emigrants and rebels.

5. Centralization of credit in the hands of the State, by means of a national bank, with State capital and exclusive monopoly.

6. Centralization of the means of communications and transport in the hands of the State.

7. Extension of factories and instruments of production owned by the State, the bringing into cultivation of waste lands, and the improvement of soil generally in accordance with a common plan.

8. Equal liability of all labor. Establishment of industrial armies especially for agriculture.

9. Combination of agriculture with manufacturing industries; gradual abolition of the distinction between town and country, by a more equitable distribution of population over the country.

10. Free education for all for all children in public schools. Abolition of children's factory labor in its present form. Combination of education with industrial production, etc., etc.

* * * * * * * *

LAW OF THE LAND

The general misconception is that any statute passed by legislators bearing the appearance of law constitutes the law of the land. The U.S. Constitution is the supreme law of the land, and any statute, to be valid, must be in agreement. It is impossible for both the Constitution and a law violating it to be valid; one must prevail. This is succinctly stated as follows:

The general rule is that an unconstitutional statute, though having the form and name of law, is in reality no law, but is wholly void, and ineffective for any purpose; since constitutionality dates from the time of enactment, and not merely from the date of the decision so branding it. An unconstitutional law, in legal contemplation, is as inoperative as if it had never been passed. Such a statute leaves the question that it purports to settle just as it would be had the statute not been enacted.

Since an unconstitutional law is void, the general principles follow that it imposes no duties, confers no rights, creates no office, bestows no power or authority on anyone, affords no protection, and justifies no acts performed under it . . .

A void act cannot be legally consistent with a valid one. An unconstitutional law cannot operate to supersede any existing valid law. Indeed, insofar as a statute runs counter to the fundamental law of the land, it is superseded thereby.

No one, is bound to obey an unconstitutional law and no courts are bound to enforce it.

Sixteenth American Jurisprudence
Second Edition, Section 256

* * * * * * * *

In CONGRESS, JULY 4, 1776.

The Unanimous Declaration
of the thirteen united
States Of America

When in the Course of human events, it becomes necessary for one people to dissolve the political bands which have connected them with another, and to assume among the powers of the earth, the separate and equal station to which the Laws of Nature and of Nature's God entitles them, a decent respect to the opinions of mankind requires that they should declare the causes which impel them to the separation.

We hold these truths to be self-evident, that all men are created equal, that they are endowed by their Creator with certain unalienable Rights, that among these are Life, Liberty and the pursuit of Happiness. That to secure these rights, Governments are instituted among Men, deriving their just powers from the consent of the governed. That whenever any Form of Government becomes destructive of these ends, it is the Right of the People to alter or to abolish it, and to institute new Government, laying its foundation on such principles and organizing its powers in such form, as to them shall seem most likely to effect their Safety and Happiness. Prudence, indeed, will dictate that Governments long established should not be changed for light and transient causes; and accordingly all experience hath shown, that mankind are more disposed to suffer, while evils are sufferable, than to right themselves by abolishing the forms to which they are accustomed. But when a long train of abuses and usurpations, pursuing invariably the same Object evinces a design to reduce them under absolute Despotism, it is their right, it is their duty, to throw off such Government, and to provide new Guards for their future security. Such has been the patient sufferance of these Colonies; and such is now the necessity which constrains them to alter their former Systems of Government. The history of the present King of Great Britain is a history of repeated injuries and usurpations, all having in direct object the establishment of an absolute Tyranny over these States.   To prove this, let Facts be submitted to a candid world.

He has refused his Assent to Laws, the most wholesome and necessary for the public good.

He has forbidden his Governors to pass Laws of immediate and pressing importance, unless suspended in their operation till his Assent should be obtained; and when so suspended, he has utterly neglected to attend to them.

He has refused to pass other Laws for the accommodation of large districts of people, unless those people would relinquish the right of Representation in the Legislature, a right inestimable to them and formidable to tyrants only.

He has called together legislative bodies at places unusual, uncomfortable, and distant from the depository of their public Records, for the sole purpose of fatiguing them into compliance with his measures.

He has dissolved Representative Houses repeatedly, for opposing with manly firmness his invasion on the rights of the people.

He has refused for a long time, after such dissolutions, to cause others to be elected; whereby the Legislative powers, incapable of Annihilation, have returned to the People at large for their exercise; the state remaining in the meantime exposed to all the dangers of invasion from without, and convulsions within.

He has endeavored to prevent the population of these States; for that purpose obstructing the Laws for Naturalization of Foreigners; refusing to pass others to encourage their migrations hither, and raising the conditions of new Appropriations of Lands.

He has obstructed the Administration of Justice, by refusing his Assent to Laws for establishing Judiciary Powers.

He has made Judges dependent on his Will alone, for the tenure of their offices, and the amount and payment of their salaries.

He has erected a multitude of New Offices, and sent hither swarms of Officers to harass our people, and eat out their substance.

He has kept among us, in times of peace, Standing Armies without the Consent of our legislature.

He has affected to render the Military independent of and superior to the Civil power.

He has combined with others to subject us to a jurisdiction foreign to our constitution, and unacknowledged by our laws; giving his Assent to their Acts of pretended Legislation:

For Quartering large bodies of armed troops among us:

For protecting them, by a mock trial, from punishment for any Murders which they should commit on the Inhabitants of these States:

For cutting off our Trade with all parts of the world:

For imposing Taxes on us without our Consent:

For depriving us in many cases of the benefits of

Trial by Jury:

For transporting us beyond Seas to be tried for pretended offenses:

For abolishing the free System of English Laws in a neighboring Province, establishing therein an Arbitrary government, and enlarging its Boundaries so as to render it at once an example and fit instrument for introducing the same absolute rule into these Colonies:

For taking away our Charters, abolishing our most valuable Laws, and altering fundamentally the Forms of our Government:

For suspending our own Legislatures, and declaring themselves invested with power to legislate for us in all cases whatsoever.

He has abdicated Government here, by declaring us out of his Protection and waging War against us.

He has plundered our seas, ravaged our Coasts, burnt our towns, and destroyed the lives of our people.

He is at this time transporting large Armies of foreign Mercenaries to complete the works of death, desolation and tyranny, already begun with circumstances of Cruelty and perfidy scarcely paralleled in the most barbarous ages, and totally unworthy the Head of a civilized nation.

He has constrained our fellow Citizens taken Captive on the high Seas to bear Arms against their Country, to become the executioners of their friends and Brethren, or to fall themselves by their Hands.

He has excited domestic insurrections amongst us, and has endeavored to bring on the inhabitants of our frontiers, the merciless Indian Savages, whose known rule of warfare, is an undistinguished destruction of all ages, sexes and conditions.

In every stage of these Suppressions We have Petitioned for Redress in the most humble terms. Our repeated Petitions have been answered only by repeated injury. A Prince, whose character is thus marked by every act which may define a Tyrant, is unfit to be the ruler of a free people.

Nor have We been wanting in attention to our British brethren. We have warned them from time to time of attempts by their legislature to extend an unwarrantable jurisdiction over us. We have reminded them of the circumstances of our emigration and settlement here. We have appealed to their native justice and magnanimity, and we have conjured them by the ties of our common kindred to disavow these usurpations, which would inevitably interrupt our connections and correspondence. They too have been deaf to the voice of justice and of consanguinity. We must, therefore, acquiesce in the necessity, which denounces our Separation, and hold them, as we hold the rest of mankind, Enemies in War, in Peace Friends.

WE, THEREFORE, the Representatives of the UNITED STATES OF AMERICA, in General Congress, Assem bled, appealing to the Supreme Judge of the world for the rectitude of our intentions, do, in the Name, and by Authority of the good People of these Colonies, solemnly publish and declare, That these United Colonies are, and of Right ought to be FREE AND INDEPENDENT STATES; that they are Absolved from all Allegiance to the British Crown, and that all political connection between them and the State of Great Britain, is and ought to be totally dissolved; and that as Free and Independent States, they have full Power to levy War, conclude Peace, contract Alliance, establish Commerce, and to do all other Acts and Things which Independent States may of right do. And for the support of this Declaration, with a firm reliance on the protection of Divine Providence, we mutually pledge to each other our Lives, our Fortunes, and our sacred Honor.

SIGNERS OF THE DECLARATION OF INDEPENDENCE

According to the Authenticated List Printed by Order of Congress of January 18, 1777   John Hancock, etc.

* * * * * * *

The CONSTITUTION OF THE UNITED STATES

We, the People of the United States, in Order to form a more perfect Union, establish Justice, insure domestic Tranquillity, provide for the common defense, promote the general Welfare, and secure the Blessings of Liberty to ourselves and our Posterity, do ordain and establish this Constitution for the United States of America.

ARTICLE I

Section 1. All legislative Powers herein granted shall be vested in a Congress of the United States, which shall consist of a Senate and House of Representatives.

Section 2. The House of Representatives shall be composed of Members chosen every second Year by the People of the several States, and the Electors in each State shall have the Qualifications requisite for Electors of the most numerous Branch of the State Legislature.

No Person shall be a Representative who shall not have attained to the Age of twenty-five Years, and been seven Years a Citizen of the United States, and who shall not, when elected, be an Inhabitant of that State in which he shall be chosen.

Representatives and direct Taxes shall be apportioned among the several States which may be included within this Union, according to their respective Numbers, which shall be determined by adding to the whole Number of free Persons, including those bound to Service for a Term of Years, and excluding Indians not taxed, three-fifths of all other Persons. The actual Enumeration shall be made within three Years after the first Meeting of the Congress of the United States, and within every subsequent Term of ten Years, in such Manner as they shall by Law direct. The Number of Representatives shall not exceed one for every thirty Thousand, but each State shall have at Least one Representative; and until such enumeration shall be made, the State of New Hampshire shall be entitled to chuse three, Massachusetts eight, Rhode-Island and Providence Plantations one, Connecticut five, New York six, New Jersey four, Pennsylvania eight, Delaware one, Maryland six, Virginia ten, North Carolina five, South Carolina five, and Georgia three.

When vacancies happen in the Representation from any State, the Executive Authority thereof shall issue Writs of Election to fill such Vacancies.

The House of Representatives shall chuse their Speaker and other Officers; and shall have the sole Power of Impeachment.

Section 3. The Senate of the United States shall be composed of two Senators from each State, chosen by the Legislature thereof, for six Years; and each Senator shall have one Vote.

Immediately after they shall be assembled in Consequence of the first Election, they shall be divided as equally as may be into three Classes. The seats of the Senators of the first Class shall be vacated at the Expiration of the second Year, of the second Class at the Expiration of the fourth Year, and of the third Class at the Expiration of the sixth Year, so that one third may be chosen every second Year; and if Vacancies happen by Resignation, or otherwise, during the Recess of the Legislature of any State, the Executive thereof may make temporary Appointments until the next Meeting of the Legislature, which shall then fill such Vacancies.

No Person shall be a Senator who shall not have attained to the Age of thirty Years, and been nine Years a Citizen of the United States, and who shall not, when elected, be an Inhabitant of that State for which he shall be chosen.

The Vice President of the United States shall be President of the Senate, but shall have no Vote, unless they be equally divided.

The Senate shall chuse their other Officers, and also a President pro tempore, in the Absence of the Vice President, or when he shall exercise the Office of President of the United States.

The Senate shall have the sole Power to try all Impeachments. When sitting for that Purpose, they shall be on Oath or Affirmation. When the President of the United States is tried, the Chief Justice shall preside: And no Person shall be convicted without the Concurrence of two thirds of the Members present.

Judgment in Cases of Impeachment shall not extend further than to removal from Office, and disqualification to hold and enjoy any Office of honor, Trust or Profit under the United States: but the Party convicted shall nevertheless be liable and subject to Indictment, Trial, Judgment and Punishment, according to Law.

Section 4. The Times, Places and Manner of holding
Elections for Senators and Representatives, shall be prescribed in each State by the Legislature thereof; but the Congress may at any time by Law make or alter such Regulations, except as to the Places of chusing Senators.

The Congress shall assemble at least once in every Year, and such Meeting shall be on the first Monday in December, unless they shall by Law appoint a different Day.

Section 5. Each House shall be the Judge of Elections, Returns and Qualifications of its own Members, and a Majority of each shall constitute a Quorum to do Business; but a smaller Number may adjourn from day to day, and may be authorized to compel the Attendance of absent Members, in such Manner, and under such Penalties as each House may provide.

Each House may determine the Rules of its Proceedings, punish its Members for disorderly Behavior, and, with the Concurrence of two thirds, expel a Member.

Each House shall keep a Journal of its Proceedings, and from time to time publish the same, excepting such Parts as may in their Judgment require Secrecy; and the Yeas and Nays of the Members of either House on any question shall, at the Desire of one fifth of those Present, be entered on the Journal.

Neither House, during the Session of Congress, shall, without the Consent of the other, adjourn for more than three days, nor to any other Place than that in which the two Houses shall be sitting.

Section 6. The Senators and Representatives shall

receive a Compensation for their Services, to be ascertained by Law, and paid out of the Treasury of the United States. They shall in all Cases, except Treason, Felony and Breach of the Peace, be privileged from Arrest during their Attendance at the Session of their respective Houses, and in going to and returning from the same; and for any Speech or Debate in either House, they shall not be questioned in any other Place.

No Senator or Representative shall, during the Time for which he was elected, be appointed to any civil Office under the Authority of the United States which shall have been created, or the Emoluments whereof shall have been encreased during such time; and no Person holding any Office tinder the United States, shall be a Member of either House during his Continuance of Office.

Section 7.   All Bills for raising Revenue shall originate in the House of Repre sentatives; but the Senate may propose or concur with Amendments as on other Bills.

Every Bill which shall have passed the House of Representatives and the Senate, shall, before it becomes a Law, be presented to the President of the United States; if he approve he shall sign it, but if not he shall return it, with his Objections to that House in which it shall have originated, who shall enter the Objections at large on their Journal, and proceed to reconsider it. If after such Reconsideration two thirds of that House shall agree to pass the Bill, it shall be sent, together with the Objections, to the other House, by which it shall likewise be reconsidered, and if approved by two thirds of that House, it shall become a Law. But in all such Cases the Votes of both Houses shall be determined by Yeas and Nays, and the Names of Persons voting for and against the Bill shall be entered on the Journal of each House respectively. If any Bill shall not be returned by the President within ten Days (Sundays excepted) after it shall have been presented to him, the Same shall be a Law, in like Manner as if he signed it, unless the Congress by their Adjournment prevent its Return, in which Case it shall not be a Law.

Every Order, Resolution, or Vote to which the Concurrence of the Senate and House of Representatives may be necessary (except on a question of Adjournment) shall be presented to the President of the United States; and before the Same shall take Effect, shall be approved by him, or being disapproved by him, shall be repassed by two thirds of the Senate and House of Representatives, according to the Rules and Limitations prescribed in the Case of a Bill.

Section 8. The Congress shall have Power To lay and collect Taxes, Duties, Imposts and Excises, to pay the Debts and provide for the common Defense and general Welfare of the United States; but all Duties, Imposts and Excises shall be uniform throughout the United States;

To borrow Money on the credit of the United States;

To regulate Commerce with foreign Nations, and among the several States, and with the Indian Tribes;

To establish an uniform Rule of Naturalization, and uniform Laws on the subject of Bankruptcies throughout the United States;

To coin Money, regulate the Value thereof, and of foreign Coin, and fix the Standard of Weights and Measures;

To provide for the Punishment of counterfeiting the Securities and current Coin of the United States;

To establish Post Offices and post Roads;

To promote the Progress of Science and useful Arts, by securing for limited Times to Authors and Inventors the exclusive Right to their respective Writings and Discoveries;

To constitute Tribunals inferior to the supreme Court;

To define and punish Piracies and Felonies committed on the high Seas, and Offences against the Laws of Nations;

To declare War, grant Letters of Marque and Reprisal, and make Rules concerning Captures on Land and Water;

To raise and support Armies, but no Appropriation of Money to that Use shall be for a longer Term than two Years;

To provide and maintain a Navy;

To make Rules for the Government and Regulation of the land and naval Forces;

To provide for calling forth the Militia to execute the Laws of the Union, suppress Insurrections and repel Invasions;

To provide for organizing, arming, and disciplining, the Militia, and for governing such Part of them as may be employed in the Service of the United States, reserving to the States respectively, the Appointment of the Officers, and the Authority of training the Militia according to the discipline prescribed by Congress;

To exercise exclusive Legislation in all Cases whatsoever, over such District (not exceeding ten Miles square) as may, by Cession of particular States, and the Acceptance of Congress, become the Seat of the Government of the United States, and to exercise like Authority over all Places purchased by the Consent of the Legislature of the State in which the Same shall be, for the Erection of Forts, Magazines, Arsenals, dock-Yards, and other needful Buildings;-And

To make all Laws which shall be necessary and proper for carrying into Execution the foregoing Powers, and all other Powers vested by this Constitution in the Government of the United States, or in any Department or Office thereof.

Section 9. The Migration or Importation of such Persons as any of the States now existing shall think proper to admit, shall not be prohibited by the Congress prior to the Year one thousand eight hundred and eight, but a Tax or duty may be imposed on such Importation, not exceeding ten dollars for each Person.

The Privilege of the Writ of Habeas Corpus shall not be suspended, unless when in Cases of Rebellion or Invasion the public Safety may require it.

No Bill of Attainder or ex post facto Law shall be passed.

No Capitation, or other direct, Tax shall be laid, unless in Proportion to the Census or Enumeration hereinbefore directed to be taken.

No Tax or Duty shall be laid on Articles exported from any State. No Preference shall be given by any Regulation of Commerce or Revenue to the Ports of one State over those of another; nor shall Vessels bound to, or from, one State, be obliged to enter, clear, or pay Duties in another.

No Money shall be drawn from the Treasury, but in Consequence of Appropriations made by Law; and a regular Statement and Account of the Receipts and Expenditures of all public Money shall be published from time to time.

No Title of Nobility shall be granted by the United States; and no Person holding any Office of Profit or Trust under them, shall, without the Consent of the Congress, accept of any present, Emolument, Office, or Title, of any kind whatever, from any King, Prince, or foreign State.

Section 10. No State shall enter into any Treaty, Alliance, or Confederation; grant Letters of Marque or Reprisal; coin Money; emit Bills of Credit; make any Thing but gold and silver Coin a Tender in Payment of Debts; pass any Bill of Attainder, ex post facto Law, or Law impairing the Obligation of Contracts, or grant any Title of Nobility.

No State shall, without the Consent of the Congress, lay any Imposts or Duties on Imports or Exports, except what may be absolutely necessary for executing its inspection Laws: and the net Produce of all Duties and Imposts, laid by any State on Imports or Exports, shall be for the Use of the Treasury of the United States; and all such Laws shall be subject to the Revision and Control of the Congress.

No State shall, without the Consent of Congress, lay any Duty on Tonnage, keep Troops, or Ships of War in time of Peace, enter into any Agreement or Compact with another State, or with a foreign Power, or engage in War, unless actually invaded, or in such imminent Danger as will not admit of delay.

ARTICLE II

Section 1. The executive Power shall be vested in a President of the United States of America. He shall hold his Office during the Term of four Years, and, together with the Vice President, chosen for the same Term, be elected as follows:

Each State shall appoint, in such Manner as the Legislature thereof may direct, a Number of Electors, equal to the whole Number of Senators and Representatives to which the State may be entitled in the Congress: but no Senator or

Representative, or Person holding an Office of Trust or Profit under the United States, shall be appointed an Elector.

The Electors shall meet in their respective States, and vote by Ballot for two Persons, of whom one at least shall not be an Inhabitant of the same State with themselves. And they shall make a List of all the Persons voted for, and of the Number of Votes for each; which List they shall sign and certify, and transmit sealed to the Seat of the Government of the United States, directed to the President of the Senate. The President of the Senate shall, in the Presence of the Senate and House of Representatives, open all the Certificates, and the Votes shall then be counted. The Person having the greatest Number of Votes shall be the President, if such Number be a Majority of the whole Number of Electors appointed; and if there be more than one who have such Majority, and have an equal Number of Votes, then the House of Representatives shall immediately chuse by Ballot one of them for President; and if no Person have a Majority, then from the five highest on the List the said House shall in like Manner chuse the President. But in chusing the President, the Votes shall be taken by States, the Representatives from each State having one Vote; A quorum for this Purpose shall consist of a Member or Members from two thirds of the States, and a Majority of all the States shall be necessary to a Choice. In every Case, after the Choice of the President, the Person having the greatest Number of Votes of the Electors shall be the Vice President. But if there shall remain two or more who have equal Votes, the Senate shall chuse from them by Ballot the Vice President.

The Congress may determine the Time of chusing the Electors, and the Day on which they shall give their Votes: which Day shall be the same throughout the United States.

No Person except a natural born Citizen, or a

Citizen of the United States, at the time of the Adoption of
this Constitution, shall be eligible to the Office of President;
neither shall any Person be eligible to that Office who shall
not have attained to the Age of thirty five Years, and been
fourteen Years a Resident within the United States.

In Case of the Removal of the President from
Office, or of his Death, Resignation, or Inability to discharge
the Powers and Duties of the said Office, the Same shall
devolve on the Vice President, and the Congress may by Law
provide for the Case of Removal, Death, Resignation or
Inability, both of the President and Vice President, declaring
what Officer shall then act as President, and such Officer shall
act accordingly, until the Disability be removed, or a President
shall be elected.

The President shall, at stated Times, receive for his
Services, a Compensation, which shall neither be encreased
nor diminished during the Period for which he shall have been
elected, and he shall not receive within that Period any other
Emolument from the United States, or any of them.

Before he enter on the Execution of his Office, he
shall take the following Oath or Affirmation: - "I do solemnly
swear (or affirm) that I will faithfully execute the Office of
President of the United States, and will to the best of my
Ability, preserve, protect and defend the Constitution of the
United States."

Section 2.   The President shall be Commander in
Chief of the Army and Navy of the United States, and of the
Militia of the several States, when called into the actual
Service of the United States; he may require the Opinion, in
writing, of the principal Officer in each of the executive
Departments, upon any Subject relating to the Duties of their
respective Offices, and he shall have Power to grant Reprieves
and Pardons for Offenses against the United States, except in

Cases of Impeachment.

He shall have Power, by and with the Advice and Consent of the Senate, to make Treaties, provided two thirds of the Senators present concur; and he shall nominate, and by and with the Advice and Consent of the Senate, shall appoint Ambassadors, other public Ministers and Consuls, Judges of the supreme Court, and all other Officers of the United States, whose Appointments are not herein otherwise provided for, and which shall be established by Law; but the Congress may by Law vest the Appointment of such inferior Officers, as they think proper, in the President alone, in the Courts of Law, or in the Heads of Departments.

The President shall have Power to fill up all Vacancies that may happen during the Recess of the Senate, by granting Commissions which shall expire at the End of their next Session.

Section 3. He shall from time to time give to the Congress Information of the State of the Union, and recommend to their Consideration such Measures as he shall judge necessary and expedient; he may, on extraordinary Occasions, convene both Houses, or either of them, and in Case of Disagreement between them, with Respect to the Time of Adjournment, he may adjourn them to such Time as he shall think proper; he shall receive Ambassadors and other public Ministers; he shall take Care that the Laws be faithfully executed, and shall Commission all the Officers of the United States.

Section 4. The President, Vice President and all civil Officers of the United States, shall be removed from Office on impeachment for, and Conviction of, Treason, Bribery, or other high Crimes and Misdemeanors.

ARTICLE III

Section 1. The judicial Power of the United States, shall be vested in one supreme Court, and in such inferior Courts as the Congress may from time to time ordain and establish. The Judges, both of the supreme and inferior Courts, shall hold their Offices during good Behavior, and shall, at stated Times, receive for their Services, a Compensation, which shall not be diminished during their Continuance in Office.

Section 2. The judicial Power shall extend to all Cases, in Law and Equity, arising under this Constitution, the Laws of the United States, and Treaties made, or which shall be made, under their Authority; -to all Cases affecting Ambassadors, other public Ministers and Consuls;-to all Cases of admiralty and maritime Jurisdiction to Controversies to which the United States shall be a Party;-to Controversies between two or more States;-between a State and citizens of another State;-between Citizens of different States;-between Citizens of the same State claiming Lands under Grants of different States, and between a State, or the Citizens thereof, and foreign States, Citizens or Subjects.

In all Cases affecting Ambassadors, other public Ministers and Consuls, and those in which a State shall be Party, the supreme Court shall have original Jurisdiction. In all the other Cases before mentioned, the supreme Court shall have appellate Jurisdiction, both as to Law and Fact, with such Exceptions, and under such Regulations as the Congress shall make.

The Trial of all Crimes, except in Cases of impeachment, shall be by Jury; and such Trial shall be held in the State where the said Crime shall have been committed; but when not committed within any State, the Trial shall be at such Place or Places as the Congress may by Law have directed.

Section 3. Treason against the United States, shall consist only in levying War against them, or in adhering to their Enemies, giving them Aid and Comfort. No Person shall be convicted of Treason unless on the Testimony of two Witnesses to the same overt Act, or on Confession in open Court.

The Congress shall have Power to declare the Punishment of Treason, but no Attainder of Treason shall work Corruption of Blood, or Forfeiture except during the Life of the Person attainted.

ARTICLE IV

Section 1. Full Faith and Credit shall be given in each State to the public Acts, Records, and judicial Proceedings of every other State. And the Congress may by general Laws prescribe the Manner in which such Acts, Records and Proceedings shall be proved, and the Effect thereof.

Section 2. The Citizens of each State shall be entitled to all Privileges and Immunities of Citizens in the several States.

A Person charged in any State with Treason, Felony, or other Crime, who shall flee from Justice, and be found in another State, shall on Demand of the executive Authority of the State from which he fled, be delivered up, to be removed to the State having Jurisdiction of the Crime.

No Person held to Service or Labour in one State, under the Laws thereof, escaping into another, shall, in Consequence of any Law or Regulation therein, be discharged from such Service or Labour, but shall be delivered up on Claim of the Party to whom such Service or Labour may be due.

      Section 3. New States may be admitted by the Congress into this Union; but no new State shall be formed or erected within the Jurisdiction of any other State; nor any State be formed by the Junction of two or more States, or Parts of States, without the Consent of the Legislatures of the States concerned as well as of the Congress.

      The Congress shall have Power to dispose of and make all needed Rules and Regulations respecting the Territory or other Property belonging to the United States; and nothing in this Constitution shall be construed as to Prejudice any Claims of the United States, or of any particular State.

      Section 4. The United States shall guarantee to every State in this Union a Republican Form of Government, and shall protect each of them against Invasion; and on Application of the Legislature, or of the Executive (when the Legislature cannot be convened) against domestic Violence.

ARTICLE V

      The Congress, whenever two thirds of both Houses shall deem it necessary, shall propose Amendments to this Constitution, or, on the Application of the Legislatures of two thirds of the several States, shall call a Convention for proposing Amendments, which, in either Case, shall be valid to all Intents and Purposes, as Part of this Constitution, when ratified by the Legislatures of three fourths of the several States, or by Conventions in three fourths thereof, as the one or the other Mode of Ratification may be proposed by the Congress; Provided that no Amendment which may be made prior to the Year One thousand eight hundred and eight shall in any Manner affect the first and fourth Clauses in the Ninth

Section of the first Article; and that no State, without its Consent, shall be deprived of its equal Suffrage in the Senate.

ARTICLE VI

All Debts contracted and Engagements entered into, before the Adoption of this Constitution, shall be as valid against the United States under this Constitution, as under the Confederation.

This Constitution, and the Laws of the United States which shall be made in Pursuance thereof; and all Treaties made, or which shall be made, under the Authority of the United States, shall be the supreme Law of the Land; and the Judges in every State shall be bound thereby, any Thing in the Constitution or Laws of any State to the Contrary notwithstanding.

The Senators and Representatives before mentioned, and the Members of the several State Legislatures, and all executive and judicial Officers, both of the United States and of the several States, shall be bound by Oath or Affirmation, to support this Constitution; but no religious Test shall ever be required as a Qualification to any Office or public Trust under the United States.

ARTICLE VII

The Ratification of the Conventions of nine States, shall be sufficient for the Establishment of this Constitution between the States so ratifying the Same.

Done in Convention by the Unanimous Consent of the States present the Seventeenth Day of September in the Year of our Lord one thousand seven hundred and Eighty seven and of the Independence of the United States of America the Twelfth. IN WITNESS whereof We have hereunto subscribed our Names,

GEORGE WASHINGTON, President, And Deputy from Virginia,

In CONVENTION,

Monday, September 17th, 1787.

PRESENT

The States of New-Hampshire, Massachusetts, Connecticut, Mr. Hamilton from New-York, New-Jersey, Pennsylvania, Delaware, Maryland, Virginia, North-Carolina, South-Carolina and Georgia:

RESOLVED,

That the preceding Constitution be laid before the United States in Congress assembled, and that it is the opinion of this Convention, that it should afterwards be submitted to a Convention of Delegates, chosen in each State by the People thereof, under the Recommendation of its Legislature, for their Assent and Ratification; and that each Convention assenting to, and ratifying the Same, should Notice thereof to the United States in Congress assembled.

Resolved, That it is the Opinion of this Convention, that as soon as the Conventions of nine States shall have ratified this Constitution, the United States in Congress assembled should fix a Day on which Electors should be appointed by the States which shall have ratified the same, and a Day on which the Electors should assemble to vote for the President, and the Time and Place for commencing Proceedings under this Constitution. That after such Publication the Electors should be appointed, and the

Senators and Representatives elected: That the Electors should meet on the Day fixed for the Election of the President, and should transmit their Votes certified, signed, sealed and directed, as the Constitution requires, to the Secretary of the United States in Congress assembled, that the Senators and Representatives should convene at the Time and Place assigned; that the Senators should appoint a President of the Senate, for the sole Purpose of receiving, opening and counting the Votes for President; and, that after he shall be chosen, the Congress, together with the President, should, without Delay, proceed to execute this Constitution.

By the Unanimous Order of the Convention,
GEORGE WASHINGTON, President.
William Jackson, Secretary.

* * * * * * * *

The BILL OF RIGHTS
As provided in the FIRST TEN
AMENDMENTS
TO THE CONSTITUTION OF THE
UNITED STATES
Effective December 15, 1791

Articles in addition to, and Amendment of the Constitution of the United States of America, proposed by Congress, and ratified by the Legislatures of the several

States, pursuant to the fifth Article of the original Constitution.

PREAMBLE

The conventions of a number of the States having at the time of their adopting the Constitution, expressed a desire, in order to prevent misconstruction or abuse of its powers, that, further declaratory and restrictive clauses should be added: And as extending the ground public confidence in the Government, will best insure beneficent ends of its institution.

ARTICLE I

Congress shall make no law respecting an establishment of religion, or prohibiting the free exercise thereof; or abridging the freedom of speech, or of the press; or the right of the people peaceably to assemble, and to petition the Government for a redress of grievances.

ARTICLE II

A well regulated Militia, being necessary to the security of a free State, the right of the people to keep and bear Arms, shall not be infringed.

ARTICLE III

No Soldier shall, in time of peace be quartered in any house, without the consent of the Owner, nor in time of war, but in a manner to be prescribed by law.

ARTICLE IV

The right of the people to be secure in their persons, houses, papers, and effects, against unreasonable searches and seizures, shall not be violated, and no Warrants shall issue, but upon probable cause, supported by Oath or affirmation, and particularly describing the place to be searched, and the persons or things to be seized.

ARTICLE V

No person shall be held to answer for a capital, or otherwise infamous crime, unless on a presentment or indictment of a Grand Jury, except in cases arising in the land or naval forces, or in the Militia, when in actual service in time of War or public danger; nor shall any person be subject for the same offence to be twice put in jeopardy of life or limb; nor shall be compelled in any criminal case to be a witness against himself, nor be deprived of life, liberty, or property, without due process of law; nor shall private property be taken for public use without just compensation.

ARTICLE VI

In all criminal prosecutions, the accused shall enjoy the right to a speedy and public trial, by an impartial jury of the State and district wherein the crime shall have been committed, which district shall have been previously ascertained by law, and to be informed of the nature and cause of the accusation; to be confronted with the witnesses against him; to have compulsory process for obtaining witnesses in his favor, and to have the assistance of Counsel for his defense.

ARTICLE VII

In suits at common law, where the value in controversy shall exceed twenty dollars, the right of trial by jury shall be reserved, and no fact tried by a jury shall be otherwise re-examined in any Court of the United States, than according to the rules of the common law.

ARTICLE VIII

Excessive bail shall not be required, nor excessive fines imposed, nor cruel and unusual punishments inflicted.

ARTICLE IX

The enumeration in the Constitution, of certain rights, shall not be construed to deny or disparage others retained by the people.

ARTICLE X

The powers not delegated to the United States by the Constitution, nor prohibited by it to the States, are reserved to the States respectively, or to the people.

ARTICLE XI

The Judicial power of the United States shall not be construed to extend to any suit in law or equity, commenced or prosecuted against one of the United States by

Citizens of another State, or by Citizens or Subjects of any Foreign State.

ARTICLE XII

The Electors shall meet in their respective states, and vote by ballot for President and Vice-President, one of whom, at least, shall not be an inhabitant of the same state with themselves; they shall name in their ballots the person voted for as President, and in distinct ballots the person voted for as Vice-President, and they shall make distinct lists of all persons voted for as President, and of all persons voted for as Vice-President, and of the number of votes for each, which lists they shall sign and certify, and transmit sealed to the seat of the government of the United States, directed to the President of the Senate;-The President of the Senate shall, in the presence of the Senate and House of Representatives, open all the certificates and the votes shall then be counted;-The person having the greatest number of votes for President, shall be the President, if such number be a majority of the whole number of Electors appointed; and if no person have such majority, then from the persons having the highest numbers not exceeding three on the list of those voted for as President, the House of Representatives shall choose immediately, by ballot, the President. But in choosing the President, the votes shall be taken by states, the representation from each state having one vote; a quorum for this purpose shall consist of a member or members from two-thirds of the states, and a majority of all the states shall be necessary to a choice. And if the House of Representatives shall not choose a President whenever the right of choice shall devolve upon them, before the fourth day of March next following, then the Vice-President shall act as President, as in the case of the death or other constitutional disability of the President. -The person having the greatest number of votes as Vice-President, shall be the Vice-President, if such number be a majority of the whole number of Electors appointed, and if no person have a majority, then from the two highest numbers on the list, the Senate shall choose the Vice-President; a quorum for the purpose shall consist of two-thirds of the whole number of Senators, and a majority of the whole number shall be necessary to a choice. But no person constitutional ineligible to the office of President shall be eligible to that of Vice-President of the United States.

ARTICLE XIII

Section 1. Neither slavery nor involuntary servitude, except as a punishment for crime whereof the party shall have been duly convicted, shall exist within the United States, or any place subject to their jurisdiction.

Section 2. Congress shall have power to enforce this article by appropriate legislation.

ARTICLE XIV

Section 1. All persons born or naturalized in the United States, and subject to the jurisdiction thereof, are citizens of the United States and of the State wherein they reside. No State shall make or enforce any law which shall abridge the privileges or immunities of citizens of the United States; nor shall any State deprive any person of life, liberty, or property, without due process of law; nor deny to any person within its jurisdiction the equal protection, of the laws.

Section 2. Representatives shall be apportioned

among the several States according to their respective numbers, counting the whole number of persons in each State, excluding Indians not taxed. But when the right to vote at any election for the choice of electors for President and Vice-President of the United States, Representatives in Congress, the Executive and Judicial officers of a State, or the members of the Legislature thereof, is denied to any of the male inhabitants of such State, being twenty-one years of age, and citizens of the United States, or in any way abridged, except for participation in rebellion, or other crime, the basis of representation therein shall be reduced in the proportion which the number of such male citizens shall bear to the whole number of male citizens twenty-one years of age in such State.

Section 3. No person shall be a Senator or Representative in Congress, or elector of President and Vice-President, or hold any office, civil or military, under the United States, or under any State, who, having previously taken an oath, as a member of Congress, or as an officer of the United States, or as a member of any State legislature, or as an executive or judicial officer of any State, to support the Constitution of the United States, shall have engaged in insurrection or rebellion against the same, or given aid or comfort to the enemies thereof. But Congress may by a vote of two-thirds of each House, remove such disability.

Section 4. The validity of the public debt of the United States, authorized by law, including debts incurred for payment of pensions and bounties for services in suppressing insurrection or rebellion, shall not be questioned. But neither the United States nor any State shall assume or pay any debt or obligation incurred in aid of insurrection or rebellion against the United States, or any claim for the loss or emancipation of any slave; but all such debts, obligations and claims shall be held illegal and void.

Section 5. The Congress shall have power to enforce, by appropriate legislation, the provisions of this article.

ARTICLE XV

Section 1. The right of citizens of the United States to vote shall not be denied or abridged by the United States or by any State on account of race, color, or previous condition of servitude.

Section 2. The Congress shall have power to enforce this article by appropriate legislation.

ARTICLE XVI

The Congress shall have power to lay and collect taxes on incomes, from whatever source derived, without apportionment among the several States, and without regard to any census or enumeration.

ARTICLE XVII

The Senate of the United States shall be composed of two Senators from each State, elected by the people thereof, for six years; and each Senator shall have one vote. The electors in each State shall have the qualifications requisite for electors of the most numerous branch of the State Legislatures. When vacancies happen in the representation of any State in the Senate, the executive authority of such State shall issue writs of election to fill such vacancies: Provided, That the

Legislature of any State may empower the executive thereof to make temporary appointments until the people fill the vacancies by election as the Legislature may direct.

This amendment shall not be so construed as to affect the election or term of any Senator chosen before it becomes valid as part of the Constitution.

ARTICLE XVIII

Section 1. After one year from the ratification of this article the manufacture, sale, or transportation of intoxicating liquors within, the importation thereof into, or the exportation thereof from the United States and all territory subject to the jurisdiction thereof for beverage purposes is hereby prohibited.

Section 2. The Congress and the several States shall have concurrent power to enforce this article by appropriate legislation.

Section 3. This article shall be inoperative unless it shall have been ratified as an amendment to the Constitution by the legislatures of the several States, as provided in the Constitution, within seven years from the date of the submission hereof to the States by the Congress.

ARTICLE XIX

The right of citizens of the United States to vote shall not be denied or abridged by the United States or by any State on account of sex.

Congress shall have power to enforce this article by appropriate legislation.

ARTICLE XX

Section 1. The terms of the President and Vice President shall end at noon on the 20th day of January, and the terms of Senators and Representatives at noon on the 3rd day of January, of the year in which such terms would have ended if this article had not been ratified; and the terms of their successors shall then begin.

Section 2. The Congress shall assemble at least once in every year, and such meeting shall begin at noon on the 3rd day of January, unless they shall by law appoint a different day.

Section 3. If, at the time fixed for the beginning of the term of the President, the President elect shall have died, the Vice President elect shall become President. If a President shall not have been chosen before the time fixed for the beginning of his term, or if the President elect shall have failed to qualify, then the Vice President elect shall act as President until a President shall have qualified; and the Congress may by law provide for the case wherein neither a President elect nor a Vice President elect shall have qualified, declaring who shall then act as President, or the manner in which one who is to act shall be selected, and such person shall act accordingly until a President or Vice President shall have qualified.

Section 4. The Congress may by law provide for the case of the death of any of the persons from whom the House of Representatives may choose a President whenever the right of choice shall have devolved upon them, and for the case of the death of any of the persons from whom the Senate may choose a Vice President whenever the right of choice shall have devolved upon them.

Section 5. Sections I and 2 shall take effect on

the 15th day of October following the ratification of this article.

Section 6. This article shall be inoperative unless it shall have been ratified as an amendment to the Constitution by the legislatures of three-fourths of the several States within seven years from the date of its submission.

ARTICLE XXI

Section 1. The eighteenth article of amendment to the Constitution of the United States is hereby repealed.

Section 2. The transportation or importation into any State, Territory, or possession of the United States for delivery or use therein of intoxicating liquors, in violation of the laws thereof, is hereby prohibited.

Section 3. This article shall be inoperative unless it shall have been ratified as an amendment to the Constitution by conventions in the several States, as provided in the Constitution, within seven years from the date of the submission hereof to the States by the Congress.

ARTICLE XXII

Section 1. No person shall be elected to the office of the President more than twice, and no person who has held the office of President, or acted as President, for more than two years of a term to which some other person was elected President shall be elected to the office of the President more than once. But this article shall not apply to any person holding the office of President when this article was proposed by the Congress, and shall not prevent any person who may be holding the office of President, or acting as President, during the term within which this article becomes operative from holding the office of President or acting as President during the remainder of such term.

Section 2. This article shall be inoperative unless it shall have been ratified as an amendment to the Constitution by the legislatures of three-fourths of the several states within seven years from the date of its submission to the states by the Congress.

ARTICLE XXIII

Section 1. The District constituting the seat of Government of the United States shall appoint in such manner as the Congress may direct:

A number of electors of President and Vice President equal to the whole number of Senators and Representatives in Congress to which the District would be entitled if it were a State, but in no event more than the least populous State; they shall be in addition to those appointed by the States, but they shall be considered, for the purposes of the election of President and Vice President, to be electors appointed by a State; and they shall meet in the District and perform such duties as provided by the twelfth Article of Amendment.

Section 2. The Congress shall have power to enforce this article by appropriate legislation.

ARTICLE XXIV

Section 1. The right of citizens of the United States to vote in any primary or other election for President or Vice President, for electors for President or Vice President, or for Senator or Representative in Congress, shall not be denied or abridged by the United States or any State by reason of failure to pay any poll tax or other tax.

Section 2. The Congress shall have power to enforce this article by appropriate legislation.

ARTICLE XXV

Section 1. In case of the removal of the President from office or of his death or resignation, the Vice President shall become President.

Section 2. Whenever there is a vacancy in the office of the Vice President, the President shall nominate a Vice President who shall take the office upon confirmation by a majority vote of both houses of Congress.

Section 3. Whenever the President transmits to the President Pro Tempore of the Senate and the Speaker of the House of Representatives his written declaration that he is unable to discharge the powers and duties of his office, and until he transmits to them a written declaration to the contrary, such powers and duties shall be discharged by the Vice President as Acting President.

Section 4. Whenever the Vice President and a majority of either the principal officers of the executive departments or of such other body as Congress may by law provide, transmit to the President Pro Tempore of the Senate and the Speaker of the House of Representatives their written declaration that the President is unable to discharge the powers and duties of his office, the Vice President shall immediately assume the powers and duties of the office as Acting President.

Thereafter, when the President transmits to the

President Pro Tempore of the Senate and the Speaker of the
House of Representatives his written declaration that no
inability exists, he shall resume the powers and duties of his
office unless the Vice President and a majority of either the
principal officers of the executive department or of such other
body as Congress may by law provide, transmit within four
days to the President Pro Tempore of the Senate and the
Speaker of the House of Representatives their written
declaration that the President is unable to discharge the powers
and duties of his office. Thereupon Congress shall decide the
issue, assembling within 48 hours for that purpose if not in
session. If the Congress, within 21 days after receipt of the
latter written declaration, or, if Congress is not in session,
within 21 days after   Congress is required to assemble,
determines by two-thirds vote of both houses that the President
is unable to discharge the powers and duties of his office, the
Vice President shall continue to discharge the same as Acting
President; otherwise, the President shall resume the powers
and duties of his office.

ARTICLE XXVI

     Section 1. The right of citizens of the United
States, who are eighteen years of age or older, to vote shall
not be denied or abridged by the United States or by any State
on account of age.

     Section 2. The Congress shall have power to
enforce this article by appropriate legislation.

* * * * * * *

FEDERAL JURISDICTION

In the United States, there are two separate and distinct jurisdictions, such being the jurisdiction of the States within their own territorial boundaries and the other being federal jurisdiction. Broadly speaking, state jurisdiction encompasses the legislative power to regulate, control and govern real and personal property, individuals and enterprises within the territorial boundaries of any given State. In Contrast, federal jurisdiction is extremely limited, with the same being exercised only in areas external to state legislative power and territory. Notwithstanding the clarity of this simple principle, the line of demarcation between these two jurisdictions and the extent and reach of each has become somewhat blurred, due to popular misconceptions and the efforts expended by the federal government to conceal one of its major weaknesses. Only by resorting to history and case law can this obfuscation be clarified and the two distinct jurisdictions be readily seen.

The original thirteen colonies of America were each separately established by charters from the English Crown. Outside of the common bond of each being a dependency and colony of the mother country, England, the colonies were not otherwise united. Each had its own governor, legislative assembly, and the Courts, were governed separately and independently by the English Parliament.

The political connections of the separate colonies to the English Crown and Parliament descended to an unhappy state of affairs as the direct result of Parliamentary acts adopted in the late 1760's and early 1770's. Due to the real and perceived dangers caused by these various acts, the First Continental Congress was convened by representatives of the several colonies in October, 1774, the purpose of which was to submit a petition of grievances to the British Parliament and Crown. By the Declaration and Resolves of the First Continental Congress, dated October 14, 1774, the colonial representatives labeled these Parliamentary acts of which they complained as "impolitic, unjust, and cruel, as well as unconstitutional, and most dangerous and destructive of American rights," and the purpose of which were designs, schemes and plans "which demonstrate a system formed to enslave America." Revolution was assuredly in the formative stages absent conciliation between the mother country and the colonies.

Between October, 1775, and the middle of 1776, each of the colonies separately severed their ties and relations with England, and several adopted constitutions for the newly formed States. By July, 1776, the exercise of British authority in any and all colonies was not recognized in any degree. The capstone of this actual separation of the colonies from England was the more formal Declaration of Independence.

The legal effect of the Declaration of Independence was to make each new State a separate and independent sovereign over which there was no other government of superior power or jurisdiction. This was clearly shown in Millvaine v. Coxe's Lessee, 8 U.S. (4 Cranch) 209 (1808, where it was held:

> "This opinion is predicated upon a principle which is believed to be undeniable, that the several states which composed this union, so far at least as regarded their municipal regulations, became entitled, from the time when they declared themselves independent, to all the rights and powers of sovereign states, and that they did not derive them from

concessions made by the British king. The treaty of peace contains a recognition of their independence, not a grant of it. From hence it results, that the laws of the several state governments were the laws of sovereign states, and as such were obligatory upon the people of such state, from the time they were enacted", 4 Cranch, at 212.

And a further expression of similar import is found in Harcourt v. Gaillard, 25 U.S. (12 Wheat) 523 (1827), where the Court stated:

"There was no territory within the United States that was claimed in any other right than that of some one of the confederated states; therefore, there could be no acquisition of territory made by the United States distinct from, or independent of some one of the states.

"Each declared itself sovereign and independent, according to the limits of its territory.

"{T}he soil and sovereignty within their acknowledged limits were as much theirs at the declaration of independence as at this hour," 12 Wheat., at 526, 527.

Thus, unequivocally, in July, 1776, the new States possessed all sovereignty, power, and jurisdiction over all the soil and persons in their respective territorial limits.

This condition of supreme sovereignty of each State over all property and persons within the borders thereof continued notwithstanding the adoption of the Articles of Confederation. In Article II of such Articles, it was expressly stated:

> "Article II. Each state retains its sovereignty, freedom and independence, and every Power, Jurisdiction and right, which is not by this confederation expressly delegated to the United States, in Congress assembled".

As the history of the confederation government has shown, each State was indeed sovereign and independent to the degree that it made the central government created by the confederation fairly ineffectual. These defects of the confederation government strained the relations between and among the States and the remedy became the calling of a constitutional convention.

The representatives which assembled in Philadelphia in May, 1787, to attend the Constitutional Convention met for the primary purpose of improving the commercial relations among the States, although the product of the Convention produced more than this. But, no intention was demonstrated for the States to surrender in any degree the jurisdiction so possessed by the States at that time, and indeed the Constitution as finally drafted continued the same territorial jurisdiction of the States as existed under the Articles of Confederation. The essence of this retention of state jurisdiction is embodied in Article I, Section 8, Clause 17 of the U.S. Constitution, which reads as follows:

> "To exercise exclusive Legislation in all Cases whatsoever, over such District (not exceeding ten

Miles square) as may, by Cession of particular States, and the Acceptance of Congress, become the Seat of the Government of the United States, and to exercise like Authority over all Places purchased by the Consent of the Legislature of the State in which the Same shall be, for the Erection of Forts, Magazines, Arsenals, dock-Yards, and other needful Buildings."

The reason for the inclusion of this clause in the Constitution was and is obvious. Under the articles of Confederation, the States retained full and complete jurisdiction over lands and persons within their borders. The Congress under the Articles was merely a body which represented and acted as agents of the separate States for external affairs, and had no jurisdiction within the States. This defect in the Articles made the Confederation Congress totally dependent upon any given State for protection, and this dependency did, in fact, cause embarrassment for that Congress. During the Revolutionary War, while the Congress met in Philadelphia, a body of mutineers from the Continental Army surrounded the Congress and chastised and insulted the members thereof. The governments of both Philadelphia and Pennsylvania proved themselves powerless to remedy the situation, and the Congress was forced to flee first to Princeton, New Jersey, and finally to Annapolis, Maryland. See Fort Leavenworth R. Co. v. Lowe, 114 U.S. 525, 529, 5 S. Ct. 995 (1885). Thus, this clause was inserted into the Constitution to give jurisdiction to Congress over its capital, and such other places as Congress might purchase for forts, magazines, arsenals, and other needful buildings wherein the State ceded Jurisdiction of such lands to the federal government. Other than in these areas, this clause of the Constitution did not operate to cede further jurisdiction to the federal government, and jurisdiction over unceded areas remained within the States.

While there had been no real provisions in the Articles which permitted the Confederation Congress to acquire property and possess exclusive jurisdiction over such property, the above clause filled an essential need by permitting the federal government to acquire land for the seat of government and other purposes from certain of the states. Such possessions were deemed essential to enable the United States to perform the powers conveyed by the Constitution, and a cession of lands by any particular State would grant exclusive jurisdiction of such lands to Congress. Perhaps the most cogent reasons and explanations for this clause in the Constitution were set forth in Essay No. 43 of The Federalist:

"The indispensable necessity of complete authority at the seat of government carries its own evidence with it. It is a power exercised by every legislature of the Union, I might say of the world, by virtue of its general supremacy. Without it not only the public authority might be insulted and its proceedings interrupted with impunity, but a dependence of the members of the general government on the State comprehending the seat of the government for protection in the exercise of their duty might bring on the national councils an imputation of awe or influence equally dishonorable to the government and dissatisfactory to the other members of the Confederacy. This consideration has the more weight as the gradual accumulation of public improvements at the stationary residence of the government would be both too great a public pledge to be left in the hands of a single State, and would create so many obstacles

to a removal of the government, as still further to
abridge its necessary independence. The extent of this
federal district is sufficiently circumscribed to satisfy
every jealousy of an opposite nature. And as it is to
be appropriated to this use with the consent of the
State ceding it; as the State will no doubt provide in
the compact for the rights and the consent of the
citizens inhabiting it; as the inhabitants will find
sufficient inducements of interest to become willing
parties to the cession; as they will have had their voice
in the election of the government which is to exercise
authority over them; as a municipal legislature for
local purposes, derived from their own suffrages, will
of course be allowed them; and as the authority of the
legislature of the State, and of the inhabitants of the
ceded part of it, to concur in the cession will be
derived from the whole people of the State in their
adoption of the Constitution, every imaginable
objection seems to be obviated.

"The necessity of a like authority over forts,
magazines, etc., established by the general
government, is not less evident. The public money
expended on such places, and the public property
deposited in them, require that they should be exempt
from the authority of the particular State. Nor would
it be proper for the places on which the security of the
entire Union may depend to be in any degree
depended on a particular member of it. All objections
and scruples are here also obviated by requiring the
concurrence of the States concerned in every such
establishment."

Since the time of the ratification and implementation of the present U.S. Constitution, the U.S. Supreme Court and all lower Courts have had many opportunities to construe and apply the above provision of the Constitution. And the essence of all these decisions is that the states of this action have exclusive jurisdiction of property and persons located within their borders, excluding such lands and persons residing thereon which have been ceded to the United States.

Perhaps one of the earliest decisions on this point was <u>United States v. Beavans</u>, 16 U.S. (3 Wheat) 336 (1815), which involved a federal prosecution for the murder committed on board the Airship, Independence, anchored in the harbor of Boston, Massachusetts. The defense complained that only the state had jurisdiction to prosecute and argued that the federal Circuit Courts had no jurisdiction of this crime supposedly committed within the federal government's admiralty jurisdiction. In argument before the Supreme Court, counsel for the United States admitted as follows:

"The exclusive jurisdiction which the United States have in forts and dockyards ceded to them, is derived from the express assent of the states by whom the cessions are made. It could be derived in no other manner; because without it, the authority of the state would be supreme and exclusive therein," 3 Wheat, 350, 351.

in holding that the State of Massachusetts had jurisdiction over the crime, the Court held:

"What, then, is the extent of jurisdiction which

a state possesses?

"We answer, without hesitation, the jurisdiction of a state is co-extensive with its territory; co-extensive with its legislative power," 3 Wheat., at 386, 387.

"The article which describes the judicial power of the United States is not intended for the cession of territory or of general jurisdiction. ...Congress has power to exercise exclusive jurisdiction over this district, and over all places purchased by the consent of the legislature of the state in which the same shall be, for the erection of forts, magazines, arsenals, dock-yards,, and other needful buildings.

"It is observable that the power of exclusive legislation (which is jurisdiction) is united with cession of territory, which is to be the free act of the sates. It is difficult to compare the two sections together, without feeling a conviction, not to be strengthened by any commentary on them, that, in describing the judicial power, the framers of our constitution had not in view any cession of territory; or, which is essentially the same, of general jurisdiction, " 3 Wheat, at 388.

Thus, in Beavans, the Court established a principle that federal jurisdiction extends only over the areas wherein it possesses the power of exclusive legislation, and this is a principle incorporated into all subsequent decisions regarding the extent of federal jurisdiction. To hold otherwise would destroy the purpose, intent and meaning of the entire U.S. Constitution.

The decision in Beavans was closely followed by decisions made in two state courts and one federal court within the next two years. In <u>Commonwealth v. Young</u>, Brightly, N.P. 302 (Pa., 1818), the Supreme Court of Pennsylvania was presented with the issue of whether lands owned by the United States for which Pennsylvania had never ceded jurisdiction had to be sold pursuant to state law. In deciding that the state law of Pennsylvania exclusively controlled the sale of federal land, the Court held:

> "The legislation and authority of congress is confined to cessions by particular states for the seat of government, and purchases made by consent of the legislature of the state, for the purpose of erecting forts. The legislative power and exclusive jurisdiction remained in the several states, of all territory within their limits, not ceded to, or purchased by, congress, with the asset of the state legislature, to prevent the collision of legislation and authority between the United States and the several states, " Id., at 309.

A year later, the Supreme Court of New York was presented with the issue of whether the State of New York had jurisdiction over a murder committed at Fort Niagara, a federal fort. In <u>People v. Godfrey</u>, 17 Johns. 225 (N.Y., 1819), that Court held that the fort was subject to the jurisdiction of the state since the lands therefore had not been ceded to the United States. The rationale of its opinion stated:

> "To oust this state to its jurisdiction to support and maintain its laws, and to punish crimes, it must be

shown that an offense committed within the acknowledged limits of the state, is clearly and exclusively cognizable by the laws and the Courts of the United States. In the case already cited, Chief Justice Marshall observed, that to bring the offense within the jurisdiction of the Courts of the union, it must have been committed out of the jurisdiction of any state; it is not (he says,) the offense committed, but the place in which it is committed, which must be out of the jurisdiction of the state," 17 Johns., at 233.

The case relied upon by this Court was U.S. v. Beavans, supra.

At about the same time that the New York Supreme Court rendered its opinion in Godfrey, a similar fact situation was before a federal Court, the only difference being that the murder committed in the case occurred on land which had been ceded to the United States. In United States v. Cornell, 25 Fed. Ca. 646, No. 14, 867 (C.C.D.R.I., 1819), the Court held that the case fell within federal jurisdiction, describing such jurisdiction as follows:

"But although the United States may well purchase and holds lands for public purposes, within the territorial limits of a state, this does not of itself oust the jurisdiction or sovereignty of such State over the lands so purchased. It remains until the State has relinquished its authority over the land either expressly or by necessary implication.

"When therefore a purchase of land for any of

these purposes is made by the national government, and the State Legislature has given its consent to the purchase, the land so purchased by the very terms of the constitution ipso facto falls within the exclusive legislation of Congress, and the State jurisdiction is completely ousted, " Id., at 648.

Almost 18 years later, the U.S. Supreme Court was again presented with a case involving the distinction between State and federal jurisdiction. In <u>New Orleans v. United States</u>, 35 U.S. (10 Pet.) 662 (1836), the United States claimed title to property in New Orleans likewise claimed by the city. After holding that title to the subject lands was owned by the city, the Court addressed the question of federal jurisdiction and stated:

"Special provision is made in the Constitution for the cession of jurisdiction from the States over places where the federal government shall establish forts or other military works. And it is only in these places, or in the territories of the United States, where it can exercise a general jurisdiction", 10 Pet., at 737.

In <u>New York v. Miln</u>, 36 U.S. (11 Pet.) 102 (1837), the question before the Court involved the attempt by the City of New York to assess penalties against the master of a ship for his failure to make a report as to the persons his ship brought to New York. As against the master's contention that the act was unconstitutional and that New York had no jurisdiction in the matter, the Court held:

"If we look at the place of its operation, we

find it to be within the territory, and therefore within the jurisdiction of New York, If we looked at the person on whom it operates, he is found within the same territory and jurisdiction," 36 Y.S., at 133.

"They are these: that a State has the same undeniable and unlimited jurisdiction over all persons and things within its territorial limits, as any foreign nation, where that jurisdiction is not surrendered or restrained by the Constitution of the United States. That, by virtue of this, it is not only the right but the bounden and solemn duty of the State, to advance the safety, happiness and prosperity of its people, and to provide for its general welfare, by any and every act of legislation which it may deem to be conductive to these ends; where the power over the particular subject, or the manner of its exercise is not surrendered or restrained, in the manner just stated. That all those powers which relate to merely municipal legislation, or what may, perhaps, more properly be called internal police, are not thus surrendered or restrained; and that consequently, in relation to these, the authority of a State is complete, unqualified and exclusive." 36 U.S., at 319.

Some eight years later, in Pollard v. Hagan, 44 U.S. (3How.) 212 (1845), the question of federal jurisdiction was once again before the Court. This case involved a contest of the title to real property, with one of the parties claiming a right to the disputed property via a U.S. patent; the lands in question were situated in Mobile, Alabama, adjacent to Mobile Bay. In discussing the subject of federal jurisdiction, the Court held:

"We think a proper examination of this subject will show that the United States never held any municipal sovereignty, jurisdiction, or right of soil in and to the territory, of which Alabama or any of the new states were formed, " 44 U.S., at 221.

"{B}ecause, the United States have no constitutional capacity to exercise municipal jurisdiction, sovereignty, or eminent domain, within the limits, a state or elsewhere , except in the cases in which it is expressly granted," 44 U.S., at 223.

"Alabama is therefore entitled to the sovereignty and jurisdiction over all the territory within her limits, subject to the common law, " 44 U.S., at 228, 229.

The single most important case regarding the subject of federal jurisdiction appears to be <u>Fort Leavenworth R. Co. v. Lowe</u>, 114 U.S. 525, 5 S. Ct. 995 (1885), which sets forth the law on this point fully. There, the railroad company property which passed through the Fort Leavenworth federal enclave was being subjected to taxation by Kansas, and the company claimed an exemption from state taxation. In holding that the railroad company's property could be taxed, the Court carefully explained federal jurisdiction within the States:

"The consent of the states to the purchase of lands within them for the special purposes named, is, however, essential, under the constitution, to the transfer of the general government, with the title, of political jurisdiction and dominion. Where the lands are acquired without such consent, the possession of the United States, unless political jurisdiction be ceded to them in some other way, is simply that of an ordinary proprietor. The property in that case, unless used as a means to carry out the purposes of the government, is subject to the legislative authority and control of the states equally with the property of private individuals," 114 U.S., at 531.

Thus, the cases decided within the 19th century clearly disclosed the extent and scope of both State and federal jurisdiction. In essence, these cases, among many others, hold that the jurisdiction of any particular state is co-extensive with its borders or territory, and all persons and property located or found therein are subject to such jurisdiction; this jurisdiction is superior. Federal jurisdiction results only from a conveyance of state jurisdiction to the federal government for lands owned or otherwise possessed by the federal government, and thus federal jurisdiction is extremely limited in nature. And there is no federal jurisdiction if there be no grant or cession of jurisdiction by the State to the federal government. Therefore, federal territorial jurisdiction exists only in Washington, D.C., the federal enclaves within the States, and the territories and possessions of the United States.

The above principles of jurisdiction established in the last century continue their vitality today with only one minor exception. In the last century, the cessions of jurisdiction by States to the federal government were by legislative acts which typically ceded full jurisdiction to the federal government, thus placing into the hands of the federal government the troublesome problem of dealing with any government scattered, localized federal enclaves which had been totally surrendered by the States. With the advent in this century of large federal works projects and national parks, the problems regarding management of these areas by the federal government were magnified. During the last century, it was though that if a State ceded jurisdiction to the federal government, the cession granted full and complete jurisdiction. but, with the ever increasing number of separate tracts of land falling within the jurisdiction of the federal government in this century, it was obviously determined by both federal and state public officers that the States should retain greater control over these ceded lands, and the Courts have acknowledged the constitutionality of varying degrees of state jurisdiction and control over lands so ceded.

Perhaps one of the first cases to acknowledge the proposition that a State would retain a degree of jurisdiction over property ceded to the federal government was Surplus Trading Co. v. Cook, 281 U.S. 647, 50 S. Ct. 455 (1930). In this case, a state attempt to assess an ad valorem tax on Army blankets located within a federal army camp was found invalid and beyond the state's jurisdiction. But, in regards to the proposition that a State could make a qualified cession of jurisdiction to the federal government, the Court held:

> "{T}he state undoubtedly may cede her jurisdiction to the United States and may make the cession either absolute or qualified as to her may appear desirable, provided the qualification is consistent with the purposes for which the reservation is maintained and is accepted by the United States. And, where such a cession is made and accepted, it will be determinative of the jurisdiction of both the United States and the state within the reservation",. 281 U.S., at 651, 652.

Two cases decided in 1937 by the U.S. Supreme Court, further clarify the constitutionality of a reservation of any degree of state jurisdiction over land ceded to the jurisdiction of the United States. In <u>James v. Dravo Contracting Company</u>, 302 U.S. 134, 58 S. Ct. 208 (1937), the State of West Virginia sought to impose a tax upon the gross receipts of the company arising from a contract which it had made with the United States to build some dams on rivers. One of the issues involved in this case was the validity of the state tax imposed on the receipts derived by the company from work performed on lands to which the State had ceded "concurrent" jurisdiction to the United Sates. In the Court's opinion, it held that a State could reserve and qualify any cession of jurisdiction for land owed by the United states; since the State had done so here, the Court upheld this part of the challenged tax notwithstanding a partial cession of jurisdiction to the U.S.. A similar result occurred in <u>Silas Mason Co. v. Tax Commission of State of Washington</u>, 302 U.S. 186, 58 S. Ct. 233 (1937). Here, the United States was undertaking the construction of several dams on the Columbia River in Washington, and had purchased the lands necessary for the project. Silas Mason obtained a contract to build a part of the Grand Coulee Dam, but filed suit challenging the Washington Income Tax when the State sought to impose such tax on the contract proceeds. Mason's argument that the federal government had exclusive jurisdiction over both the lands and such contract was not upheld by either the Supreme Court of Washington or the U.S. Supreme Court. The latter Court held that none of the lands owned by the U.S. were within its jurisdiction and thus Washington clearly had jurisdiction to impose the challenged tax; see also <u>Wilson v. Cook</u>, 327 U.S. 474, 66 S. Ct. 663 (1946).

Some few years later in 1943, the Supreme Court was again presented with similar taxation and jurisdiction

issues; the facts in these two cases were identical with the
exception that one clearly involved lands ceded to the
jurisdiction of the United States. The single difference caused
directly opposite results in both cases. In pacific <u>Coast Dairy
v. Department of Agriculture of California</u>, 318 U.S. 285, 63
S. Ct. 628 (1943), the question involved the applicability of
state law to a contract entered into and performed on a federal
enclave to which jurisdiction had been ceded to the Untied
States. During World War II, California passed a law setting
a minimum price for the sale of milk, which law imposed
penalties for sales made below the regulated price. Here,
Pacific Coast Dairy consummated a contract on Moffett Field,
a federal enclave within the exclusive jurisdiction of the
United States, to sell milk to such federal facility at below the
regulated price. When this occurred, California sought to
impose a penalty for what it perceived as a violation of state
law. But, the U.S. Supreme Court refused to permit the
enforcement of the California law, holding that the contract
was made and performed in a territory outside the jurisdiction
of California and within the jurisdiction of the United States,
a place where this law didn't apply. Thus, in this case, the
existence of federal jurisdiction was the foundation for the
ruling. However, in <u>Penn Dairies v. Milk Control
Commission of Pennsylvania</u>, 318 U.S. 261, 63 S. Ct. 617
(1943), an opposite result was reached on almost identical
facts. Here, Pennsylvania likewise had a law which regulated
the price of milk and penalized sales of milk below the
regulated price. During World War II, the United States
leased some land from Pennsylvania for the construction of a
military camp; since the land was leased, Pennsylvania did not
cede jurisdiction to the United States. When Penn Dairies
sold milk to the military facility for a price below the
regulated price, the Commission sought to impose the penalty.
In this case, since there was no federal jurisdiction, the

Supreme Court found that the state law applied and permitted the imposition of the penalty. Thus , these two cases clearly show the different results which can occur with the presence or absence of federal jurisdiction.

A final point which must be made regarding federal jurisdiction involves the point, as to when such jurisdiction ends or ceases. This point was considered in S.R.A. v. Minnesota, 327 U.S. 558, 66 S. Ct. 749 (1946), which involved the power of a state to tax the real property interest of a purchaser of land sold by the United States. Here, a federal post office building was sold to S.R. A. pursuant to a real estate sales contract, which provided that title would pass only after the purchase price had been paid. In refuting the argument of S.R.A. that the ad valorem tax on its equitable interest in the property was rally an unlawful tax on U.S. property, the Court held:

> "In the absence of some such provisions, a transfer of property held by the United States under state cessions pursuant to Article I, Section 8, Clause 17 of the Constitution would leave numerous isolated islands of federal jurisdiction, unless the unrestricted transfer of the property to private hands is thought without more to revest sovereignty in the states. As the purpose of Clause 17 was to give control over the sites of governmental operations to the Untied States, when such control was deemed essential for federal activities, it would seem that the sovereignty of the United States would end with the reason for its existence and the disposition of the property. We shall treat this case as though the Government's unrestricted transfer of property to non-federal hands is a relinquishment of the exclusive legislative power", 327

U.S., at 563, 564.

Thus it appears clearly that once any property within the exclusive jurisdiction of the Untied States is no longer utilized by the government for governmental purposes, and the title or any interest therein is conveyed to private interests, the jurisdiction of the federal government ceases and jurisdiction once again reverts to the State.

The above principles regarding the distinction between State and federal jurisdiction continue thorough today; see Paul v. United States, 371 U.S. 245, 83 S. Ct. 426 (1963), and United States v. State Tax Commission of Mississippi, 412 U.S. 363, 93 S. Ct. 2183 (1973). And what was definitely decided in the beginning days of this Republic regarding the extent scope and reach of each of these two distinct jurisdictions remains unchanged and forms the foundation and basis for the smooth workings of state governmental systems in conjunction with the federal government. Without such jurisdictional principles which form a clear boundary between the jurisdiction of the States and the United States, our federal governmental system would have surely met its demise long before now.

In summary, jurisdiction of the States is essentially the same as that possessed by the States which were leagued together under the Articles of Confederation. The confederated States possessed absolute, complete and full jurisdiction over property and persons located within their borders. It is hypocritical to assume or argue that these States which had absolved and banished the centralized power and jurisdiction of the English Parliament and Crown over them by the Declaration of Independence, would shortly thereafter cede comparable power and jurisdiction to the Confederation

Congress. They did not and they closely and jealously guarded their own rights, powers and jurisdiction. When the Articles were replaced by the Constitution, the intent and purpose of the States was to retain their same powers and jurisdiction, with a small concession of jurisdiction to the Untied States for lands found essential for the operation of that government. However, even this provision did not operate to instantly change any aspect of state jurisdiction, it only permitted its future operation wherein any State, by its own volition, should choose to cede jurisdiction to the United States.

By the adoption of the Constitution , the States jointly surrendered some 17 specified and well defined powers to the federal Congress, which related strictly to external affairs of the states. Any single power, or even several powers combined, do not operate in a fashion as to invade or divest a State of its jurisdiction. As against a single State, the remainder of the States under the Constitution have no right to jurisdiction within the single state absent its consent.

The only provision in the Constitution which permits jurisdiction to be vested in the United States is found in Article I, Section 8, Clause 17, which provides the mechanism for a voluntary cession of jurisdiction from any State to the United States. When the Constitution was adopted, the United States had jurisdiction over no lands within the States, possessing jurisdiction only in the lands encompassed in the Northwest Territories. Shortly thereafter, Maryland and Virginia ceded jurisdiction to the United States for Washington, D.C.. As time progressed thereafter, the States at various times ceded jurisdiction to federal enclaves within the states. Today, the territorial jurisdiction of the United States is found only in such ceded areas, which encompass Washington, D.C., the federal enclaves within the States, and such territories and possessions which may be now owned by the United States.

The above conclusion is not the mere opinion of the author of this brief, but it is likewise the opinion of the federal government itself. In June, 1957, the government of the United States published a work entitled Jurisdiction Over Federal Areas Within the States: <u>Report of the Interdepartmental Committee for the Study of Jurisdiction Over Federal Areas Within the States, Part II</u>, which report is the definitive study on this issue. Therein, the Committee stated:

"The Constitution gives express recognition to but one means of Federal acquisition of legislative jurisdiction -- by State consent under Article I, Section 8, clause 17 ... Justice McLean suggested that the Constitution provided the sole mode for transfer of jurisdiction, and that if this mode is not pursued, no transfer of jurisdiction can take place," Id., at 41.

"It scarcely needs to be said that unless there has been a transfer of jurisdiction (1) pursuant to clause 17 by a Federal acquisition of land with State consent, or (2) by cession from the State to the Federal Government, or unless the Federal Government has reserved jurisdiction upon the admission of the State, the Federal Government possesses no legislative jurisdiction over any area within a State, such jurisdiction being for exercise by the State, subject to non-interference by the State with Federal functions," Id., at 45.

"The Federal Government cannot, by unilateral action on its part, acquire legislative jurisdiction over any area within the exterior boundaries of a State," Id., at 46.

"On the other hand, while the Federal Government has power under various provisions of the Constitution to define, and prohibit as criminal, certain acts or omissions occurring anywhere in the United States, it has no power to punish for various other crimes, jurisdiction over which is retained by the States under our Federal-State system of government, unless such crime occurs on areas as to which legislative jurisdiction has been vested in the Federal Government," Id., at 107.

Thus, from an abundance of case law, buttressed by this lengthy and definitive government treatise on this issue, the "jurisdiction of the United States" is carefully circumscribed and defined as a very precise portion of America. The United States as the body politic is one of the 51 jurisdictions existing in the United States of America.

Notes

Notes to Chapter Four

1. Thomas McConnell, "The Report From Iron Mountain: The Blueprint for Absolute Tyranny - Part I," *Monetary & Economic Review* (October 1994), 1.

1. Thomas McConnell, "The Report from Iron Mountain: The Blueprint for Absolute Tyranny - Part II," *Monetary & Economic Review* (November 1994). 1.

Notes To Chapter Six

1. Marilyn Brannan, "The Dumbing Factor: GOALS 2000," *Monetary & Economic Review* (September 1994), 1.

2. Cynthia Barnes, "Whites stole this land and they'll reap a bitter harvest," *The Denver Post* (December 9, 1994), 14-B.

Notes to Chapter Nine

1. Kishore Jayabalan, "Rooting out workplace evils is a growing concern," *The Rocky Mountain News* (December 18, 1994), 109-A

Notes to Chapter Ten

1. Faludi, Susan. *BACKLASH; The Undeclared War Against American Women.* New York: Anchor Books, 1991, 14.

2. Id.

3. Id.

Notes to Chapter Twelve

1. Primer on Rheumatic Diseases, p. 190

2. Id.

Bibliography

Bailey, Ronald. *ECO-SCAM The False Prophets of Ecological Apocalypse.* New York, St. Martins Press, 1993.

Barnes, Cynthia: "Whites stole this land, and they'll reap a bitter harvest." *The Denver Post*, Friday, December 9, 1994: p. 14-B.

Bates, Larry. *THE NEW ECONOMIC DISORDER, Will You Survive?* Creation House, a division of Strang Communications, 600 Reinhart Road, Lake Mary, Florida 32746, November, 1994. (1-800-336-7000).

Bender, David L. & Bruno Leone. *CIVIL LIBERTIES, OPPOSING VIEWPOINTS.* San Diego, California: Greenhaven Press, Inc., 1994.

Bender, David L. & Bruno Leone. *Social Justice, Opposing*

Viewpoints. San Diego, California: Greenhaven Press, Inc., 1990.

Bailey, Ronald. *ECO-SCAM: THE FALSE PROPHETS OF ECOLOGICAL APOCALYPSE.* New York: St. Martin's Press, 1993.

Bodansk, Yossef. *TARGET AMERICA, Terriorism in the U.S. Today.* New York: S.P.I. Books, 1993.

Brannan, Marilyn. "The Dumbing Factor: GOALS 2000." *Monetary & Economic Review,* A division of FAMC, Inc., September, 1994. Address: 3500 JFK Parkway, Fort Collins, CO., 80525. Telephone 1-800-336-7000.

Clark, Judith Freeman. *ALMANAC OF AMERICAN WOMEN IN THE 20TH CENTURY.* New York: Pentice Hall Press, 1987.

Cuddy, Dennis Laurence, Ph.D. *NOW IS THE DAWNING OF THE NEW AGE NEW WORLD ORDER.* Oklahoma City, OK: Hearthstone Publishing, Ltd., 1991.

Faludi, Susan. *BACKLASH; The Undeclared War Against American Women.* New York: Anchor Books, 1991.

Ferguson, Marilyn. *THE AQUARIAN CONSPIRACY, Personal and Social Transformation in the 1980s.* Los Angeles, California: J.P. Tarcher, Inc., 1980.

Fiorenza, Elisabeth Schuussler. *But SHE Said, Feminist Practices of Biblical Intrepertation.* Boston, Massachusetts: Beacon Press, 1992.

French, Marilyn. *The War Against Women.* New York: Summit Books, 1992.

Haydon, Albert Eustace. *The Quest of the Ages.* New York: Harper and Publishers, 1929.

Herrnstein, Richard J., & Murray, Charles. *THE BELL CURVE; Intelligence and Class Structure in American Life.*

New York: The Free Press, 1994.

Hick, J. & Sakari, H. *The Experience of Religious Diversity*, Grover, 1986.

Huxley, Julian Sorrell, Sir. *Man Stands Alone.* Freeport, New York: Books for Libraries Press, 1970.

Lewes, Kenneth. *The Psychoanalytic Theory of Male Homosexuality.* New York: Simon & Schuster, 1988.

Mayer, Jane & Abramson, Jill. *STRANGE JUSTICE; The Selling of Clarence Thomas.* Boston: Houghton Mifflin Co., 1994.

McConnell, Thomas. "The Report From Iron Mountain: The Blueprint for Absolute Tyranny - Part I." *Monetary & Economic Review*, A division of FAMC, Inc., October, 1994. Address: 3500 JFK Parkway, Fort Collins, Co 80525. Telephone: 1-800-336-7000.

McConnell, Thomas. "The Report From Iron Mountain: The Blueprint for Absolute Tyranny - Part II." *Monetary & Economic Review*, A division of FAMC, Inc., November, 1994. Address: 3500 JFK Parkway, Fort Collins, Co 80525. Telephone: 1-800-336-7000.

McCuen, Gary E. *The Religious Right.* Wisconsin: GEM Publications, Inc., 1989

Newton, David E. *Gay and Lesbian Rights.* California: ABC-CLIO, Inc., 1994.

O'Neill, William L. *The Woman Movement: Feminism in the United States and England.* New York: Barnes And Noble, Inc., 1969.

Palmer, Ezra. *Everything You Need To Know About DISCRIMINATION.* New York: The Rosen Publishing Group, Inc., 1994.

Robertson, Pat. *THE TURNING TIDE: THE FALL OF*

LIBERALISM AND THE RISE OF COMMON SENSE. Texas: Word Publishing, 1979.

Santayna, George. *Reason and Religion.* New York: Collier Books, 1962. (Originally published in 1905).

Scarce, Rik. *ECO-WARRIORS: Understanding the Radical Environmental Movement.* Chicago: The Noble Press, Inc., 1990.

Schwarz, John E. *THE FORGOTTEN AMERICANS.* New York, London: W.W. Norton & Company, 1992.

Sellars, Roy Wood, and Ten others. "Towards a New Humanist Manifesto." *The Humanist* (Jan-Feb, 1973).

Seredich, John. *Your Resource Guide To Environmental Organizations.* Irvine, California: Smiling Dolphins Press, 1991.

Sowell, Thomas. *CIVIL RIGHTS: Rhetoric or Reality?* New York: William Morrow & Company, Inc., 1984.

Thoreau, Henry David. *Walden and Civil Disobedience.* New York: Penguin Books, 1983.

Tillich, Paul. *Theology of Culture.* Edited by Robert C. Kimball. London: Oxford University Press, 1959.

Wilcox, John George & Laird. *Nazis, Communists, Klansmen, and Others on the Fringe.* Buffalo, New York: Prometheus Books, 1992.